LOW PROFILE

a life in
the world of books

Frank Herrmann

LOW PROFILE

A LIFE IN THE WORLD OF BOOKS

The Plough Press

NOTTINGHAM, ENGLAND

2002

First Edition
Published by **The Plough Press**
13 Carlton Business Centre, Station Road,
Carlton, Nottingham NG4 3AA, UK
Web: www.ploughpress.com

ISBN: 0-902813-18-8 (UK)

Title: Low Profile
Author: Frank Herrmann
Typography: Andrew Burrell
Indexer: Douglas Matthews

British Library Cataloguing-in-Publication Data
A CIP Record is available from The British Library

This work was printed in the United States of America on 60# archival,
acid-free paper meeting the requirements of the American Standard for
Permanence of Paper for Printed Library Materials.

FOR

PIERS RAYMOND

WHO SHOULD HAVE BEEN

THE FIRST TO READ IT

Contents

Acknowledgements

Most of the photographs and illustrations come from the family archive. My mother was an early user of the Leica. My son Paul, a professional photographer, is responsible for my favourite shot of Patricia (p.104), Wulkow in winter (p.280) and the double portrait of the Spender brothers (p.362), as well as the photograph on the jacket. I am grateful to Norman Thelwell for allowing me to use his drawing on page 109 and to Dick Bruna for the use of 'Miffy' on page 113. Mary Bland supplied the photograph of David (p.35) and Rosemary Raymond of Piers on page 127. John Bodley kindly found the photographs of Richard de la Mare (taken by Mark Gerson) and of Sir Geoffrey Faber (by Douglas Glass) in the Faber archive. I apologise if, inadvertently, I have failed to make acknowledgement for any other illustrations.

My deepest gratitude must go to my secretary of twenty-five years, Sheila Phillips, for the typing of endless drafts dictated over the telephone, and then producing virtually error-free disks for the typesetter; to Paul Wakeman, then of Oak Knoll Press, who first put the idea of an autobiography forward, and to John von Hoelle, Paul's successor, for unstinting encouragement; to Andrew Burrell for the painstaking work of putting the book together so that it could be printed; and to Douglas Matthews for a superb index.

Ultimately few of my adventures would have succeeded without my dear wife, Patricia's, astute powers of analysis and ardent background support and, of course, another very warm thank you must go to all those many collaborators, named and unnamed, in a long life in the world of books.

LOW PROFILE

a life in
the world of books

CHAPTER ONE

Growing Up

In 1935 I had my appendix removed in a Berlin hospital. I can, even today, feel the mask being lowered over my face and the chloroform putting me to sleep. I was eight. Thereafter my memory moves in flashes, but in essence things have never stopped happening.

Early in 1936 I was attending a general knowledge class in the gaunt, nineteenth-century primary school in the Babelsberger Strasse. This was a short walk from my parents' flat in the Freiherr-von-Stein Strasse in Berlin-Schöneberg. A particularly reptilian lady supply teacher was telling my class of some forty-five children how despicable the Jews were and how we should avoid contact with them. One small boy stood up and said, 'My grandfather is Jewish. He's a lovely man. There's nothing the matter with him. You shouldn't say things like that'. Other boys got up and said similar things. The first small boy was me. Shock, horror, drama, hysteria. My parents had to withdraw me from the school. The headmaster tried to calm things down and hush them up. But the poor man was sacked for his pains.

Looking at family photograph albums of that period today, it is striking how the joy and innocence on my mother's face was gradually replaced by strain and sadness between 1935 and 1939. My father had been prohibited from working as an architect as early as 1935 because he was of half-Jewish descent. He wanted to get that prohibition rescinded but my mother could see the writing on the wall all too clearly and persuaded my father to start planning their exodus from Germany. It was my reference to her father in my school which had precipitated the trouble.

In order that we should have some continuing degree of education, my brother and I were sent to a children's home, called Solaria

Alpina, high above the Suvretta House Hotel in St Moritz in Switzerland which my parents knew from their skiing holidays. We must have been there for between six and nine months. It was also beneficial for the boyhood asthma from which I suffered quite severely.

The children's home near St Moritz.

We learned to ski and skate and the fine art of tobogganing. On one occasion we nearly caused a diplomatic incident when my brother and I (Luke is five years younger than me), on a single toboggan, careered down the icy road to Campfer. As we came round a sharp bend we saw a large group of people straddled across the road, who seemed unwilling to move when they saw us approaching. Unable to stop, we knocked a young girl on skis flying, even though she was supported on either side by an instructor. It was only when we got back to the 'home' that we learned that our brief encounter had caused great excitement as the girl we had careered into was one of the younger sisters of King Farouk of Egypt, whose entourage had taken over an entire floor of the Suvretta House Hotel. Fortunately, no one discovered that we were the culprits.

After many months the news arrived at last that we could re-join our parents, who had finally settled in England in the summer of 1937. The Swiss couple who ran the children's home drove us by car all the way to London, through Switzerland and France. As we passed near Verdun, the Swiss owner pointed out a part of the Maginot Line to us and said, 'That, boys, will keep the Germans out of France for ever'.

In August of that year my parents parked their brand-new car outside Peter Robinson, the department store in London's Oxford Circus: an inconceivable thought today. It was 'half-price' sale day and we were buying a school uniform for my new prep school – grey suit with short trousers, grey shirts, blue-and-yellow striped tie and a cap to match. A policeman was standing by our car when we came out of the store. 'How long have you been here, sir?' he asked my father, whose knowledge of English was still very perfunctory. 'Since early June', said my father. The policeman smiled, closed his notebook and gave my father a severe ticking off. The incident became part of family history.

*

My parents had bought a house in Hampstead Garden Suburb. This was an area planned and built between 1907 and 1915: one of England's first deliberately constructed garden suburbs, brain-child of Dame Henrietta Barnett, a great social reformer. Sir Edwin Lutyens and Raymond Unwin had been the architects and they had made a wonderful job of it. My father had known of the Suburb because of his interest in such communal housing projects. Our house, No. 14 North Square, was right in the centre. There were sixteen houses in the Square and we gradually got to know the occupants of every single one of them. Some became my parents' closest friends.

Between them they taught my family about life in England. We could not have wished for a better tutorial college.

The Levetuses lived at No. 1. He exported bicycles to India. Mrs Levetus looked like the younger of the 'Potato Eaters' in Van Gogh's famous painting, and made the most delicious lemon barley water. My brother and I often stayed in her house when our parents travelled out of London. She taught us English words we did not know and even took us to a couple of the famous Robert Mayer children's concerts. But above all, Mrs Levetus introduced me to English children's books that her own children had read. My absolute favourite was the *Adventures of Professor Branestawm*, by Norman Hunter[1], with illustrations by Heath Robinson. Until then my best-loved reading matter had been the books about Dr Dolittle, by Hugh Lofting, in German. I practically knew them by heart.

Their place was now taken by *Swallows and Amazons* and the rest of Arthur Ransome's enthralling series, which Mrs Levetus provided though I think I only got as far as *Pigeon Post*. 'Pemmican' became our staple diet.

The Millar-Craigs lived at No. 2. Sir Marshall was the most retiring of men and a senior legal draughtsman at the Scottish Office. We all listened to his magnificent bass voice echoing across the Square as he shaved in the mornings. The Millar-Craigs had a seaside cottage in Old Hunstanton in Norfolk, which they loaned to my parents for some of their early English holidays. The Almonds lived at No. 5. He was Professor of Chemistry at Kings College, London, and his wife was French. After thirty years in England she still spoke with a very strong French accent. Her ancient father helped my mother in the garden. The widowed Mrs Kauffman at No. 6 was very special. Something of a martinet, she made sure that my brother and I wore our school uniforms correctly. She had an enchanting daughter,

---

1 Thirty years later I persuaded Kaye Webb to re-publish Professor Branestawm as a Puffin book. I received a charming letter of thanks from the ageing Norman Hunter.

14 North Square: my parents' first home in England. The left-hand part
is 'The Manse' where the Ballards lived.

Francesca, who must have been fifteen years older than me, whose
amazing beauty never came to the fore until she took part in local
amateur theatricals. Mrs Kauffman's two sons were both killed in
the last week of the war in two quite different theatres of operation.
Colonel Maude at No. 8 was in charge of the manufacture of 'Standard' cars and advised my father on motor vehicles. Mrs Tout at No.
11 lent my mother her house during the Blitz. Professor Lionel
Robbins of the London School of Economics was rather awe-inspir-
ing, but often provided intellectual conversation, and Fred Taylor in
'The Studio', almost hidden by trees in one corner of the Square,
painted scenic posters for railway companies. To visit him and to
watch him at work was always a special treat.

But the most important family by far were the Ballards in the other
half of our semi-detached house, the Manse. Frank Ballard was minister of the huge Free Church at the bottom of our garden. Ia, his
wife, was a hyperactive, wonderfully disorganised friend who taught

us the art of 'muddling through'. She was part of a large academic family in Cambridge, the Omans, and her many sisters all became close friends too. Frank was very dignified and infinitely serene, and later became Moderator of the Free Churches. His study contained the first substantial library in which I was allowed to browse. My father even became a lodger in the Ballards' household during his three-year stint as an emergency ambulance driver in London during the war.

Ia Ballard, my father, Frank Ballard and Luke in Cambridge.

I ought to explain that we lived at No. 14 from 1937 to 1940, and my father bought No. 4 North Square in 1943, when it had become vacant. He paid £2,000 for a ninety-nine year lease on the house, and later an extra £200 for a garage and a lease extended to 999 years. The house changed hands not long ago for just under one million pounds. Ultimately, my parents were North Square residents for nearly fifty years and became part of the Suburb fabric.

As the earlier occupants of the Square moved away, their successors continued to become friends. I never realised until much later how many of the pre-war families had been staunch supporters of the Fabian Society. Domestic politics never seemed to enter our conversations before the war: we were all totally pre-occupied by international events.

*

Probably on the advice of our North Square neighbours, my parents undertook frequent explorations with picnics of the major tourist sites around London, such as Hatfield House, Whipsnade Zoo, Hampton Court and a spot in Buckinghamshire they became very

4 North Square: my parents' home for 42 years.

fond of called Chenies. Then there were occasional holiday forays further afield, like the New Forest and Beaulieu Abbey, and a summer holiday in Cornwall: briefly on a chicken farm near St Agnes (the chickens were too much for us), and then as the first visitors to a newly-opened and delightfully furnished guest house at Prah Sands. This is now an extremely popular and crowded tourist area. In 1938 my father hired horses for himself and me and we galloped up and down the totally empty beach for hours with not another soul in sight. Thereafter holidays ceased.

The Munich crisis dawned. My London prep school, Leas House, was evacuated to the neo-Gothic Luscombe Castle, outside Dawlish in Devonshire. The surroundings were lovely, but as things turned out we got to know them all too well: the entire school caught scarlet fever, for which the quarantine was four weeks. Just as we thought it was all over, our rather prim headmaster, Mr J Myddleton Evans, who had told everybody that he was immune from the infection, caught it too. It meant another month of imprisonment.

However, small boys' horizons are not those of the adult world. Whatever agonies of worry my parents must have suffered – and I

My father as riding instructor. Me on the horse. At Prah Sands, Cornwall, 1938.

became very ill indeed with rheumatic fever to top my scarlet fever –
like the rest of the school, I became gripped by a passion for stamp
collecting. We all knew the fat, single volume, Stanley Gibbons' Catalogue, by heart. Watermarks, perforation width, mint and used values
and all. My particular interest became Heligoland and, as luck would
have it, there was an elderly, permanently bed-ridden gentleman who
lived in Dawlish who was an expert on Heligoland stamps and owned
a large collection of them, something like twelve to fifteen albums.
My father had not yet succeeded in finding work as an architect so it
was a relatively simple matter for my parents to visit Dawlish before
the scarlet fever struck. Every one of their visits meant another blissful afternoon with the Heligoland stamp collector. My father enjoyed
those occasions as much as I did.

On Sundays I was allowed to have lunch with my parents in their
hotel in Dawlish. It was on one such occasion that I learned an un-
forgettable lesson. For some inscrutable reason my parents
discouraged me from drinking at mealtimes. Even water. At the table next to ours sat a girl of my own age from another school with
her parents. Imagine my astonishment when, at the end of the meal,
her parents said to her in loud tones with some degree of consternation, 'Susan, you have been very naughty. You have not drunk any of
your water while you were eating'. It dawned on me from that moment that people could have totally divergent views on precisely the
same subject.

A year later we were back in Luscombe Castle. On 3 September
1939 the headmaster called us all together to listen to the wireless in
the main hall of the castle, adorned on all sides with stags' antlers
and depressing family portraits. Mr Chamberlain, the Prime Minister, announced that as from that moment we were at war with
Germany. It became another period when contact with my parents
was entirely by letter: there were no telephones. Looking at some of
the letters I had written then I found they were in perfectly acceptable English. And even the spelling was correct. I had picked up the
language very rapidly as if by osmosis. My only difficulty was having

to change from the sloping, old-style German script I had been taught
in Berlin to the upright Roman script in use in England. My handwriting never really recovered from the switch, gradual though it
was, and has been regarded as characterful, but illegible to most people, for the whole of my subsequent life.

*

My mother was determined that I should go to Westminster School.
She had read about it years earlier and with its position in the centre
of London, next to Westminster Abbey and close to the Houses of
Parliament, she considered it an ideal environment for the education
of her sons. She worked hard to get an introduction to the Head
Master, John Christie. She went to an interview with him, accompanied by a friend in case her English was not up to it – which it certainly
was – and got my name put on the books to enter the school in the
summer term of 1940. After I survived an interview on my own and
passed a written test, I was kitted out with a minute set of 'tails',
white shirts and loose, stiff collars, a top hat and a tuckbox with my
name on it, at the school's venerable outfitters, J G Plumb in Victoria Street. My father must have had a hard time trying in advance to
find the necessary school fees.

There still exist files devoted to the efforts put into rescuing enough
of the family's resources to buy a house in London and to found a
new life in England after paying the enormous taxes the Nazis demanded before allowing my parents to emigrate from Germany. The
seemingly precarious transfer was organised with considerable inge-
nuity by my father's German attorney through investment in a farm
in South West Africa, a former German colony. I knew nothing of
this at the time of course, and only learned about it after reading the
surviving papers forty years later.

Another major catalyst in my parents' move was my father's first
cousin, Maxwell Wimpole, an Englishman by birth and a barrister
by profession. Maxwell was a confirmed bachelor, a tiny figure with
a distinct stoop, much given to wearing bow ties and straw hats, a

character straight out of the 1910 world. He had been born Maximilian Wimpfheimer of an American father who traded in Liverpool as an importer of textiles, and had invented this ingenious Anglicisation of his name for himself. Maxwell had been caught in Germany when the First World War broke out in 1914, visiting his mother and my father's parents who together shared a large house in Pretzfeld in Franconia (of which more later). He did not have a passport, which was not then strictly necessary, and together with several thousand Englishmen in the same predicament, was interned in Ruhleben race course for the whole of the war. He became camp librarian and was

In my new 'tails' ready to go to Westminster. My father looks on in amazement.

rewarded for the work with some major distinction soon after his release at the end of hostilities. He did not much enjoy the legal world and moved to Monte Carlo with his aged father, living on his earnings as a professional bridge player. But he regarded it as a solemn duty to assist my parents in their emigration to England and went to enormous lengths to help them move. I remember the frequent cry when a problem arose after we were installed in North

Square, 'We must ring Maxwell, we must ring Maxwell'.

Maxwell didn't so much talk, he buzzed with a sort of nasal twang. It has to be said, however, that his advice was not always reliable where money was concerned, which my father learned to his cost. Maxwell himself had the great good luck to own a major share in a semi-dormant coalmine in Leicestershire, for which he received a huge sum in compensation when the Labour government, after the war, decided to nationalise the coal mines. From that time on he lived in a delightful central London guest house and settled down to a comfortable routine consisting of playing bridge, lunching at the National Liberal Club and going to the cinema with his friends in the afternoon. I often joined him for the last two during the school holidays. The tables were finally turned when, in his old age, my mother had to look after *him*. But he too seems to have had a hand in getting me into Westminster.

In early May, 1940, I duly joined the school, not in London as had been intended but on the Sussex coast. My part of the school had been evacuated to Lancing College, near Shoreham-by-Sea; the rest to Hurstpierpoint.

My parents travelled down there in order to meet C H Fisher, the House Master of Busby's the 'house' that had been selected for me. I do not know to this day what the initials stood for. He was universally known as 'Preedy', after a pipe tobacco he had once smoked. He taught maths to the senior part of the school. John Carleton, his deputy, was what was known as a house tutor and taught history and some English. He, in fact, became Head Master of Westminster School after the war. My parents' visit that winter of 1940 coincided with a cold spell of such ferocity and so much snow that they were forced to spend the night in the school. This cemented a firm and lasting friendship beyond the mere teacher/parent relationship with both Messrs Fisher and Carleton.

Half way through that brilliant summer term of 1940, France fell and the proximity of the German army just across the Channel forced us all to move again: in addition, the Admiralty needed the Lancing

College buildings for purposes of their own. We saw various Dutch and Belgian government ministers-in-exile arriving by plane at the tiny Shoreham airport and we spent hilarious nights on the incredibly uncomfortable pews of the Lancing chapel crypt awaiting German bombs that fortunately never came near us.

A few of the friendships I made in my first term lasted a life time, but I did not distinguish myself in class. I was joint bottom of the Transitus, the school's lowest form, with another boy, who later in life also went into publishing. I suppose we played cricket, but I don't remember doing so, although I had had to buy the necessary white flannels. What I do recall is an outing by bicycle to the seaside resort of Littlehampton with my close friend, Henry Myhill, in the dying days of the local funfair. We each won an enormous coconut. We had no baskets or bags in which to put them and had to balance them precariously on our handle bars. Every mile or so we were forced to dismount at road blocks put up by the Local Defence Volunteers (later the Home Guard) and show our identity cards. Our coconuts aroused great suspicion. They looked as if they might conceal bombs.

Westminster's next move – it must have been a fantastic feat of organisation – was to Exeter University. I was quartered in an elderly hall of residence called Reed Hall. We were constantly warned that the benign and rather soporific climate of the Devonshire environment was not conducive to school work, and certainly it was difficult to apply oneself to irregular Latin verbs at a time when a possible German invasion was uppermost in everybody's minds.

But in fact, Exeter turned out to be another temporary stop. After the school broke up for the summer holidays, the governors decided in their wisdom that the much-heralded bombing of London would never take place and that the school should return to its natural habitat, positioned beside Westminster Abbey. No sooner had all the school property been moved back to London when the bombs began to fall in earnest. I seem to recall that my one and only day of tuition in London was spent in the boilerhouse of the Abbey, the local air raid shelter.

My mother, on the other hand, had closed and sold her house in North Square and rented No. 11 from Mrs Tout who had moved to the country. My mother had to cope with all this because my father had now been interned as an enemy alien – in common with almost all German refugees, first in Huyton, outside Liverpool, and then on the Isle of Man. He was released as an 'artist of eminent distinction' after about a year. Every night there were air raids and the anti-aircraft guns on Hampstead Heath kept us awake. My mother used to put up her umbrella to shield the two of us from the falling shrapnel as we hurried to a shelter in the nearby Free Church Hall. Occasionally we were called out to deal with the incendiary bombs that fell all around the area. We got very good at putting them out with nothing more than long-handled shovels.

London was clearly not a healthy place as the Blitz continued. Westminster masters searched the rural areas of Britain high and low to find somewhere safe we could move to that had not already been allocated for some other purpose. But it took time. My mother was strongly advised to get out of London and to take us with her. So suddenly there was a brief and unexpected interlude. Another prominent Suburb personality was Dr Joan Fry of the Quaker community. She had worked tremendously hard to help German refugees. She suggested a Quaker guest house in Wensleydale, where rooms were available and my mother might find refuge at a very reasonable cost. So off we went to catch a train to Matlock in Derbyshire, the nearest station. But our train was so greatly delayed that we arrived at the station after midnight, in complete darkness. A lone porter had been waiting for the last train. We were the only people to get out. All the local hotels proved to be full. My mother poured out her troubles to the middle-aged porter and when he heard of our predicament he offered to put us up in his own house, where two bedrooms were unoccupied because his sons were in the forces. He led the way through the blacked-out town, pushing a barrow with our luggage on it. Such kindly gestures were part of the wartime spirit and my mother never forgot. She continued to send our porter friend and his wife cards and presents at Christmas for many years until the old boy died.

Life in Wensleydale, beautiful though the area was, was healthy but monotonous without transport. We were glad to get back to London after a few weeks when we heard from Westminster that a new location for the school had been found. This time we were to move to a small town in Herefordshire called Bromyard. My 'house', Busbys, was quartered in a large brick-built, eighteenth-century mansion called Buckenhill. It was semi-derelict. There were no bathrooms

Buckenhill: restored after the war.

and little in the way of a kitchen. The house had no mains electricity supply and generators had to be installed. The water supply came from an ancient, temperamental hydraulic 'ram' at some distance from the house. We were surrounded by a huge park in which most of the magnificent trees had recently been felled, and a farm where the living conditions seemed medieval. One drive from the front of the house led towards Bromyard; another from the back, towards the Bromyard Downs and Worcester. Each was three-quarters of a mile long; both were badly rutted by the timber lorries and in appalling condition. No motorist would drive down them if they could avoid it. Our building and its many outhouses had been a Barnado's home thirty years earlier and the slightly dotty local squire who owned it had pulled down a good many walls to search, unsuccessfully, for what was thought to be hidden treasure. There were creepers growing *inside* the dining room.

*

I certainly didn't realise until many years later how important our house master now became in our upbringing during the nearly five years Westminster School spent in Herefordshire. I had hardly been aware of Preedy at Lancing or in Exeter. In Herefordshire he was omnipresent. We needed his constant guidance as the boys adjusted to this strange, primitive environment. The man was physically strong; he had rowed at Cambridge; he could, and did, lift enormous loads. He exuded an atmosphere of calm in a crisis and never seemed flustered. He very rarely spoke in anger, though he could be quite sarcastic, a potent weapon when dealing with the young. I don't think of him as much of a conversationalist: his incessant pipe-smoking probably got in the way. He said what was necessary: sometimes it was quite brief, though when the occasion demanded it he could hold forth at length in well-construed paragraphs that followed logically one after the other, just what young minds wanted. I was never taught by him. Those who were thought highly of him as a teacher, though those who were outstandingly brilliant tended to look for other intellects among the teaching staff, and Westminster was very strong in mathematics.

Preedy became so important in the rural, almost feudal Herefordshire setting because he himself had been brought up in it. His mother and sisters lived in a small cottage in a tiny, remote village called Drabbington, near Thornbury, not very far from Bromyard. I had tea there once or twice. It was charming. Wherever Preedy went, he went by bicycle: I don't believe he could drive a car. So by example, we all moved around on bicycles. They gave us mobility, which with the general shortage of petrol and the great distances from one place to another, we would simply otherwise have lacked. A broken bicycle was a disaster for there were no spares to borrow.

Westminster had a sort of sub-culture language all its own. The word 'station' means a period when one rows or plays games. In our first year or two there was little in the way of sport in Bromyard, except athletics and long-distance running, both of which I hated: though later we were able to row, using the boats and boathouses of the Blind School in Worcester, and eventually there was cricket and even football. So our 'station' for many months after our arrival consisted largely of gardening. Buckenhill had a huge walled kitchen garden. At first it was so densely overgrown after decades of neglect that it took some time even to open the great old doors that led into it, and then it took months of chopping and clearing until we got to the dilapidated greenhouses at the far end. We all became experts with the billhook. It was even longer before the soil was dug and cleared of weeds, so that planting and sowing could begin. Once it did, we produced a goodly proportion of the vegetables we consumed.

At first the academic side of the day involved walking a couple of miles across muddy fields and crossing a stream over a shaky bridge to Saltmarshe Castle, a vast neo-Gothic stone pile put up in the 1830s. Together with all the land around – including Buckenhill – it belonged to the Barnaby family. It was said that their landed possessions were such that one could walk to the sea on the Welsh coast without ever leaving land that belonged to them. I believe old Mr Barnaby, with his shock of white hair, his tattered but well-cut jackets and his multitude of dogs, thoroughly enjoyed this invasion by a few hundred schoolboys to his lonely monastic property every morning. He was often in evidence and usually chatted to us. His butler served milk and biscuits in the central baronial hall in the middle of the morning before we streamed back into the myriad bedrooms which had been turned into classrooms. At lunch time we all trooped back to Buckenhill.

*

There was also, of course, a strong military element in school life. What before the war had been the Officers' Training Corps had now, more democratically, become the Junior Training Corps. But the uniforms were still those in the style of 1918, with ghastly khaki breeches and puttees which one had to roll from the ankle above the boots to just below the knee. It was necessary to wear pyjama trousers beneath them so that the beastly things would grip. Fortunately, it was not too long before we were issued with new-style battledress, though the quality of the material of the old uniforms was infinitely better. The generic term for military training at school was 'Corps'.

Everybody had to belong to the JTC or the Air Force equivalent (ATC), or the Boy Scouts. At Lancing I had belonged to the scouts in a troop led by Tony Benn's older brother, who not much later died as a Spitfire pilot. But the scouts gradually disappeared, and I joined the JTC.

All the arms and military equipment – mostly ancient .303 Lee-Enfield rifles – were kept in superb order by a professional ex-Guards sergeant major, Sergeant Major Stewart, he of the waxed moustaches and the twinkling eye, and father of an enormous family. But he was brilliant, almost inspirational, with the young. He tolerated their inevitable clumsiness and guided them to professionalism. He also kept a jackdaw, which he had trained to talk during the lonely business of cleaning rifles.

Later, during the war, all the older boys joined the Home Guard. The Buckenhill contingent formed a mobile platoon on bicycles, with special clips which held our Lee-Enfield rifles, and further clips to hold our heavy field wireless sets (it was a minor miracle when they worked). On alternate Sundays we went to Matins – in tails – to

Bromyard Parish Church, on bikes, of course. On the other Sundays we had Home Guard exercises all round the countryside within a radius of about fifteen miles from Bromyard. It was a wonderful way of getting to know what is a very beautiful and rather sparsely popu- lated county, and brought us into close contact with the local population, who formed other nearby Home Guard units. Preedy became a Lieutenant, and eventually a Captain; another house mas- ter a Captain, and later a Major. The Head Master, John Christie, who with his family lived in a remote farmhouse by the Bromyard Downs, two or three miles from Buckenhill, was a Corporal. On the rare occasions when he was seen wearing his uniform it looked as if it had come straight from the washing line without being ironed.

On one celebrated occasion, the focus of a particularly extensive Sunday exercise (i.e. it continued over lunch and we had to take sand- wiches) was to pretend that the German invasion had started, so that our knowledge of what to do would be fully tested. As a special messenger it was my duty to bicycle as fast as I could to the Christie's farm to break the news to the Head Master that the invasion had started. Hardly able to speak because I was so out of breath, I rang the bell, and when John Christie's lanky frame appeared in the door- way in his tatty uniform, I blurted out: 'The invasion has started, sir'. Christie replied, 'I know, boy, I know. They telephoned me.' It was a terrible let-down.

On another occasion, in common with various other Home Guard units mostly made up of farm workers and local shopkeepers, we were to have a 'battle' (it was, of course, called an operation), against a unit of American troops stationed near Bromyard. We decided that the only way we could win, because of the Americans' vastly supe- rior equipment, was by capturing their commanders from where we knew to be their headquarters. We had by then been issued with Sten guns – a small, highly unreliable automatic weapon, made in garages all over England – and to the American senior officers' total astonishment and disbelief, we rounded them up with these (un- loaded) weapons pointed at their midriffs, and marched them,

blindfolded, to a hideout. As far as I can remember, we won the
battle because the remaining American troops were totally confused.
But we got a severe reprimand from some very high-up officers – it
may even have been the War Office – for 'cheating'.

*

After a year or two, the daily peregrination to Saltmarshe Castle was
abandoned and we had lessons, on alternate days, at Buckenhill, where
space had now been converted into classrooms, and at Whitbourne.
The latter was a charming, small village in a valley in Worcestershire,
six miles from Buckenhill, cross-country, along tiny, gated roads
through the most scenically beautiful landscape. The most exhilarating stretch was an incredibly steep hill with a sharp bend at the
bottom, nicknamed 'the Precipice', which we were eventually ordered
to walk down because so many boys had been injured in bicycle acci-
dents. Whitbourne Court, Manor and Rectory housed the King
Scholars, Rigauds and other houses – that is, half the school. They
were all in much better shape structurally than Buckenhill and, ac-
cordingly, life there was less spartan. The classrooms also were more
elegant.

Despite all the handicaps, cultural life continued to play a role.
Preedy and other masters were inveterate theatrical producers and I
played minor roles in *Hamlet*, *Macbeth*, *As You Like It*, and various
plays by Bernard Shaw. I was no actor, but there were boys among
us who were really brilliant actors, though most of them became
accountants in later life. What was more important, I became involved in the literary life. Busbys had a house paper, the *College Street
Clarion* (in London, Busbys was situated in College Street). Unlike
other house papers, which came out once a term, or even once a
year, the *Clarion* appeared every two weeks. For some years I contributed articles. Then I became a member of the *Clarion* staff. For
the last year in Herefordshire I was editor. It was without doubt
wonderful training for a publishing career. One had to drag articles
out of unwilling authors; these had to be edited; all the pages had to

be typed onto wax stencils. These had to be given to Preedy on a Wednesday. He would duplicate the requisite number of each page, and we worked late into the night on Thursdays assembling, collating and stapling the whole magazine – of eight to twelve foolscap pages – so that it could be sold to the boys (at 3d a copy) on Friday mornings.

A large number of copies also had to be wrapped and sent to boys who had left the school but wanted to stay in touch and to know what their former fellows were up to. This involved a great deal of correspondence with them to find out what they were doing. A large majority, of course, were in the Forces and we would often publish first-hand accounts from them of battles in distant places. Sometimes we published articles from former masters, as well as people with Westminster connections. The *Clarion* was also the first publication to divulge to the world in 1941 that some of the famous school buildings at Westminster had been virtually destroyed by fire bombs.

*

Inevitably, we were asked from time to time to help farmers with harvesting and other work. Even though some of them had assistance from 'Land Girls' and Italian prisoners-of-war, there was a desperate shortage of labour. Very often the work to which – unskilled as we were – we were allocated, was stooking. In the days before combine harvesters, wheat, barley and oats were cut and each sheaf tied automatically with string, but six such sheaves had to be stood up together, by hand, so that they would dry out. This was called a stook. English fields, not only those in Herefordshire, usually produced a rich crop of thistles among the cereal. The thistles played hell with your hands unless you were as horny-handed as many of the farm workers, or wore thick gloves, and thick gloves were not always available. Potato-picking was back-breaking, and another punitive chore was hoeing turnips. What was fun was loading the wagons with the dried-out stooks at harvest time, and even driving the tractors. I worked on many farms in Herefordshire but each summer there was, in addition, a harvest camp near the Welsh border, where forty or fifty boys would spend two weeks getting in the harvest. Preedy was very much in charge – and in his absolute element. We visited the same huge farm year after year. It was gruelling hard work; we slept in large chicken houses (hell on hot summer nights) but the farmers' wives gave us the most wonderful food (and cider) which, in contrast to the normal monotonous wartime diet, was a great treat.

What constantly appalled me were the terrible conditions to which the farms and farm buildings had degenerated. Liquid manure covered most of the yards where cows were kept for milking. Pigs existed in conditions which today would be considered criminal and barn roofs were so poorly maintained that the rain spoiled a goodly proportion of the harvested crops. When the Herefordshire War Agricultural Committee offered a prize for an essay of two thousand words on the subject of 'Farming After the War' to any boy who had been to a harvest camp, I regarded this as a wonderful opportunity to suggest improvements. I took great trouble over the piece and it really was the most exciting moment in my life when Preedy called to me one day across the vast Buckenhill staircase, and said, 'Oh Herrmann. By the way. You have won the farming essay prize'. Even in those drear days, I was interviewed by the local newspapers and the entire essay was published in *Farmers Weekly*, and led to a long correspondence. I found myself as a speaker on several farming brains trusts all over the county but, best of all, I won £50. It was fame of the most fleeting kind.

*

After my father's release from internment, he volunteered to drive emergency ambulances. As the bombing continued throughout the winter of 1940 and into 1941, he felt very firmly that my mother and brother (then only eight) ought to be somewhere safer. They came, provisionally, to Bromyard – and stayed. My mother found pleasant rooms in an ancient Bromyard pub called 'The King's Arms'. It was run by a vivacious and forceful Cornish woman named Mrs Pengelly; Mrs Pen for short. She cooked well and took trouble over her guests. The only disadvantage was the permanent smell of beer throughout the pub. Surprisingly, my mother, who had the most sensitive sense of smell, got used to it. Her fellow guests were a strange mixture, reminiscent of one of those BBC Radio plays where incompatible characters get locked in together. There were Lord and Lady Strabolgi (he was a Labour peer); the glamorous divorced mother of another Westminster boy, who worked in a local bookshop started by one of the school's modern language masters, Mr Claridge (nickname Hippo); Mr and Mrs Bonhote (he was Westminster's senior modern language master; his wife was American and a distinctly pyrogenic character), and my mother and brother. Mrs Pen had to be called in from time to time to re-establish peace. John Christie and his wife Lucy had been resident for a while before they found the farm on the Bromyard Downs.

Imagine my surprise and, above all, my embarrassment, when some time in 1941 various boys came up to me at Buckenhill and said 'Did you know that your mother is up here, teaching French?', and indeed there she was, an hour later, in a white fur jacket and a broad-rimmed red hat, carrying a number of French grammars under her arm. What had happened was that Tom Bonhote was stricken with severe pneumonia. It was clear that he would be away for weeks. John Christie (nickname 'Legs') called on my mother early one morning and asked whether she would take his place – immediately. He knew that she had excellent French, perfect German and passable Italian, but she had never taught a soul. With trembling heart and much encouragement, she took Tom Bonhote's classes one after the other. It turned out that she was a natural teacher. The boys liked her highly unconventional teaching methods. It became the happiest period of her life and she stayed on for many years, even when Tom Bonhote returned. In 1943 she went back to London where my father had now bought 4 North Square, and became one of the four founding teachers of Westminster Under School for boys up to the age of thirteen, including Luke.

Years later I discovered that she was paid an absolute pittance for her teaching work. In gratitude for the opportunity to make her mark as a teacher however, she left the school a sum of money many times greater than her collective earnings. To the surprise of us all, she left it to encourage music: she always enormously enjoyed the school concerts and the choral singing, when I became a member of the school Choral Society.

*

After the D-Day Landings and the Germans' disastrous campaigns in Russia, it gradually became clear that an Allied victory was assured. This meant that the school could slowly begin to plan its return to London. By now it had established a much more sophisticated approach to rural life generally and to teaching in particular, even though there was a shortage of masters. (For example, I never learned any geography: there was no one to teach it.) We were also back to playing most games: fencing became particularly popular. The *Clarion* devoted its pages to reminding readers of what life in the school had been like before the war, which, by now, hardly any boys could remember; and the correspondence columns discussed what sort of dress should become obligatory instead of the corduroy shorts and open-neck shirts which we had all become used to.

During my last two years I had opted to specialise in science. I would have preferred modern languages or history. But a general mood prevailed that the country needed scientists. As far as I was concerned it soon became evident that I had made a big mistake. I simply lacked the mathematical foundations which were an essential requirement in physics. Chemistry I could cope with easily. During the holidays I visited or worked in various firms where chemists were needed, and got on well. On one occasion I visited an East End firm in London, during the period when Hitler was launching his V-1s, and later V-2 rockets (*Vergeltungswaffen*: weapons of retaliation). The firm in question manufactured paint. I had just arrived and was being interviewed by the managing director. We sat on either side of a magnificent partner's desk. V-1s (or doodlebugs, as they were known) could be detected by a distinctive propulsion sound which cut out just before they descended. We both heard one such rocket approaching when the sound of its engine ceased. The managing director disappeared below his partner's desk. I went on sitting on the other side. The subsequent explosion rocked the building and some panes of glass fell out of the windows. We then carried on talking, and I looked around the slightly damaged paintworks as if nothing had happened.

I had to begin planning what I was going to do after I left Westminster. John Christie suggested that I should go to his old Oxford college, Magdalen. I expressed doubt about my academic ability as a scientist, but just at that stage I won another coveted essay prize with a long paper on enzymes. This persuaded the powers-that-be that I would have no problems. I was despatched to Oxford to be interviewed by the redoubtable president of Magdalen, Sir Henry Tizard. A most distinguished scientist and scientific administrator, he had been the principal progenitor of developing radar, which had been one of the factors that had helped to withstand Hitler's 1940 air onslaught on Britain. I found him a daunting personality but he seemed to regard me as a perfectly acceptable student. I was enrolled to go up to Magdalen in the autumn of 1945.

I was allocated a pleasant room in the 'New Building' overlooking Magdalen's deer park. I had a Welsh 'scout', Taffy, who looked after my basic needs. The complete intake of new students assembled on our second day to meet the Dean. Among us was Kenneth Tynan, later a luminary in the theatrical world. He was light years ahead of those of us who had just left school, but there were also among us many who had just been demobilised from the forces. Theirs was a maturity which Tynan's brilliance lacked. One of the newly-arrived academics on my staircase was the first Professor of Italian Studies to join Oxford from Italy after the war, A P d'Entreves. He did my soul a power of good. Frequent informal conversations with him were wonderfully intellectually stimulating where literature, painting and architecture were concerned. Walking a parallel course to mine to breakfast each morning was C S Lewis, then famed as the author of the broadcast *Screwtape Letters*. He wore dark brown corduroys, sports

Magdalen College, the New Building: too good to be true.

coats too short for him, and was rarely without a pipe. But our conversations, so far as we had any, were confined to banalities. Another distinguished, long-legged don whose rooms were very near, was Professor G R Driver. His subject was Hebrew Studies and he was known to be at work with others on a new translation of the Bible. But I do not think he even noticed new undergraduates.

I believe my spartan years in Herefordshire were good for me in that they encouraged self-sufficiency which, with Westminster's own dislike of pretentiousness, left one with a view that one lived in a world of equals. Oxford was not like that. True, there was a wonderful sense of freedom, but there was also a mass of individuals who gave themselves airs. I found this inhibiting and it took some getting used to.

I joined various societies that seemed to espouse interesting causes. One was the Cosmos Society, whose concern was international affairs and whose president was Gilbert Murray. I don't know how it was that I rose so quickly up the committee ladder but I became editor of its magazine, the *New Cosmopolitan*, in my second term. I also wrote articles for both the University magazines, the *Isis* and *Cherwell*. Much the most appealing society was the 'Author Critics' Society. Members would read aloud short stories they had written and others there would criticise them. It was excellent training for would-be authors and the standard of the contributions was high.

Communication among the student community was by small cards, hand-written and hand-delivered, inviting one to tea, to committee meetings, to the cinema to see classic films, advising one of postponed tutorials and consisting of exhortations to pay up for this and that. The tone was generally flippant: very much a cross between Evelyn Waugh and Nancy Mitford. I rowed as I had at Westminster. Magdalen Boat Club did incredibly well. We over-bumped twice in the relevant regattas, but unfortunately there was a great shortage of oars and I never received mine. My rowing also led to a blister that turned badly septic and I nearly lost the middle finger of my right hand.

Academically I progressed very slowly. I loved working in the various magnificent libraries, but I didn't care for the time that I had to spend in the laboratories. My chemistry tutor seemed pleased; but the physics was hell. It was too mechanistic for me. I treated it with too much awe and reverence to achieve complete understanding, which my fellow students didn't seem to bother about. It was quite clear that I was not that sort of scientist, if I was a scientist at all. On

the other hand, immersion in the sciences did teach me to be analytical and to set my thoughts down in a logical manner. My essays were
full of 'therefores' and 'howevers', and my reasoning was neatly divided into 'firstly', 'secondly' and 'thirdly'. It took years to shake this
off. When I saw what my friends, who were reading English, were
having to do, despite the inclusion of Anglo-Saxon in their course, I
longed to make a change to do the same. But the pressure of students waiting for admission after years in the forces precluded any
such change. Magdalen and I decided pretty well simultaneously that
it would be folly to go on for a lifetime doing what did not come
naturally to me. To my parents' great distress, Sir Henry Tizard and
I parted company, but so impressed was I by his career and personality when I found out more about him, that, not many years later at
Methuen's, I encouraged the publication of a biography about him
(Ronald Clark, *Tizard*, 1965), which won considerable acclaim and
became a lasting monument to his brilliant and often contentious
career.

The question now for me was what to do next. I had no hesitation
about this whatever. I wanted to get into publishing.

It is a vague phrase, much used, but I had heard people employed
in publishing talking about what they did and the thought of being
a link between authors and the reading public appealed to me enormously. I began to investigate what was actually involved. I studied
Sir Stanley Unwin's *The Truth About Publishing* very closely. In my
local public library I regularly read the trade paper, the *Bookseller*, to
see what actually went on in the book world and who were the principal participants. I compiled lists of publishers who brought out
the sorts of books that I would have liked to publish, and then I
started to write letters asking if these firms had a vacancy for the likes
of me. In all, I ultimately wrote to forty-one publishers. To do them
justice, they almost all replied. Most said no at once: they needed
someone with experience. A few asked me to come for interview and
then said no. In the end, I wrote to Geoffrey Faber, chairman of
Faber & Faber, but more to the point, father of a son who had been

My mother with her father, Alfons Jaffé, celebrating his 85th birthday on an outing to Woodstock.

My father, a few years later, with his sons. Luke on the right was on leave from his army service.

at school with me. Dick Faber had short, curly, red hair and a wonderful tenor/alto voice; he was, in fact, a King's Scholar and became Head of the School. I had got to know him quite well at a forestry camp years earlier and he was one of my mother's star pupils. His father, Geoffrey Faber, said 'Come and see me'. I explained that I had written to a multitude of publishers but without any success. He asked to see my standard letter of application and corrected it, to its detriment I thought, but I hardly ever had to use it again because he gave me an introduction to Kurt Maschler, for whom I began to work. But the whole business of finding a post in publishing was such that I felt that if ever I should write an autobiography I should entitle it 'No Entry'!

All this searching for work took many weeks. I used the time to undertake my first journey to France in the company of my Westminster friend, Henry Myhill. He had been called up and became what was called a 'Bevin Boy'. Instead of serving in the armed forces he had been drafted into working in a coalmine. He absolutely hated it because for months on end he had virtually nothing to do. He had become a student at Grenoble University which specialised in teaching disgruntled English students, and during his vacations he travelled round France exploring the country. His garb consisted of his old football shorts and shirt. He carried about an aged suitcase which contained one change of clothing and material for cooking his breakfasts, including a small Primus stove. Henry became an eccentric and later, after acting as a tour guide for some years, he lived in a campervan, travelling around the world. But he was a most faithful friend and later in life I encouraged him to become a travel writer and Faber's published a whole series of his books on European islands.

I also enrolled on a London University three-year diploma course of evening classes for the study of English literature, at the City Literary Institute in Holborn. It gave me a wonderful grounding in the whole vast subject, and my copious reading stood me in very good stead, not only in publishing but also later in book auctioneering. I had the luck to have the same very good tutor, Lillian Haddikin, for the three whole years – starting from Chaucer right through to T S Eliot. The consistency of tuition alone was very beneficial. Finally, this unfettered period gave me an opportunity to see more of my aged grandparents, my mother's parents, who lived near Oxford. At this stage they resided in a guesthouse in Boars Hill, outside Oxford, in the house of the almost-forgotten, one-time Poet Laureate, Robert Bridges. I was given a camp bed in what had been his library. This still contained all his books and, more important, all his working papers. I really enjoyed myself at night time, reading his prolific correspondence. There was one file that particularly intrigued me. It concerned Bridges' spell on the newly-formed British Broadcasting Company's pronunciation committee. Bernard Shaw had been a fellow member of it, and had frequently written to Bridges to say how much he disagreed with the Poet Laureate's opinion on pronunciation. I had never previously read letters that were so unbelievably direct and *rude*. Shaw's blunt epistolary style contrasted wonderfully with Bridges' elegant responses. The letters made a deep impression on me and engendered a fascination for archival material that never deserted me and really came into its own later in life. It also made me hesitant ever to throw away old files.

CHAPTER TWO

The Faber Years:
An Apprenticeship

I joined the production department of Faber & Faber in January 1947. The firm was still where it had started, at 24 Russell Square right next to Senate House of London University. The production department was in a large, airy room on the first floor facing on to the Square. David Bland was the production manager and there were six of us working under him.

David Bland and Vivian Ridler (later renowned as the printer to the University Press at Oxford) had been students together at Bristol. They had founded and run a small private press, the Perpetua Press. David had then joined Faber's in 1937. In 1940 he had been called up into the RAF and became a navigator in Bomber Command. He had only recently returned to Faber's after four years as a prisoner of war. He had been shot down over Germany and badly injured by burns. In his absence the department had been run by Sean Jennett who had recently left to look after production at the newly-founded Grey Walls and Falcon Presses.

In my eyes David was the ideal boss. He was totally unflappable. He explained things with a minimum expenditure of words. When he delegated responsibility he trusted you completely to see the job through. Although a man of few words, his personality was warm and friendly. On my first day at Faber's, he took me to lunch at Schmidt's in Charlotte Street. And Charlotte Street, with its great multitude of (then cheap) international eating houses was where I went for lunch every day during the next eight years.

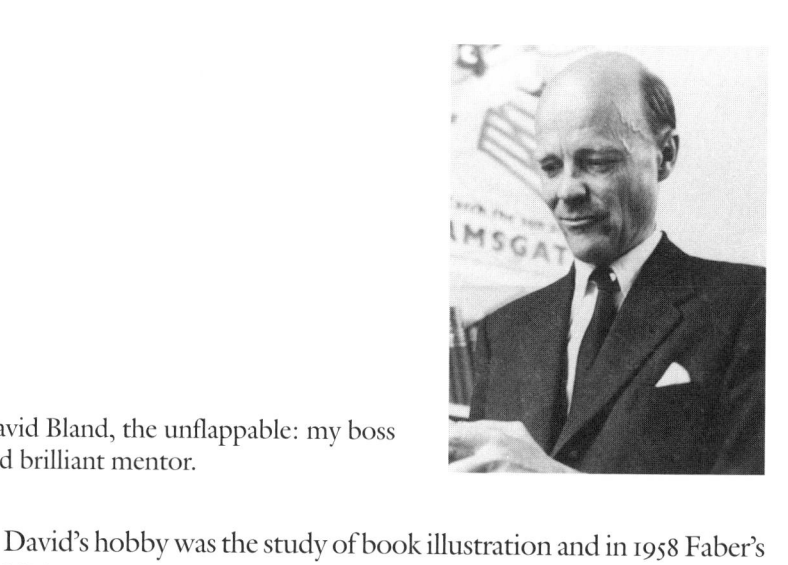

David Bland, the unflappable: my boss
and brilliant mentor.

David's hobby was the study of book illustration and in 1958 Faber's
published his major work on the subject, *The History of Book Illustration*. It followed several years after his shorter and more practical
Illustration of Books which had been reprinted regularly in the interim.

David had a unique, ranging walk in which his legs seemed to curl
round each other, and he was inordinately attached to the raincoat
he had been given on demobilisation from the RAF and a little fluffy
pork pie hat with which he concealed his balding pate out of doors.
He was undoubtedly one of the nicest people with whom I have
worked in a long career and I greatly missed his amazingly
commonsense approach to problems when I moved to greater
responsibility elsewhere.

Our work at Faber's was organised in such a way that we were
responsible for most aspects of the design, typography, estimating,
progress chasing, picture research and often, indeed, editorial work.
Everything stemmed from a weekly Book Committee, later called
'Black Book' meeting, which was really the firm's nerve centre. On
the very few occasions when I was allowed to penetrate this holiest
of holies in order to bring one of the directors some paper they had
forgotten to take with them, it became clear to me that it was a com-

bined management and editorial meeting, chaired with a very light and light-hearted touch by Geoffrey Faber. Faber's then had no editors as such. Indeed, I well remember Geoffrey Faber remonstrating – again on one of the few occasions when I was allowed to see the great man – that he would not allow such American concepts into his firm (in fact they did creep in fairly soon afterwards!). In 1947 there were six directors – plus Alan Pringle, known as 'the reader'. Each of them was responsible for one or other of the well-known aspects of the firm's list.

Richard de la Mare, son of the poet, begetter of the Faber house look - and master of the deep sigh.

Richard de la Mare, deputy chairman to Geoffrey Faber (not then knighted) specialised in books on the arts, particularly those relating to pottery and porcelain, organic husbandry and gardening – all great personal enthusiasms of his own. He had amassed a large collection of Japanese and, to a lesser extent, Chinese porcelain and had a fourteen-acre garden around his beautiful Queen Anne house in the middle of Much Hadham. Indeed, in my early days, Dick de la Mare seemed so engrossed with the activities of the Soil Association that I was not sure whether that or Faber's was his principal occupation. Dick had joined the firm, arriving from Selwyn & Blount, in its very early days in 1925, when it was still Faber & Gwyer, and it was his far-reaching and revolutionary ideas on book design, typography and print buying that we were now putting into practice. Almost any pre-war Faber book was a model example of what Dick was able to achieve. I believe it is now generally agreed that it was he and Wren Howard of Jonathan Cape who initiated the revolution in standards of book production for commercial firms made possible by advances in type design from the Monotype Corporation and other sources, as well as improved printing processes.

For me, Dick became something of a father figure. I might have worked for Fabers, but I really worked for him. With hindsight I don't believe he realised how highly the world regarded him.

Morley Kennerley was another director of whom I saw a great deal. He was the son of the American auctioneer and publisher, Mitchell Kennerley. Morley was tall, handsome and debonair and if he had gone into films he would certainly have rivalled the careers of Stewart Granger or Cary Grant. He constantly amazed me by the speed with which he would reach a decision, often on complex matters; while others hummed and hawed and pondered, Morley, when presented with the facts, simply said 'do this and that'. It was only later that I realised he was often wrong and that taking one's time to make up one's mind was no bad thing. His areas of interest were wide and embraced books originating in America which included a large hobby section on bridge, canasta, chess, travel, sports, cookery and health. One of his star authors was Gayelord Hauser, whose bestseller, *Look Younger, Live Longer*, was one of my personal headaches in that the printing number grew from 30,000 to 80,000 as orders increased while the book was still in production.

Old 'Papa' Crawley presided over sales in a large room above our heads. Another particularly tall figure, he had formerly been Methuen's London traveller. His earnings there were on a commission basis and he had been so successful that his take-home pay greatly exceeded that of Methuen's managing director, E V Lucas. When Lucas thereupon endeavoured to reduce Crawley's commission, Crawley promptly left and joined Geoffrey Faber's fledgling firm as its first sales manager. Bill Crawley was also responsible for children's books, an increasingly important feature of the Faber list. In the early post-war days he managed this with two secretaries, one of whom doubled up as a reader for children's books. Of considerable importance to this list were the illustrators, in which I took a particular interest.

Faber's was a natural port of call for any budding artist who wanted to illustrate books or design jackets. So there was a constant stream of artists who arrived at 24 Russell Square to show us the portfolios of their work. They hardly ever came by appointment. In my early days David Bland interviewed most of these himself: later this duty – most of my colleagues regarded it as rather a chore – was spread to any member of the production department who was not on the phone at the time. Eventually I rather specialised in the work because I enjoyed meeting the artists and judging their work, and also perhaps because I started a card index of the people we had seen with notes on their particular talent, or lack of it. So that when Papa Crawley suggested an illustrator whom we had already used many times, I wanted instead to give someone unknown but talented a chance, and this led to arguments. Mr Crawley was the only director with whom one could (or perhaps I could) argue, so I eventually got my way. Thereafter it was often my job actually to find and commission a suitable illustrator.

T S Eliot was another director. But if Geoffrey Faber and Dick de la Mare seemed remote, it was three years before I discovered that Mr Eliot actually worked in the building and didn't still reside in America. It was only when I heard visitors asking for him at the reception desk that I realised he was not just a feature of the firm's letter heading. When eventually I had to go to see him from time to time with some editorial query or other, he always sat hunched on a small, low armchair in his cluttered office, with a heap of papers on his lap. He would look up quizzically after one had knocked and entered, and seemed to regard the intrusion of a mere mortal from the production side of the firm as an irritation which reflected on his efficiency in filling up the Editorial Form. This vital document was completed by every director and accompanied a manuscript on

T S Eliot OM, joined the firm in its very early days, not as an outside literary adviser but as a full-time director. I took this photograph of him when compiling a photo-essay on Bloomsbury for *LIFE* magazine.

its way from them, to the Book Committee where a printing number was decided on after the Committee had sanctioned publication, and then to Dick de la Mare who took it back into his office, and later decided at a bi-weekly meeting with David Bland on a suitable printer. TSE's instructions on the editorial form were more complete and detailed than those of any of his colleagues, but he sometimes asked for the impossible: it was then that a visit to his office became imperative.

In my later days at Faber's I went in for a photographic competition organised by *LIFE* magazine. The subject I chose was Bloomsbury. I mentioned this one day to Mr Eliot and at once the diffidence became transformed into lasting enthusiasm. He gave me lots of introductions to famous Bloomsbury figures then still living in the area; he posed for me at the top of Faber's staircase (and Faber's used my photograph for publicity purposes for years after, without payment, of course); he insisted on seeing all my photographs and in reading and correcting my accompanying essay. He thought it was good, but *LIFE* magazine didn't. The prize went to a man who had photographed seagulls.

The firm's youngest director at the time of my arrival was Peter du Sautoy, who had only recently joined Faber's himself after being de-mobbed from the RAF as a Squadron Leader in administration at the Air Ministry. I was told that before the war he had been on the cataloguing staff at the British Museum, but that after many years work they had still not got far into the letter 'B'. Peter seemed as shy as I felt, and looked after contracts. He also dealt with Faber's all-important nursing list. At that stage our paths didn't often cross. He had, in fact, been taken on by the firm to replace C W Stewart, one of Geoffrey Faber's original co-directors, who had been killed towards the end of the war when he fell under a tube train in Hampstead station.

I have left Geoffrey Faber till last. He was obviously the man who mattered most: the firm was his creation. I would never have got to Faber's if it had not been for him. But as far as the staff was concerned he was remote, possibly because the firm had grown so much

The old Reading Room in the British Museum (as it then was). Part of my Bloomsbury photo-essay.

The bible racks in the old British Museum Iron Library: an early interest in antiquarian books?

in size since he had founded it. Occasionally when one saw him socially he suddenly seemed quite different: there was a warm and human side to him. He would often chortle with delight when something pleased him. I always felt that it would be very interesting to see him at the High Table at the Oxford College of All Souls where he was Estates Bursar, which kept him out of the office a great deal. I was once a silent witness to a lively debate between him and Dick de la Mare on the merits of a breed of cows of especially small stature, called Dexters, on which Dick wanted to publish a book but Geoffrey thought the market too confined. We published the book.

Sir Geoffrey Faber, founder of the firm, but also poet, biographer, one-time brewer, farmer, estates bursar of All Souls - with a gift for delegation tantamount to genius.

When he wrote, he wrote with great elegance, but with strongly held commercial convictions. His volume of 1934, *A Publisher Speaking*, is a collection of five separate talks he had given to booksellers over the years. He was obviously proud of them, and most of his arguments in the book are still valid today.

These then were the Faber directors: for most of us in the production department they were Titans, a race apart. We were there to labour; their job, it certainly seemed to us, was to direct. In all my years at Faber's Dick de la Mare, who was ultimately responsible for all matters of production, never once came into our office. Indeed, he confessed shortly before my departure that he was not quite sure where our office was, or indeed who was in it. Geoffrey Faber was hardly ever seen by any member of staff. When he sent round a memorandum in 1951 on time keeping, admonishing us in the gentlest, most coaxing terms, to get to the office by 9.45 and not to leave before 5.45, we thought the world was coming apart. We only read about TSE in the newspapers or sometimes got the gossip from Miss Swann, our telephone operator/receptionist, but more about her later. Morley Kennerley was an occasional visitor. Peter du Sautoy we saw weekly because he came round on Fridays with envelopes that contained our weekly wages.

One of the things I found frustrating was that the Faber management was secretive about anything that might give staff who were not directors any idea at all how well a book had sold or how the firm was faring in financial terms. When I asked David Bland how a book had sold, he never knew the answer. The reason probably was that he was so relieved and delighted that it had finally seen the light of day that he took no further interest in it after its publication. Dick de la Mare instantly clammed up when asked about the money side of things, so my sly little questions about the commercial success of some of the books on way-out subjects that interested him personally were met with nothing but deep sighs.

I soon discovered, however, that sales figures could be established if one moved to the very top of the building and entered a little private empire run by Mr Barclay. Mr Barclay was small and rotund and almost totally bald. He wore stiff white collars which didn't match his shirts, and he took off his shiny dark suit jacket when he came to the office and donned an old, brown cardigan with holes at the elbows. Mr Barclay was Austrian and had done something exciting and intellectual before he had arrived in England as a refugee. He now ran the royalty department with a staff of three or four elderly ladies. He entered the figures into the ledgers with an old-fashioned pen which he constantly dipped into a special, cracked inkwell. His entries were in an elaborate cursive hand but the pages were filthy, dog-eared and covered in blots.

Mr Barclay was delighted that anyone should take an interest in the details of his tattered ledgers and it was from these that I learned the seemingly classified information of what royalties not only our best-selling Mr Eliot had received and how his latest drama had sold, but also that our star nursing author, Evelyn Pearce, sister-tutor at the Middlesex Hospital, actually earned more money from her books than the famous Mr Eliot. But there simply was not the time nor the opportunity to visit Mr Barclay more than once in a while.

There was a general exodus from the production department each day at 4.00 pm – tea break. This took place in the office of the firm's three senior secretaries and was a wonderful and rare opportunity to meet people from other parts of the firm, and for gossip. Queen of the gossip was Polly Perkins, a tall, rangey, beak-nosed but vibrant personality with a sharp tongue. Her function was to sieve through all the unsolicited manuscripts that arrived unendingly every day at 24 Russell Square. It was said to be a poor week when there were fewer than thirty or forty. Polly had to find the nuggets among the dross and report on anything with merit to the Book Committee. I forget how many authors she had discovered: what sticks in the memory is that she initially turned down William Golding's *Lord of the Flies*. It was the new boy, Charles Monteith, who had rescued the manuscript from her rejection pile, cut and edited it with consummate skill and turned it into a best seller. Charles, with whom I had overlapped at Magdalen, had been brought into the firm with some éclat from Oxford by Geoffrey Faber.

The fact that Polly Perkins also looked after the firm's advertising and publicity under the aegis of Morley Kennerley (a brilliant natural publicist) and wrote a vast number of our promotional blurbs, didn't emerge until much later. It was obviously a side of her work which she found much less interesting than looking at manuscript material.

The tea breaks also underlined that there was a discernible class distinction between parts of the firm. The production, publicity and sales staff belonged to the upper echelon. The accounts, trade, packing and post departments – all squashed into other parts of Russell Square – did not. They were allowed to bring tea cups into their offices and on to their desks. For us this was strictly forbidden.

Faber's had done staggeringly well during the second world war. There had been a desperate shortage of paper and only firms that had bought paper extensively before 1939 received a quota. Almost every book printed sold, and sold very quickly. A proportion of the resulting profits had been siphoned off by the State in the form of an excess profits tax, but relatively large sums still stuck. With his expertise on property, and uncanny foresight, Geoffrey Faber had bought a vast building in Grosvenor Place just off Hyde Park Corner and overlooking the gardens of Buckingham Palace, as a future home for an expanded Faber's after the war. He was said to have paid very little for it. I worked there for a memorable month and remember it as a desperately gloomy environment.

My employer there was Kurt Maschler (little-known father of a famous son, Tom Maschler of Cape's) who had been a publisher in Germany and had come to England as a refugee. It was my first experience of publishing, the seemingly closed world which I had been so anxious to enter. Yet after only two or three days it was clear to me that Mr Maschler and I could not work together for long. The problem was that he thought too quickly. I simply could not keep up with him. He was also exceedingly dogmatic and had great difficulty in delegating or communicating clearly.

During and immediately after the war there was a great public hunger for colour in books, particularly on the arts. Kurt Maschler had been clever enough to buy a vast stock of old four-colour half tone blocks and the relevant 'progressives' which had been reproduced by *Apollo* magazine in the late nineteen twenties and thirties. He sorted these out into the work of specific artists and schools of painting and approached Faber's with an idea for a joint publishing venture, eventually called FAMA Limited. The result was the 'Faber Gallery', a series of large format, limp books of no more than thirty-two pages, into which various binders tipped ten to twelve colour plates that had been printed separately. Each volume carried an introduction and lengthy captions by a well-known authority in the art world. 'The Faber Gallery' sold in large numbers at 7s 6d (35 pence) and was a success. It was phased out some years later as colour printing developed.

I parted with Kurt Maschler after four weeks. We remained good friends for many years afterwards and exchanged Christmas cards which carried brief, annual reports on what we had each been doing, and I received a succinct congratulatory note from KM every time the trade press reported on some move or achievement in which I had been involved.

FAMA was not the only Faber subsidiary that had been found a home in the back of Grosvenor Place and Headfort Place. Dick de la Mare had used part of Faber's under-utilised reserves in starting a block-making firm called Fine Art Engravers. This was to overcome another production bottle-neck – getting half tone and line blocks made more speedily for Faber's many illustrated books and series. Again there was, after the war, a great shortage of blockmaking capacity, and publishers had to wait many months to turn photographs and line illustrations or diagrams into printing blocks – a cause of serious delays in the whole book production process.

Fine Art Engravers was run by two skilled, quick-witted characters whom Dick de la Mare had fished out of some other firm of process engravers. Ernie Blann was the salesman and managing director; Reg Hawkins was the technical manager who ran the processing plant. The difficulty which Faber's board, who had backed the venture, had overlooked was that, in order to establish viability, FAE would have to get work from many other publishers as well as from Faber's, and when they did, Faber's work had to go to the end of the queue.

So relations between the production department at 24 Russell Square and FAE were at best strained and at worst tantamount to open warfare. It was certainly the biggest cross poor David Bland had to carry, and even his fantastic degree of tolerance sometimes snapped; the rest of us in the department would listen with amazement at the viciousness of his end of telephone conversations with FAE's works, which were down at the Royal Mills, Esher, in an unused part of James Burn's bindery, another principal supplier to

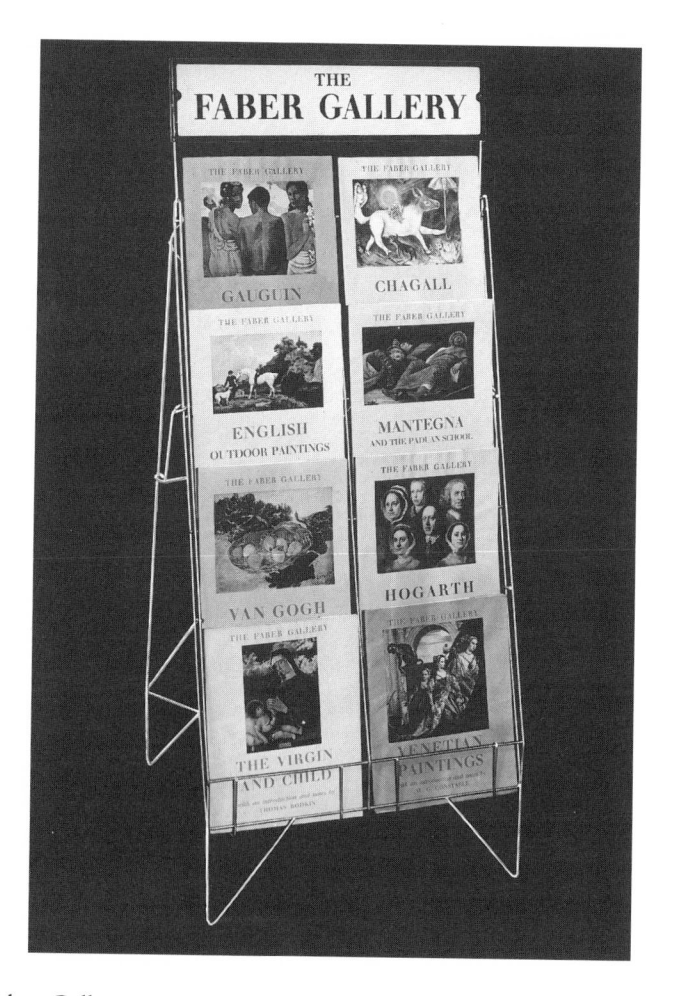

The Faber Gallery: Kurt Maschler's brilliant invention. My first shot at designing a display unit.

Faber's. The problem was not only that FAE was slow, but that from time to time they also produced inferior blocks which would be fiercely condemned by our expert authors (and our printers). They frequently lost – or mislaid – valuable originals. They made errors on their invoices, which we had, therefore, religiously to check because they never redounded to Faber's but always to their own credit. From my point of view, dealing with Fine Art Engravers was a most valuable object lesson in production management that stood me in good stead for ever afterwards.

Ernie Blann was the most brilliant salesman and the most accomplished liar I had ever come across, and I soon learned that the only method of avoiding a head-on collision course was by resorting to a bantering, teasing approach which required a strong sense of humour. It was only later that I learned that Reg Hawkins performed miracles of improvisation on poor and inadequate processing plant, equipment and materials, and it was a wonder that we got any blocks at all. Ernie Blann was only doing his best to protect the set-up and keep it afloat.

Faber's sold the building at Grosvenor Place shortly before I left them. Various ambitious publishing ventures, such as huge, multi-volume art encyclopaedias to be edited by R H Wilenski, and an enormous new anatomical textbook to rival *Gray's Anatomy* by the terrifyingly dynamic and short-tempered Professor Lockhart of Aberdeen University, had absorbed capital wildly beyond anyone's calculations, and sales generally in the years after the war slowed down as other goods and forms of entertainment that had been in short supply or completely unobtainable during the war came back into circulation. So the Faber board must have been faced with something of a cash crisis. We heard rumours to this effect, but nothing precise, from David Bland. The sum realised for the building was said to be £80,000, an enormous figure in those days and enough to give Faber's a welcome injection of capital to increase its publishing programme quite considerably.

Perhaps it's worth mentioning at this stage that economic

considerations in the late-1940s and early-1950s seemed quite different from any we know today. Money mattered less; there was much less interest in material values; things cost much less in real terms: an evening paper cost one penny; a novel cost 7s 6d (35 p); an average non-fiction work 10s 6d (55 p); a relatively expensive one 15s (75 p); an extensive demy 8vo with thirty-two pages of monochrome half tone plates, perhaps a guinea (£1 05p). Even giant firms measured their turnover in hundreds of thousands; journalists rarely wrote about projected profits; no one knew precisely what a billion was; the word 'cashflow' had never been heard of; accountants were simply book-keepers; a new Ford 'Popular' cost just over £200; I started life at Faber's on £4 a week and got married on £750 a year – and we collected polychrome English delftware!

So living was cheap, if haphazard. The workload that each of us in the production department managed in the early post-war years was enormous by today's standards. At the end of each month we completed an up-dated 'Work Return'. This was simply a list of the titles for which we were responsible. Against each we made brief notes on the latest state of play: the stages of production that had been completed and those that still had to be carried out.

Our direct dealings with authors were extensive. It was Dick de la Mare's formidable secretary, Mary Grenside, who was responsible for sending proofs to the authors. It was our job to get them back on time and to deal with authors' queries and complex corrections. In this way we got to know a vast spectrum of writers, both factual and creative, and many became close permanent friends, and it was often to us that they turned for advice on what to write about after a title was completed and published. Thus a job in Faber's production department was a curious and wholly absorbing amalgam of typographical design, production and editorial work. David Bland usually saw to it that an author's second, third or fourth book would be handled by the same member of staff. It saved time, simplified communications and built up a relationship of trust – and responsibility.

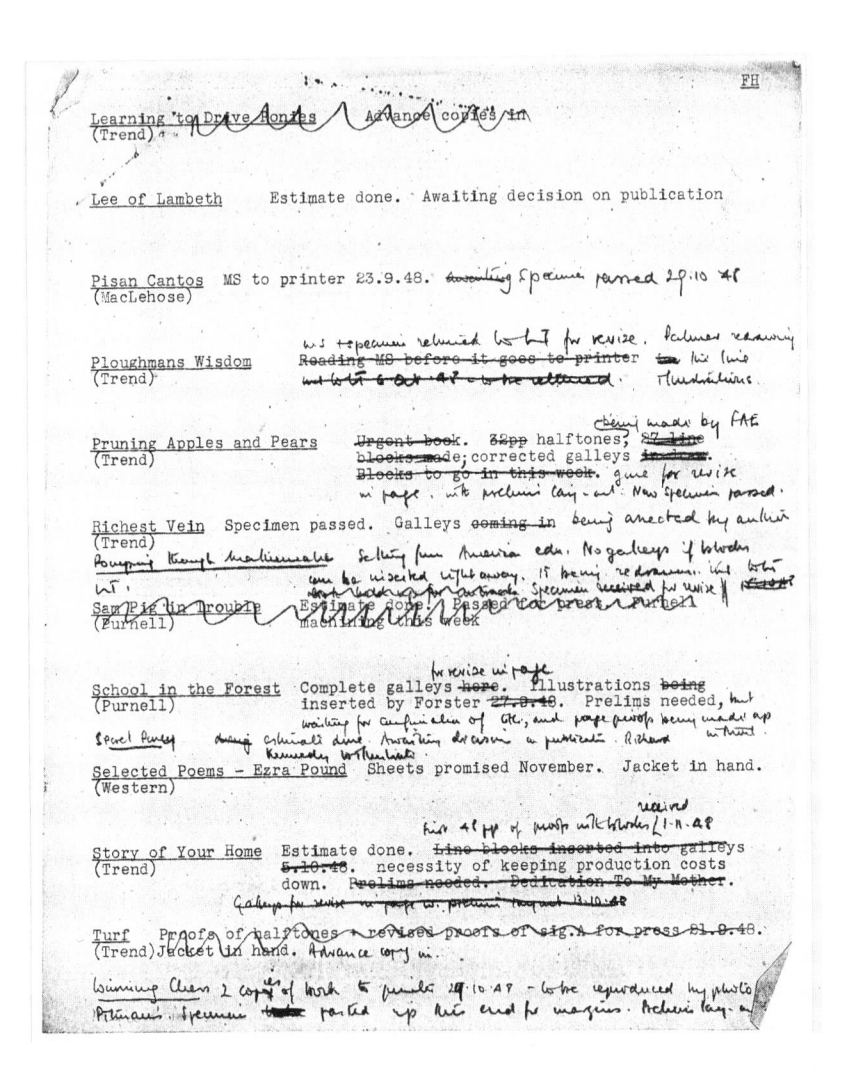

A page from a 1948 monthly 'work return'. I was looking after no more than 25 titles.

'My' authors were as diverse as anyone could imagine. I received rude postcards from Ezra Pound about corrections in his *Pisan Cantos*. I got charming letters from Alison Uttley. I formed a close friendship with the doctors Phillis and C Willett Cunnington, who, at my suggestion, wrote a whole series of handbooks on 'costume during the ages' after I had nursed their *English Women's Clothing in the Twentieth Century* through the press. One of my more trying acquaintances was Beryl de Zoete for whom we were producing a new edition of *Dance and Drama in Bali*. Her proofs were always behind schedule and were brought in by a wholly delightful elderly man who arrived at Russell Square on a bicycle, never removed his cycle clips from his corduroy trousers, and never wore a tie. At first we thought he was just a particularly well-read and knowledgeable gardener/handyman; it was only on one of his final visits that I learned he was Arthur Waley, famed in his own right as author and translator from the Chinese, but modest beyond belief. There were novelists, poets, gardeners, farmers, beekeepers, fly fishermen, eminent colonial civil servants (the latter all authors in a series edited by Margery Perham), chess players, cooks (Jean Conil), puppeteers, experts on stagecraft (Richard Southern), philosophers (C E M Joad), children's authors, astronomers (Patrick Moore – part-author of an early *Atlas of the Moon*), art historians (I was the only person at Faber's who got on well with Edgar Wind, even though we had to send his Reith Lectures through five sets of revised proofs – he and I shared a passion for informative footnotes), ballet dancers, plastic surgeons and politicians.

By some quirk of fate I kept the entire set of annotated work returns compiled during my time at Faber's. We never looked after less than forty titles at a time, often more, and these would probably change at least twice during the course of a year. So that each of us produced something of the order of sixty to eighty titles a year. I recall that David Bland's own list usually exceeded a hundred titles, but there were many that remained dormant for years while the author completed his manuscript or found his illustrations. The title

FH 4

The Last Chukker
(Trend)

Ms to Trend 8.1.51. Revised specimen in.
Drawings in drawer. Unsuitable for line?
Galleys promised April 2nd. *Est. done*

Life History of our Earth
(W.P.S.)

~~Some~~ page proofs in.

Look Younger, Live Longer
(Purnell)

~~Title page approved. Estimate for 20000
done. Page proofs for press:~~, index for
~~press 26.2.51.~~ *Advance copies in.*

Main Fleet to Singapore
(Trend)

Ms to Trend 5.2.51. New Russell Grenfell
fairly urgent. Illustrations finally
settled with author. Palmer to re-draw
maps.

Making of the National
Theatre
(Bowering)

Halftone blocks being made ~~a plan to come
Prelims to Bowering with galleys for revise in page.~~ Book must be out in May.
Copy for appendix 15.2.51. ~~Bowering
chasing up proofs.~~ *Page proof 17-208 p.
pm. Fg A + T for revise.*

Man or Matter
(Trend)

All blocks made and originals returned to
author. Estimate done. Dutch printer
going ahead with colour blocks. Have
asked for early proofs. Page proofs
being ~~corrected. Revise prelims.~~ *press. Prelims
for revise. Index being set. Plates for press.*

Meaning of Art
(MacLehose)

New edition. Estimate done. Page galleys
passed for press. Details about 1000 US
edition sent to MacL 28.12.50.

Millenium of Hieronymus Bosch
(Shenval)

Ms to Shenval 4.9.50. 24pp plates, four
colour plates 196pp. Composition est.
from Shenval. New estimate done including US edition. Colour blocks made.
Prelims to be numbered separately; told
Atterwill 12.1.51. Galleys in. Translator
putting illustrations in correct order
and line blocks in text. Have sent him
detailed instructions.

A page extracted from a 1951 'work return'. By now there were 50 or more titles on my list every month.

had crept on to David's list after he had prepared a preliminary costing to see if the book was a commercial proposition at not too enormous a price.

*

Sitting beside me when I started work was Rowley Atterbury who had joined Faber's after being phased out of the RAF. He had been interviewed in the first instance by Morley Kennerley, had joined on a three-month back-into-industry scheme and had then returned to Russell Square permanently after completing his service in the Air Force. Rowley impressed me deeply with his vast interest in and extensive knowledge of type faces. Even then he had a particular penchant for those of the early nineteenth century and began to collect the relevant typefounders' specimen books. However, his real passion in life was printing rather than typography and he had recently started printing on a small hand press in his aunt's garage over the weekends. He produced beautifully illustrated programmes for the City Music Society run by a friend of his, a tea broker called Ivan Sutton, to whom he seemed to speak on the telephone at least three times a day. I remember constantly passing messages from one to the other. Rowley's typography was meticulous and his knowledge of printing technicalities such that printers addressed him with great respect. Faber's nursing books were his special responsibility, and nursing students all over the world must have benefited from the care with which he designed the text books and differentiated between the numerous levels of crossheads with which nursing authors structured their manuals.

Nursing books brought Rowley into touch with the only specialist editor whom Faber's then employed, because, of course, a considerable medical and nursing knowledge and background were required in the preparation of the manuscripts. In the late 1940s this post was occupied by Miss A M K Watson SRN who had been found a tiny, ill-lit office in Faber's basement. Miss Watson was small, moustachioed and grey haired, and it was rumoured that she really did use a pudding basin when her hair was cut. She was also extremely short-sighted and wore thick, pebble-lens glasses. She frequently lost vital pages of her MSS, and on one occasion I was, in my innocence, extremely perplexed to find a collection of not nearly empty whisky bottles in the bottom of one of her manuscript cupboards, when I had been deputed to find some vital nursing diagrams in her absence. I mentioned this later to Rowley who seemed not at all surprised.

Rowley left Faber's in 1950 in order to set up the Westerham Press, which eventually became one of Britain's, if not Europe's, most technically advanced, fine quality printing houses.

Berthold Wolpe on the other side of the room was Faber's in-house jacket designer and he also designed most of the binding brasses, as well as the occasional particularly important book. (Towards the end of my career I was allowed to design a few brasses too.) Berthold had joined Faber's in 1941 from the Fanfare Press where

I frequently photographed Berthold Wolpe when he needed portraits of himself for overseas typographical journals. Here is a card of himself he sent me in return.

he had designed a remarkable range of ornaments and little-known type faces such as Tempest and Cyclone. He had also been responsible for designing the display faces Albertus and Pegasus for the Monotype Corporation, and Hyperion for Bauer's type foundry in Frankfurt in the mid-thirties, having studied lettering and type design under Rudolf Koch. He was a brilliant letterer and his powers of invention never ceased to amaze me, but he found it difficult to keep to schedules and worked the strangest conceivable hours. He usually arrived in mid-morning; then had a late but enormously long lunch hour, mostly spent hunting for rare books, particularly examples of early lithographic printing, and then stayed behind for hours, long after we had all gone home. One of Berthold's problems was that he had to show every jacket design to Mr Crawley, the sales director, for approval, and Mr Crawley did not arrive at the office until four o'clock in the afternoon because he did all his detailed paperwork at home. Therefore one usually found poor Berthold hanging around Mr Crawley's office waiting to see him from tea time until we all left.

Miss Randall's desk was right next to the door. She was a large young lady, with strong left-wing views and supported some political theatre group, which seemed to involve all her working hours when she was not at Faber's.

It was Arthur Thompson who had, surprisingly, allowed my entry into this select group. Arthur was a nephew of Dick de la Mare's, and suffered badly from asthma. It was his temporary departure from the department to go on an asthma cure in Switzerland that created a vacancy at a moment when the department's work load was particularly heavy. Arthur's journey to Switzerland took place at the exact moment when I had informed Geoffrey Faber that I did not feel that I could continue to work with Kurt Maschler. When I asked him if he, perchance, knew of any other vacancies in publishing, he came back with the reply that if I would like to help out in his own production department during the four weeks when Arthur was in Switzerland, it might be useful experience for me. I jumped at the chance and reported for duty at precisely 9 am on the following Monday morning. Nobody had told me that work didn't officially start until 9.45 am. I was put to work cutting up blockproofs to prepare a paste-up for the pages of one of the first in a new series Faber's had recently started of monographs on pottery and porcelain. The book in question was *English Delftware* by Professor F H Garner. It was to play an important role in my life, and Professor Garner not only became a friend but also introduced me, some years later, as a member to the English Ceramic Circle. Arthur Thompson's asthma cure turned out to need not four weeks but twelve weeks. And after three months of extremely hard work and able tuition by David Bland and Rowley Atterbury, I was beginning not only to grasp the essentials of typography and book production but also to enjoy the work and to realise that this was a career I wanted very much to continue.

I was getting very anxious about what would happen to me after Arthur's return. Nobody seemed to want to discuss the matter with me. Eventually I plucked up the courage to ask David Bland about it. 'Oh,' came the memorable reply, 'if you can find yourself a desk somewhere, you can stay.' I found myself a desk and stayed eight years.

So it came about that I found myself sitting next to Arthur Thompson for some years. He lived in a dream world: a slight, delicate, sensitive, gifted person who found it difficult to cope with the practical things of life. He wrote poems in a post-Eliot fashion as well as dreamy novels which he had the greatest difficulty in getting published, despite his trade connections. Eventually, some years after he left Faber's, Gollancz brought out one to the delight of all his friends. Arthur was a latterday Denton Welch: the dilettante personified, and yet whenever anyone saw him out of the office he was accompanied by the most beautiful girls. They obviously found his remote persona and his deepset grey eyes fascinating and invitingly attractive. He died at an early age soon after I had left Russell Square.

Our team was completed by a departmental secretary and a remote member of the staff who played a significant role in our lives.

This was Miss Swann. A tiny, dumpy lady of uncertain years who sat just by Faber's entrance in 24 Russell Square and doubled up as receptionist and telephone operator. It has to be remembered that, in those days, any outgoing or incoming call had to go through Miss Swann's switchboard and it was only she who could obtain any number we wanted. It also has to be remembered that there were probably no fewer than sixty members of the firm's staff who wanted to use the telephone. So in retrospect one can see Miss Swann's difficulties. But the greatest impediment to an effective use of the phone – the most vital instrument in the production department – was Miss Swann's insatiable curiosity. She had to know precisely what was going on in every part of the firm, and even listening only to snatches of other people's conversation seriously impeded the dialling – or even recalling – of numbers that we in the production department desperately needed. It added to the spice – and frustrations – of life. My suggestion some years later that we should have a direct line in the department for the sake of greater efficiency was considered outrageous, and Geoffrey Faber himself sat on it for many months. In the end David Bland boldly decided to ignore higher authority and our life became a lot easier.

Miss Swann knew everybody who was anybody in the literary world. She had a fabulous memory for facts and faces, and many of Mr Eliot's famous poetical friends looked upon her as a confidante in their troubles. I always regarded it as a great loss to publishing history that Miss Swann never wrote or published her memoirs.

In order, at least in part, to overcome the problems of telephonic conversations, our suppliers, the printers and binders, called on the production department with great regularity. The representatives were mostly people with interesting personalities and were passed around the department like parcels in order to discuss with each of us the problems on the books for which we were responsible.

The Reverend E O Beck was our most frequent visitor in the early post-war days. He looked after the interests of Latimer Trend and Bowering Press, both of Plymouth. He was what was called a 'print farmer', that is he was a commission salesman for firms who employed him. Mr Beck often came up with new names of firms he persuaded us to use, but this was rarely a success in view of Faber's pernickety demands for high quality, and these newcomers usually dropped out very quickly.

Latimer Trend, in fact, was owned by Faber's. Printing capacity too was well below the demands made on it by book publishers during the war and so Trend printed a high proportion of our books. They were cheap and efficient and run by a brilliant elderly ex-comp called Mr Williams, whom only later in life I recognised as one of the world's organising geniuses. He never fussed; he frequently did the impossible, and he always remained good tempered. The fact that Trend's worked for a good many other publishers never seemed to cause us any problems. This was probably due to the Reverend Beck's diplomatic skills. So they were a most important adjunct to Faber's publishing capacity: in total contrast, one has to say, to Fine Art Engravers.

The Bowering Brothers printed the occasional book and most of Faber's jackets. Faber's owned a small stake in the firm (so did Mr Beck) together with the two immensely tall, ginger-haired brothers. The one who ran the works we were rarely allowed to see, or even talk to. To this day I am not certain whether he really existed. The Bowering brother we did see was full of funny stories, extremely fond of the bottle and really came to discuss progress over printing jackets with Berthold, but in view of Berthold's unpredictable lunch hours, we often had to 'entertain' Mr Bowering until Berthold arrived.

In my early days Mr Beck also acted on behalf of Western Printing Services, a West Country firm located in Avonmouth outside Bristol where they were housed in a series of First World War wooden sheds. Run by another totally unflappable manager, Mr Manley, WPS had remarkably high standards of typesetting, proof reading and, particularly, machining. For this reason they were obviously more expensive than Trends and we were not allowed to send them more than a few titles at any one time. The entire factory was destroyed by fire in the early 1950s, a matter which involved one of my authors in something of a personal trauma. L A Wilding was senior classics master at the Dragon School in Oxford. Faber's had decided to enter the educational market and had persuaded him to write a *Junior Latin Course*. This he had done, and because of the special vowel sounds and of the book's complicated typographical structure, he had written the whole thing out in an exceedingly neat hand in blue and red inks. So there was only a single copy of the manuscript. I had spent a long time studying existing Latin text books, and then designing a simple, easily intelligible but good looking layout. Both the MS and my elaborate layouts went up in smoke in Avonmouth. The author took the blow amazingly well and set about re-writing the book at once. In fact, he was charitable enough to say that the second version was an improvement on the first. To my amazement his own domestic insurance policy covered the disaster and he got a small payment in compensation from them. The book went into many editions after the first printing and stayed on Faber's list for years, though the adventure in educational publishing on a bigger scale was soon abandoned.

MacLehose were our grandest printers. Also called the Glasgow University Press, they were still family owned and controlled. They were much slower, more complicated to deal with and vastly more expensive than any of our other suppliers but their quality was high and, for some reason which none of us ever understood, Dick de la Mare was prepared to tolerate all this. When it came to arguments about invoices, and particularly the cost of corrections, he often took up the cudgels with the Glasgow office himself, his only direct form of involvement in all our myriad activities. We often thought he did so because he was the only person who could, from years of earlier experience, understand the complexities of MacLehose's estimates. Day-to-day matters in Glasgow were dealt with by Donald MacLehose; really serious matters became the province of John Easton, a great philatelist and author of two books on the subject that Faber's had published. Only once during my time at Faber's the chairman of the company, the redoubtable Hamish MacLehose, a tall, impressive and dignified old man, said to be closely related to the Macmillan family, called on us in person. As he entered the room, David Bland asked all of us to STAND UP, which we solemnly did as he went round shaking us each by the hand and then departed for lunch with Dick de la Mare. It made a deep impression on me and puzzled me greatly. No one was prepared to explain this degree of reverence. But it did occur to me years later that publishers had had to woo and wine and dine their printers to get any work done at all during the war, and though MacLehose had certainly worked for Faber's for many years, perhaps this was a hangover of respect from those difficult wartime days.

There was no doubt in our minds why Faber's used Purnell's of Paulton. Their capacity was enormous; their prices were reasonable and they had been able to help Faber's out during the war with extra supplies of paper. Paulton had been a small Somerset mining village. Soon after the First World War the mines had closed and a brilliant Bristol accountant, Wilfred Harvey, had bought up the tiny local stationer's and printing shop there, and with the help of government grants had turned the ex-miners into printers and built up a vast and busy plant. We dealt with various younger members of the Harvey clan and they were friendly and efficient. Theirs was really the only printery we dealt with who could cope with long runs for the occasional best-selling novel, and they could bind with amazing speed. The London representative was an ex-England rugger player called Clifford Gibbs, another brilliant salesman, though one was slow to realise that he was actually selling; he larded the conversation with so many extraneous matters. He was a lay preacher for a sect with a strongly evangelical bent. It always seemed to me an excellent outlet for his persuasive powers.

Books originating in America, of which we published many, were usually reprinted without alteration except to the prelims, by our two photo-litho printers, Pitmans and Bradford & Dickens. There

could not have been two more contrasting outfits. Pitmans was part
of the shorthand family's empire. Their London representative was
Ivor (Peter) Parley, a hard-drinking, fast-living character who drove
the first ever Mini Cooper, a hotted-up version of Mr Issigoni's original Mini car. He was completely out of my league. Pitmans were in
Bath, regarded Faber's as a difficult, marginal customer and there
were always problems over punctual deliveries. Bradford & Dickens, on the other hand, was a self-effacing, easy-to-deal-with outfit
in Northampton, represented by the very serious, moustachioed Mr
Bradford who found print selling a little below his dignity. He collected antiques, particularly Chinese porcelain, which established a
kinship and I enjoyed dealing with him.

Shenval Press of Hertford was an organisation like no other, nur-
tured to success, if not actually founded, by a charismatic individual
with a strong Scottish background who has rarely received the credit
due to him in the printing world. James Shand had brilliant entrepreneurial gifts; he was far-sighted and, more than any other printer
we dealt with, he appreciated and cared about good design. He had
a flair for recognising talent in the most unexpected places, and relations with James were stimulating to a degree exceeding all other
suppliers. But it was not all milk and honey. Getting a book produced by the Shenval Press required a very special approach. First,
the money side: Shenval's initial estimate was always much too high.
The firm dealt with a host of advertisers who didn't control their
costs as tightly as Faber's. So the book was sent to another printer,
who quoted a much lower price. One would then confront James
with his estimate and the other, and a compromise would be reached.
The important thing was to get this confirmed in writing otherwise
it would not count.

Faber's got specimen pages for every book we put in hand to show
all the typographical variants, like chapter heads, footnotes, headlines, cross heads and the correct type size, leading and type area.
When we passed the specimen page in due course we specified the
inside and the head margin before (and after) the binder's trim. The

generality of typographical specification and instructions were included on an enormously detailed, pre-printed form (of which we
kept a carbon copy) which had been evolved by Dick de la Mare and
David Bland over the years. It was a wonderfully economic and concise way of giving instructions and, under a careful production
assistant, it brooked no divergences or errors.

The Shenval Press never followed our instructions in detail. James
would say 'We thought this was an improvement'. It often was, and
I, for one, was pleased to be corrected. A precise printing schedule
followed the approval of the specimen page and the printer's estimate. The costs quoted had, in the meantime, been incorporated
into a complicated in-house estimate form for varying printing numbers, with the addition of paper, binding, jacket, illustrations and
any other costs. This would have been scrutinised by David Bland,
and subsequently by Dick de la Mare. A final printing and binding
number, the retail price, break-even point and profit would then have
been calculated and the combined factors approved (or not, as the
case might be) by the Book Committee. The whole process took
many weeks, partly because Dick de la Mare did not come into the
office on Mondays and only occasionally on Fridays, and David Bland
found it difficult to have his weekly conference with Dick. In his
three days in the office, Dick had to attend the Book Committee,
which took up most of a Wednesday, and interview binders and
papermakers (he insisted on ordering every sheet of paper we used
himself), as well as many authors and overseas publishers. He also
kept up a vast and voluble correspondence. Dick de la Mare wrote
the most wonderfully cogent, detailed and lucid letters of any publisher I have encountered in my long career in that world. He
managed to do so by the use of complex dictaphone equipment at
home and by thinking about the letters (he once told me) during his
long drives back to Much Hadham from Russell Square (in an ancient open sports car, a 1930s Lagonda). Because of this unpredictable
and lengthy time lag, we could not get schedules of proofing and
printing details from our suppliers until everything was approved.

So getting these details involved another period of waiting. Shenval promised dates which had to be taken not with a pinch, but with a large bran tub of salt. It involved dealing with the wholly delightful but elusive Fred (F W) Atterwill, Shenval's works manager.

Shenval were not bad in their timing of producing proofs: the obstacle was getting the sheets actually printed. All our suppliers sent us monthly work returns of progress with the titles entrusted to them – which we then incorporated onto our own work returns. These printers' schedules were kept on a bulldog clip hanging on the side of David Bland's desk and were our most important working tool. Shenval had invented a wonderfully meaningless phrase which they continually used, saying that a book was 'at machine'. This meant that the proofs of the book had all been passed for press and that the type had been corrected and that they might start machining when the spirit moved them. It could involve any period from two weeks to six months. This particular form of frustration was the reason why one could not afford to send Shenval more than one or two titles at any given moment. Although there was another final hurdle to cross.

Shenval's invoices for a book bore only a marginal relation to their agreed estimate. The composition price would have gone back to James's first – and not the revised, compromise – estimate. It was Fred Atterwill who taught me the art of polite, good-tempered haggling. I would have to spend hours on the telephone arguing with him, until we got the price back to the one on our house estimate, but allowing for a small extra sum which we had already included as the 'Shenval Factor'. But when all was said and done, books printed by Shenval achieved a quality in their composition and machining which only MacLehose could approach.

While we stuck to this limited selection of favoured suppliers, David Bland was granted the luxury of using more *recherché* and famous firms from time to time. Thus that magnificent lithographer, T E Griffits of the Baynard Press, was a not infrequent visitor to the department, because when Barnett Freedman did a job for Faber's –

whether it was a jacket, a Christmas card or a special endpaper – only Tom Griffits was able to print it. Occasionally, highly illustrated books would go to Lund Humphries or Balding & Mansell. And in one or two exceptional cases, Herbert Simon came in to talk about a Rolls Royce job that the Curwen Press would print for us. The nursing books would often go to Clays of Bungay and Clowes of Beccles. In fact, through the brilliant salesmanship techniques of little Willy Clowes, they eventually became one of our regulars. A man whom I greatly enjoyed dealing with was Alan Steel of Butler & Tanner. God knows how Alan had drifted into becoming a printer's salesman. He had in his early days owned a book shop, Joyner & Steel in South-ampton Row, and had been one of the early publishers of D H Lawrence until he got into trouble with the authorities for import-ing some of Lawrence's prohibited books from Italy. Alan Steel was one of the most talented and memorable gossips in the literary and production world. He usually knew long before anyone else who had had a row with whom, who had been fired and what better jobs could be had. He always promised to write his memoirs after his retirement but never did so, perhaps because they were too libellous for publication.

Last but certainly not least among the regular visitors to the pro-duction department were the bookbinders who worked for us. We would keep them abreast of the progress of titles which they knew they would have to bind. We, or Dick, had usually suggested them when it came to preparing the house estimate for a book. We had enormously detailed schedules within the department from which we could calculate precisely what the cost of binding a book in any of the standard sizes would come to. We took into account the length of the text (calculated as the number of sixteen or thirty-two page signatures); the number of pages of plates that had to be included, how and where they were to be wrapped round or inside signatures; the weight of boards; the sort of cloth and its cost per yard; whether we or the binders would supply the endpapers; in how many col-ours and what material the brass was to be blocked on the spine (and perhaps the front board). We still used real gold foil on most of the expensive titles; whether the book was to have a plain top, a colour-washed top or, very occasionally, a real gold top, and any other of a multitude of variations that would crop up.

A matter which Faber's took extremely seriously was the quality of the 'rounding and backing' of the spine, and the prominence of the grooves between the boards and the spine. Dick hated square backs, a cheaper form of binding, and I remember Rowley Atterbury's delight when Dick had permitted him to have a square back on some specially abstruse title. This passion for our traditional form of binding and the hatred of any alternatives (like square backs) meant that for years Faber's rejected any book bound on the continent. The consequence was that such titles, which were part and parcel of a most important development in publishing, the European co-edition, which most often originated at the annual Frankfurt Book Fair, passed Faber's by for many critical years to the particular chagrin of Morley Kennerley, who regarded them as an easy and useful way of making money.

The two binding firms Faber's used most extensively were James Burn of the Royal Mills, Esher, and Leighton-Straker, whose works were in North London. The Burn's representative, Lionel Darley, later a director of his company, who died as recently as 1991 in his mid-nineties, was the most enchantingly sympathetic person who crossed our path, and mornings would be cheered up by his prompt arrival at 11 a m. Physically, Lionel Darley was small and looked exactly like a humanised version of the portrait of Mr Punch that used to appear at the head of the contents page of that magazine. Every utterance he made seemed to express surprise at whatever he was recounting. Binding was a slow business. At that stage, capacity nowhere near matched the demands made on it. Wartime bombing had destroyed many binders' works, including those of James Burn. There was a desperate shortage of materials, machines and, indeed, people to work them. Binders found themselves in the galling position of having to reject profitable new orders because they had literally mountains of uncompleted, often unprofitable, backlog orders.

The absolute minimum time for getting a book bound at Esher was four weeks, but twelve weeks was nothing out of the way. This would play havoc with our schedules and Faber's publishing plans, but Lionel took all the criticism in good part. 'I'll see what I can do' was his favourite phrase. He much preferred to discuss the merits of the latest of the Sitwells' autobiographies, which he would read before anyone else because he also bound books for Macmillan who published them. Indeed, his firm had been binding books for Macmillan regularly since 1851. He was also a great Maurice Collis fan, an author whom we published, and for some reason Lionel had made a detailed study of Somerset de Chair's long biography of Napoleon. This had originally been published by the Golden Cockerel Press, but we published a revised edition. To me it seemed that he knew most of Dickens and Hardy by heart. It was his enthusiasm that fired me to read their works myself, and the same went for other of his favourites: Compton Mackenzie, Charles Morgan, Siegfried Sassoon, E M Forster and Michael Sadleir.

He had taken up hand-binding as a hobby late in life in order, he would cheerfully explain to us, to have a better understanding of what the works were up against. He later bound some of my antiquarian bargains most beautifully in particularly refined buckrams but would never accept payment for the work.

Occasionally matters with Burns would reach a crisis point. Dick de la Mare and David Bland became tired of trying to apply pressure to the works at Esher where the formidable works manager, Mr Freshwater, ruled supreme. For some reason I had got on particularly well with this ferocious and permanently harrassed character on a visit to the bindery. I had made some casual suggestion for improving the 'flow' in the bindery, which had been put into practice and had achieved an improvement in time-saving out of all proportion to its apparent significance. I was therefore wheeled in to plead with Mr Freshwater for improvements of delivery. I always got myself very carefully briefed by Mr Darley beforehand. When something was achieved he would mutter repeatedly, 'I don't know how you do it, boy! I really don't know how you do it'.

For many years Lionel had been collecting information on the history of James Burn which had been founded in 1781. His reading towards that end was omnivorous. It included Trevelyan's *English Social History* and he would exclaim on the wonders revealed for months on end as he ploughed through it. Lionel wrote very slowly in a left-handed scrawl and the book was many years in the making, appearing finally in 1959 under the title of *Book Binding Then and Now: a Survey of the First 178 Years of James Burn and Company*. There was a generous acknowledgement to Sir Geoffrey Faber for practical advice and criticism 'which at a time of complete stagnation fired the project with new life'. Rowley Atterbury, in his new role as a printer, printed it; David Bland had designed it; Berthold had been responsible for the brass and the jacket. But the finest tribute was to Mrs E M (Ella) Hatt. 'If at any point the narrative achieves lucidity the hand of Mrs Ella Hatt may be suspected. She read the manuscript twice and though she failed to move it far towards sublimity, at least she earned my gratitude for nudging it a pace or two away from the ridiculous.'

Mrs Hatt was another important Faber institution. The widow of a Bristol journalist who died when their son was in his infancy, she had come to seek her fortune in London and had been employed by Faber's as their proof reader and indexer. Ella was an early victim of union intransigence. Both she and her husband worked at Western Printing Services. When he died unexpectedly, the union forced her to leave the company. It was Mr Manley, the manager, who had persuaded Faber's to employ her. She had a tiny office just beneath the roof in 24 Russell Square – not far from Mr Barclay – and almost every final proof of every book had to pass through her hands and receive her spindley scrawled initials in red ink before we were allowed to send it back to the printer. Her speed of reading was sensational and her genius at spotting literals amazing. Her indexes tended to be abbreviated. She loved to gossip, and visits to her office in order to collect vital proofs or to give her some forgotten element of a book, always proved informative and rewarding. She eventually wrote a successful series of illustrated books for young children which Faber's published.

George Paul from the binders Leighton-Straker came into the office much less often than Lionel Darley, and he had certainly not developed Lionel's proficiency in distracting one from the main issue. Indeed, he always seemed to expect the worst – criticism, ferocity, displeasure, the nearest thing to a whipping anyone could manage, and seemed to take positively masochistic pleasure in anticipating it. The consequence was that we felt so sorry for him that we laid off. One wondered whether it was simply another technique of achieving the same objective as Lionel Darley?

*

I have not, perhaps, stressed sufficiently how quality conscious we were at Faber's. Dick de la Mare had started a tradition for excellence before the war which had inevitably been dented by wartime hardships, and collectively we strove to get back to those standards. Unless we were under even greater pressure than normal, it was expected of us that we should have a pretty good idea of what our manuscripts were about. I had certainly read most of my books before I began to translate them into a typographic design. We all did our utmost to match a book's character with its physical presentation, and endeavoured to make certain that whoever bought the book got good value for money. Much of the procedure was, of course, standardised but we had a vast range of Monotype type faces we could choose from, and we were encouraged to use decorative material and typefounders' founts for display. We cared passionately about letterspacing, correct margins and impositions and took immense care over the sizing of all our illustrations and the way they were fitted into the text. Halftones, of course, were always – in those almost exclusively letterpress days – printed separately; so was colour. So one might well find that the text would be printed by printer A; the monochrome plates by printer B; the colour plates by printer C, and the decorative endpapers by printer D. We rarely used printer-binders (except Purnell's and later Clowes) so there was also a separate binder, a separate jacket printer, and a brass cutter (invariably Mackrells). We would – that is, Dick de la Mare would with Mary Grenside's assistance – order paper specifically for all these individual elements, so the logistical problem alone of getting all the disparate components of the book to arrive wherever they were required at the right time, took a good deal of organisational skill, and much of our time and energy were devoted to this.

The quest for knowledge on the typographical repertoire, on methods of design and the techniques of production did not stop when we were outside the office. I attended some fascinating evening lectures on these subjects at the St Bride's Institute and thoroughly enjoyed hearing one's idols, such as Sir Francis Meynell (of Nonesuch Press fame) or Beatrice Warde (she of the Monotype Corporation, who had posed in the nude so often for Eric Gill) speak of their experiences. We looked at every exhibition on book design and printing – and there were many at that time. I spent hours in the King's Library in the British Museum poring over early examples of fine printing, and – best of all – I managed to get permission for myself, David Bland and one or two others to use the magnificent reference library in Senate House just across the road. London University had a huge collection of books on all these matters that no one, except Faber's production department, seemed to use. Some of our finest decorative borders originated in some of the early 19th century typefounders' specimen books, which we were allowed to borrow and photograph.

I also collected every new book even remotely concerned with book production, printing and publishing, as it was published, and bought the earlier classics in the field when I could afford them. I began to write odd articles on the subject, and David and Berthold were asked to give public lectures from time to time which all of us in the department religiously attended. I found them particularly interesting because they revealed David Bland in quite a different light from the character I knew so well in the office. He would display a light-hearted authority and certainty which the hazards of daily hassle in the office didn't permit.

Within the department we were incredibly self-critical. Everything was scrutinised and commented on. It could be heartbreaking but it was healthy. David Bland was pretty tolerant. The most he would say was 'I should try this', having looked at a very satisfactory but perhaps rather more stereotyped version of what one had contrived with infinite care, but not total success, and of course it worked. We all tried hard never to repeat ourselves, to be original within severely limited constraints, to avoid formula design. But being different could lead to clumsiness, and one hated nothing more than a little pencilled comment from Dick de la Mare on one's specimen page saying 'Try 11/12 pt Garamond' when one had gone to great pains to use Walbaum effectively, or 'The rule is too fussy'. I once risked a face-to-face confrontation but got nowhere at all, so it was not an experiment I ever repeated. Dick never once commented favourably or with pleasure on a finished book that had come out well and he had an amazing facility for asking questions which threw one into confusion, even when one had prepared oneself most carefully for a meeting with him.

It was only many months after I had left Faber's that David Bland told me how much Dick had lamented my departure because he thought it would take years to train up another designer in the Faber ways.

The world outside generally did appreciate that Faber books were well produced, though I was sad that book reviewers hardly ever commented on this. But there was an annual testing place which we took very seriously: that was the National Book League selection of the best books of the year (in a design and production sense). Faber's figured prominently in this annual selection and I can remember even now my *frisson* of sheer delight when David Bland told me that one of 'my' books had got into the exhibition. In 1947 there were twelve

Faber titles among the 76 chosen. Walter Lewis, printer at Cambridge University and that year's adjudicator, commented that over 800 books had been submitted by 101 publishers. In 1952 there were only fifty British books among selections from a host of other countries. Interesting, incidentally, that the then rates of exchange were quoted to explain foreign book prices: these were DM 11.70 to the £1 and 12.18 Swiss francs to the £1. How the mighty have fallen, when one considers that English money is worth only one-fifth now of what it was worth in Switzerland then!

Faber's firmly, and rightly, rejected the increasing pressure from various 'outside' sources to include the house designers' names among other details given in the catalogues of each of the design exhibitions. We all felt that this anonymity was perfectly correct. Although we had had a major share in the design and production of individual titles, the total effort was very much a case of team work involving Dick de la Mare, David Bland, Berthold Wolpe and a good many others.

It gave me great pleasure to be chosen as one of the three selectors some years later (in 1968). We chose 155 titles out of the 950 submitted. We included nine of Faber's; Cambridge was down to four; Oxford and Clarendon combined were up to thirteen; my own company, Methuen, had thirteen also (chosen, of course, by my fellow selectors and not by me!): the Faber lessons had been well and truly learned – and put into practice.

Faber's collective judgement of the commercial merits of the material submitted to the firm seemed to me rather rigid and, in consequence, sometimes fallible. I very soon became interested in the editorial process, and with Morley Kennerley's help and a few snide asides from Polly Perkins, began to be allowed to 'read' MSS on which reports were needed. At first it was largely novels originating in America, but when the directors discovered that I was bi-lingual in German, a good deal of the increasing stream of books emanating from Germany came my way as that publishing industry recovered. But my advice was rarely heeded. Dick de la Mare didn't like the look of Martin Hürlimann's *English Cathedrals* which had been edited by a Swiss friend of my father's. It became one of Thames & Hudson's very first major successes. Similarly, a French volume on Picasso which I thought a particularly able summary of the painter's work was turned down because there had been other recent books on Picasso. That too joined the T & H list and frequently reprinted. One of the very few German war novels I recommended eventually finished on Michael Joseph's list and became one of that season's best sellers. A novel with a hospital background and a very strong story line, written by a young doctor with whom I played squash, was not considered up to Faber standards. At my suggestion the author did a lot more work on it and sent it to André Deutsch, who took it avidly, and it reprinted several times before it passed into oblivion. Conversely, books I condemned did get taken on. Thus we published a Swiss book on animal morphology with delightful drawings. I considered the text incredibly boring. It did well as a remainder some years later.

If all this was bad for Faber's it was good for me. It taught me in particular the difficulties of dealing with committees at a distance and the over-riding importance of commercial judgement vis-à-vis purely literary appreciation. However, there was one outstanding instance when my views were heeded and prevailed. In the course of my ordinary production work, a manuscript arrived on my desk that was the first work by the then unknown brother of one of Alan Pringle's literary friends, then also not widely known. The subject was the capture of rare animals for zoos in remote parts of Africa, and it seemed to me that the author was a brilliant raconteur. The suggested printing number was two thousand copies, which made it an expensive book. I pleaded that here was a book that would really sell in large numbers if we had the nous to push it properly. Old Papa Crawley read it and agreed with me. So it was submitted to the Book Society and became one of their monthly choices (which meant a sale of 30,000 copies in those days), and it reprinted regularly for many years. For all I know it is still in print. The author was Gerald Durrell: its title *The Overloaded Ark*.

In some respects Faber's had a well defined publishing philosophy. Titles had to be as explicit as possible. If there was a shadow of doubt about this precision, a sub-title was essential. I had that from Geoffrey Faber direct. I can see him now, elegant cigarette holder clenched between his teeth, peering over the rim of his glasses while pondering on the answer to some query I had presented to him. My contacts with him were so few that I suppose he remembered at such moments my anguished enthusiasm to learn about publishing before he had employed me. So he would make a special point of a few moments of general conversation about some aspect of the business.

Much more often I was intercepted by his extremely intelligent secretary, Constance Sheldon, who tolerated me with warm, maternal ferocity and typed whatever I wanted to say to the great man on a thin slip of paper, which was subsequently returned to me with a beautifully concise answer in his own hand.

Dick de la Mare's view (at that time, at any rate) was that it was one's duty to publish (non-fiction) titles principally if one had spotted a gap in the literature, either because the previous standard title had become wholly archaic or because the book described new developments or experiences, or because a subject needed a book on it. If an acceptable title on a subject already existed, Dick was most reluctant to consider another book on the same theme even if the proposed author was a great authority on it and a gifted writer. Publishing, in his view, necessitated originality. Often, in fact, this meant that Faber's would publish a book before the market was ready for it. Thus two books on the adventures of escaping prisoners-of-war and the bombing of the Mohne Dam were brought out by Faber's quite soon after the war. When precisely the same subjects were treated in a more popular way only a little while later as *The Wooden Horse* (Eric Williams) and *The Dam Busters* (Paul Brickhill) they sold by the hundred-thousands. Faber's versions had each sold about fifteen hundred copies.

I believe that while Morley Kennerley's attempts to break out of this rather rigid literary corset were often successful, it was only

Geoffrey Faber himself who did not regard such books as beneath Faber's literary dignity.

Often there were attempts to combine a subject with a particular author looking for a theme for his next book. Indeed, this led to some of Faber's most successful titles. In my later days there I had met – I believe through one of Margery Perham's stable of colonial civil servant authors – a High Commissioner of Cyprus (this was before the troubles started) and during some rather informal conversation at a party he told me that there was a need for a good Baedeker type guide to Cyprus. I sent a little note to Dick de la Mare. He brought it up at the Book Committee meeting. Pringle was deputed to deal with the matter.

Alan Pringle, an infinitely serious man whom one always suspected of having been born with grey hair, was another lonesome plodder who sat in a tiny office at the very top of the building. Like David Bland he had been on the firm's staff before the war. One of his tasks was to prepare Faber's seasonal lists. He collected all the blurbs, grouped them in the relevant categories and was always bothering us in the production department for information about the format of a book, its precise number of pages and what illustrations it was going to have – long before these things were known with any degree of certainty. Pringle trained me in the art of accurate guesswork: because by the time his catalogues were distributed to the outside world many weeks later, the guesswork was often established as fact and one was not supposed to make mistakes or there would be trouble from Mr Crawley's librarian customers.

Alan Pringle and I conferred upon the Cyprus guide. He thought that one of his particularly indigent authors might well be interested in tackling the project. He was, said Pringle, in any case looking for a subject to write on. I had brought along an old Baedeker and pointed out that a great deal of work, some of it hack work, would be required. Whoever took on the job would need a long time to do the leg work and would run up considerable expenses. Pringle thought £100 advance would cope with that. I was aghast. I enquired the name of the author Pringle had in mind: it was Law-rence Durrell. His last book for Faber's had been (I think) *Reflections on a Marine Venus*. This was long before the publication of *Bitter Lemons*. I was even more aghast. Pringle thought he would write to Durrell and put the idea to him. I never saw the reply, but in any case nothing much happened. The project went into limbo, but the Book Committee liked the idea of a guide to Cyprus and little prodding reminders kept coming to Pringle and myself. I then learned that the High Commissioner who had given us the idea was retiring and thought of writing the guide himself. But, and this was an emphatic but, he showed us a book on the antiquities of Cyprus published by Methuen's and he wanted us to enquire from Methuen's whether they would give permission to our ex-High Commissioner to utilise the historical bits he wanted to incorporate.

The reply from Methuen's was one of the most scorching letters I had then seen in my brief business career. The writer stated in no uncertain terms that Methuen's had no intention whatever of allow-ing our author to use the material in his book and if they found that there was even the faintest hint of plagiarism, they would have his guts for garters. The tone and crispness of the letter contrasted sharply with the relative gentleness of the correspondence that emanated from Faber's or came our way, and I was most intrigued by the character of the Methuen's director who had written it, one Peter Wait. I could have had no inkling then that I would be working closely with the said Peter Wait for many years only a short time later. The Cyprus guide never got any further. (Peter Wait, one of the greatest academic publishers of our time, died in 1992.)

Yet if I sound critical, the Faber publishing formula worked, and worked brilliantly. One book seemed positively to support another: people seemed to buy Faber books as such. Titles became classics and remained in print for years to come. Many of the pre-war books hung around for decades after the war with minimal revision and regular reprints. In the days when backlists really counted, Faber's had a wonderful and growing backlist. Old Papa Crawley saw to that. The word 'backlist' (and its importance) was in constant use when one talked to him. That and originality, the other key concept. The reading public liked originality, the avant-garde. New books really were a topic of conversation at social gatherings. Faber books always got reviewed: we could not understand why other publishers grumbled about lack of review coverage. We almost seemed to get too much of it. Even though the reviews were often acutely critical, they helped to sell the books and I continued to be amazed how often and how quickly reprints were called for.

But *how* they were sold, I never knew. The one aspect of our world about which I was almost totally ignorant was the sales side. From discussions within the production department we knew, of course, that Mr Crawley ran the sales side, but how he did so was a complete mystery, which we were not allowed to penetrate. Questions on the subject were not welcome. We heard occasionally that it was quite impossible for us to see Mr Crawley because 'the travellers were coming in'. The only traveller we ever saw was the delightful and very Welsh Mr Jones, who used occasionally to come into our office and ask for extra copies of jackets. Our Trade Manager, who ran the trade counter, Mr Wortham, he of the beautifully cut suits and hunched shoulders, who functioned somewhere to the right of our front entrance, often came in to see us on the same quest. But apart from the need for spare jackets for grumbling customers, no one was prepared to tell us how selling was organised.

*

Nineteen-fifty was a year of change. For one thing the production department moved. This represented a major upheaval – even though we only moved down a flight of stairs into the room below the one we had previously occupied, as it had been vacated by the accounts department. David Bland, knowing that my father was an architect, asked me to have a whole lot of special cupboards designed and made for each member of the production department so that at long last we would have somewhere to put the great multitude of papers which normally piled up below our desks for lack of space anywhere else.

Miss Randall had left; then Arthur Thompson departed to a cottage in rural Essex in order to write; Rowley Atterbury had already taken the plunge and set up as a printer. We acquired a new secretary who achieved fame later in life by marrying her brother (they were unrelated offspring of step-parents). There were a number of birds of passage who stayed only a season or so and moved on. Generally the workload was simply too much for them, or they could not cope in some other respect. Ultimately we were joined by three new members of staff who became permanent fixtures: Monty Shaw took Arthur Thompson's place; Michael Wright came as a book designer, and finally there was Patricia Robinson – the latter a striking girl with deep set eyes and a pert little nose, who made her entry into the office wearing very high heeled shoes and a huge floppy hat. Her initial function was to look after the nursing books and to chase up Berthold over the production of jackets.

David Bland had been made a director and now sat in a separate room next to ours, with Berthold beside him. But the unceasing pressure of work of the previous years was beginning to take its toll. David was frequently ill and finally stayed away for several weeks with shingles. I was left in charge in actuality, though this was not officially recognised until I was suddenly designated assistant production manager. This meant that the vital weekly liaison meeting with Dick de la Mare became my responsibility. This experience was like a series of advanced driving lessons: one learned to take corners at greater speed without going into a spin; life generally moved at an accelerated pace; co-ordination became paramount – not just co-ordination of my own lot of books but of everything that was going through the production department. Dick, of course, had seen it all before and knew precisely what needed to be done. He was there with advice when it was really needed, but he expected you to come to him with all the problems solved, or there would be heavy frowns and deep sighs. Despite all this, I thought he was a wonderful man.

But after a couple of years the fates caught up with me too. I was beginning to suffer from appalling stomach cramps that seemed to have no precise medical cause. I was consigned to bed for a month and it took me two more months to recover completely. I grew a beard and became engaged to Patricia Robinson, she of the high heels and floppy hats. Her parents lived near mine. At first she had visited me with queries from David Bland. Then her calls became less purposive and more social. We kept our engagement secret for some time after my return to the office. It was difficult at first, but later on we became such supreme actors that we called this 'frigid-in, passion-out' state of affairs 'Equity', after the actors' union. Little notes flew between us when sometimes we weakened, saying, 'Remember Equity'.

Just before I became ill there had been an honourable exception to Faber's inevitable rule of rejecting German books I had recommended for publication. I felt most enthusiastic about a relatively slight volume Morley Kennerley had sent me. Its title was *Die Unsichtbare Flagge* (*The Invisible Flag*). It told the story of a German army surgeon who had served on the Russian front for three years during the war. He

The author, temporarily bearded, seven years into his career at Faber's and about to embark on matrimony.

Turning Peter Bamms's classic into English gave me a lifetime's respect for translators.

had been in charge of a horse-drawn front line operating theatre. He had treated Germans, Russians, even civilians. The author had written it under a pseudonym, Peter Bamm, because he did not want any success the book might have to interfere with his professional career. Originally a series of broadcast episodes, the German edition became an out-and-out best seller while Faber's were pondering about whether to accept it. When the decision to go ahead with the translation was finally reached, I believe it was Geoffrey Faber who had suggested that I might tackle this while I was recuperating from my illness. I found the greatest difficulty in dealing with the multitude of obscure medical terms. I got wonderful help from my school friend, Robin Bannerman, who had become a doctor after training at St Thomas's. But it was really Patricia who provided the ultimate help when she discovered that the BBC had published privately a little German-English dictionary of medical and military terms at the beginning of the war. We spent a lot of time during our engagement puzzling out the text. Fortunately, the author was pleased with the translation after it had been brilliantly edited by Charles Monteith. Charles excised all the purple prose Peter Bamm had used, Patricia had not liked and I had so laboriously translated. The book sold quite well, and although it reprinted once it never became anything approaching a best seller. There was an American edition and Penguins later published it, but I was inordinately proud of it as my first publication.

It was a nice pat on the back when one day I had a letter out of the blue from the author, Len Deighton, saying how much he had enjoyed the book and liked my translation.

Faber's were very generous to us when we got married. Convention demanded that Patricia and I could not continue to work for the same company, so she left. My pay was raised spontaneously by £100 a year. Previously salary increases had come only as a result of a good deal of agitation. Many from the firm came to our wedding and we received memorable presents.

After house-hunting vigorously all over central London we eventually found a charming flat four minutes walk from Faber's. That too ultimately came to us through the book trade. Estate agents didn't seem interested in our plight, so in desperation I inserted the following advertisement among the classified ads in the back pages of the *Bookseller*: 'Impecunious young publisher about to embark on matrimony seeks somewhere to live at a rational rent'. It worked. We had only one reply and finished up supremely happy on the top floor of No 1 Bloomsbury Street. Our progressively superior landlords were, in reverse order of seniority: the formidable Margery Towers of Richmond Towers, a literary and advertising agency; Bob Lusty of Michael Joseph (our flat had been MJ's pied-à-terre during the war, and the basement and ground floor still housed MJ's packers, stock and trade counter), a mysterious and elusive property company owned by an East End furrier and, finally, the Bedford Estate. We came to know them all well, particularly when we had to obtain permission from them to install a skylight (at our expense) above the roof of a garret room, unused since the early nineteenth-century, in order to turn it into a nursery for our first born, Camilla.

Tourists' most popular view of the British Museum, but also my short-cut to Faber's from our Bloomsbury flat on wet mornings.

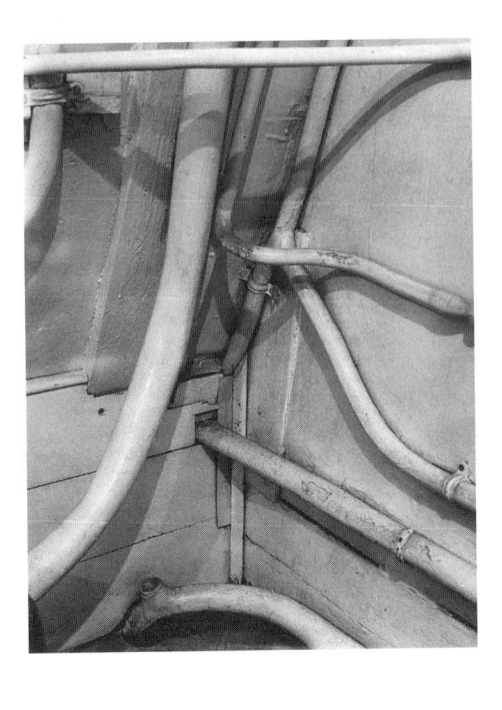

Our flat at No.1 Bloomsbury Street was a wonderful place in which to start married life, but the plumbing was primitive.

For some years I had been a member of the recently founded Society of Young Publishers. It was interesting to meet people from other firms doing the same or related work. It stopped one from feeling that our own activity was unique, though it also demonstrated that Faber's *did* do things differently. People in other production departments could not believe that we were responsible for the design side as well.

The Society met monthly at the National Book League at its splendid offices in Albemarle Street to hear the wise old men of publishing, as well as aspiring or distinguished authors. Thus on one occasion TSE addressed us on publishing poetry. It was then that he came out with the classic comment, 'If it doesn't *sing*, I am not going to publish it'. We also listened to a bright young man who had recently published a book with Gollancz which had caused something of a furore, called *The Outsider*, who told us calmly and with complete conviction how he was going to become the most brilliant and successful author of his generation. His name was Colin Wilson.

Anthony Forster, an editor on the academic side of Methuen's editorial team, became a particular friend. We met occasionally for lunch. One day he phoned to say that Methuen's only recently-appointed young production manager, Nigel Viney, had been snaffled by Shell for their public relations side, at some astronomical salary. Would I be interested in taking over his job at Methuen's? I had a two-hour interview with Methuen's MD, Alan White, during lunch time at Methuen's old offices in Essex Street. We didn't eat: we talked; not so much about book production as the future of the novel, and what the effect of Kingsley Amis and John Braine was going to have on it. At the end of our discussions, which I thoroughly enjoyed, I was not in the least certain where I stood. 'What would you like me to do?' I asked. 'Oh, I'd like you to join us as soon as you can. How soon will Faber's let you go?'

I joined Methuen's as production manager a month later (in 1956)at a salary fifty percent higher than my Faber pay, £1,250 a year, *and* a pension. It seemed riches.

I was sad to leave Faber's, particularly to part from David Bland. He had been the most congenial teacher, much more by example than by direct instruction, and my eight years at Faber's had been the most marvellous training ground for a career in publishing. Many people there remained friends for years to come. Dick de la Mare became Camilla's godfather and continued to sigh whenever I saw him from time to time and explained what I was doing, and that Methuen's was flourishing.

In these days, when the publishing landscape changes almost weekly and a man will achieve promotion or get a better job elsewhere at a higher salary because he has found one good author or thought of one good series cover design, the post-war Faber world is almost unimaginable. Our loyalty and commitment to the firm were total. Many of us bubbled over with ideas which the management filtered out to suit its own ideas and image. So much that was worthwhile was discarded and rejected that I was able to use it in my next job for several years after I left. Faber's were generally pleased that they had been put into practice. David Bland rang up quite frequently to discuss them: his difficulty was to get Dick de la Mare to accept them.

Our final memory of Faber's had a special enchantment: David Bland had asked Patricia whether she would be prepared to undertake editorial work on difficult manuscripts in a freelance capacity. We liked the idea and soon Patricia's desk in our flat at No 1 Bloomsbury Street was piled high with Faber work. This involved frequent visits to 24 Russell Square even after our daughter Camilla was born. Patricia would wheel the pram across Russell Square and leave it outside Faber's front steps, and ask Miss Swann to keep an

Patricia, freelance editor, at work in our flat.

eye on Camilla while she went inside (such was the tranquility of the times!). After a particularly prolonged visit on a wintry day, Patricia came downstairs to find the *pram missing*. Panic! Miss Swann was endlessly on the phone. 'Where has the pram gone?' Patricia at last shouted. 'Oh', said Miss Swann, 'Camilla had kicked off all her blankets when Mr Eliot came by on his way out to lunch. So he tucked her up and is pushing the pram round the Square.' Pram pushing was not a role in which one easily envisaged Mr Eliot. We often wondered whether the experience was a vicarious substitute for unfulfilled parenthood. Camilla has been dining-out on that story ever since.

CHAPTER THREE

The Old Methuen's: 'Butter or Jam, Mr Hubner?'

The atmosphere at Methuen's could not have been more different. The offices were in Essex Street, just off the Strand. I was king of the second floor which housed the production department. The beginnings of the firm had been particularly fascinating. Its founder was a headmaster and owner of a small private school in Surrey who wrote successful text books. These were published by George Bell. But on seeing how well they sold, he began to think that he should publish them himself. He did indeed have the two gifts which are essential to the making of a great publisher: a flair for knowing what the public wanted to read and an outstanding mastery of organisation.

Thus, Algernon Methuen Marshall Stedman set up in business as a publisher on his own, at the age of thirty-three, in 1889. And when after a few years the publishing venture – which he had called Methuen & Company – became successful, he changed his name to Algernon Methuen and gave up schoolmastering. After five years he had done so well that he was able to move from his two little rooms in Bloomsbury to substantial offices in Essex Street. Not only did he buy back his copyrights from Bell, but he also discovered popular novelists, now long forgotten, such as E F Benson, Stanley Weyman (author of *Under the Red Robe*), Anthony Hope and, above all, Marie Corelli whose romances, although much despised by the critics, sold by the thousand. By 1911 the first printing of her *The Life Everlasting* was 100,000. Methuen also had on his hands an enormous success with Kipling's *Barrack Room Ballads*. Later, Arnold Bennett, Joseph

Conrad and Henry James were published under his imprint. These established his reputation for books of quality, even if such authors didn't produce run-away best sellers every time. Edgar Rice Burroughs with his Tarzan series, on the other hand, did, and brought enormous rewards. Later on, H V Morton's travel books became immensely popular, as did Methuen's extensive series of 'Little Guides' to the counties of England. *The Sacred Wood*, T S Eliot's first prose work, was another Methuen discovery. He had acquired it simply by writing to the author, c/o *The Times Literary Supplement*.

Methuen's children's list got off to a wonderful, but apparently unexpected, start with Kenneth Grahame's *Wind in the Willows*, and later became famous with A A Milne's *When We Were Very Young*, *Now We Are Six*, *Winnie-the-Pooh* and *The House at Pooh Corner*.

However, Sir Algernon (he was made a baronet in 1916) was cautious in a financial sense to a degree that would be called mean today. I soon learned two interesting examples of this outlook. There was a distinct paucity of filing cabinets in my department. The splendidly efficient, but slightly fussy secretary I inherited, Minnie Caddell, who had already worked for the firm in Sir Algernon's time, explained how he always felt that large, old envelopes, stacked and labelled in alphabetical order on windowsills would do the job just as well and take up less space. And on a famous occasion when another elderly member of my production department, Paul Hubner, was asked to tea at the Methuens' rather grand house along the River Thames somewhere in Surrey on a Sunday afternoon, Lady Methuen, on offering him thinly sliced bread, had asked, 'Would you like butter on your bread, Mr. Hubner, or jam?' Sir Algernon had died in 1924 and unexpectedly had left all his shares in the company to be divided among the staff. He also stipulated who was to be chairman and managing director. Thirty years after his death, his sense of method and the tradition of thorough-going efficiency were still clearly discernible throughout the firm.

The standards of design and production, however, had not moved with the times and remained largely as those of the twenties and early thirties. In my negotiations before accepting the job I had had the nerve to say to Alan White, the managing director, that I would only join Methuen's if I was going to be given a completely free hand over all matters relating to the design and production of the firm's books. To my astonishment he assented, and to his everlasting credit he kept his word. I soon discovered that in many ways such total responsibility made my job more difficult because I could not consult my colleagues over problems as they arose. I was supposed to know all the answers.

So the contrast between Faber's standard of book production and Methuen's was stark. It was as if the same product was being manufactured simultaneously in two quite separate time warps, fifty years apart.

In 1956, when I joined Methuen's, their publishing activities – unlike Faber's – were targeted much more towards the educational market in schools and particularly in the universities, though the firm also had a small general list, largely at that time of books on humour and travel. There was also, of course, the famous backlist of children's books, the keystones of which were A A Milne and *Wind in the Willows* – both vastly enhanced by the charm of Ernest Shepard's illustrations – and the more recent Laurent de Brunhoff's *Babar* books.

Although my shortlived immediate predecessor had begun to make efforts to change this, books were generally printed on bulky featherweight paper in the insipid typography of the twenties and thirties. My task was to design and produce the new books in a style more appropriate to the time, and more marketable. However, though the books may have looked drab, their authorship and scholarship was superb and widely admired.

I had a number of brilliant and unsung colleagues who made sure that what we produced was of the best. Peter Wait was the senior academic editor. I believe at the height of his career Peter published five new books by Nobel prizewinners in one publishing season. He was the talent-spotter supreme. Greatly venerated in the academic world, distinguished scholars were delighted to be published by him. He was a member of the Athenaeum Club. Indeed, this was the source of many of his authors. I was told by one such putative author that when he was being taken to lunch there one day by Peter, the conversation ceased entirely as they entered the dining room, with all eyes fastened upon Peter. He had joined the firm before the war in 1935 as educational manager and had made a major impact. Peter had bright blue eyes with a wicked twinkle; he was of medium height, with curly hair, and looked the ex-Wykehamist and ex-naval officer that he was. A man of great charm, he would get incredible efforts out of those who worked for him. Yet his own business methods were bizarre. He only dealt with what he considered important, and ignored the rest. His desk was a graveyard of the second best, which his assistants had to bury as best they could.

There is no doubt that the firm's high academic reputation was the result of Peter's shrewd eye for the scholarly book which had a touch of the innovative, and he liked it even better if it had an element of popular potential. This was particularly so in the case of one of his most successful discoveries, Konrad Lorenz, author of *King Solomon's Ring* and *On Aggression*. There was another side to Peter which hit me on my very first day with the firm. I wandered around the department in the evening to see whether anyone was still about. Just by the gloomy, green-tiled main staircase was a very large office where three young ladies toiled over binding orders and stock records. In a separate little glass fronted cubicle in one corner dwelt a refugee from the editorial department who occupied the floor below us. She was an enchanting, tiny, snub-nosed blonde and her job was to sieve the unsolicited manuscripts that poured into our offices day after day. Peter was sitting on her seat. She was on his lap and they were kissing passionately. I retreated silently and, I hope, unseen. It was nice to realise that there was a very human side to the firm as well as its august reputation. The lady in question later married a distinguished author and had a large family. When Peter's first marriage eventually broke up, he married our equally enchanting red-headed receptionist and the union was blessed with twins.

John Cullen was responsible for our general list, which included a good many well-known travel writers and novelists. But his real claim to fame was to build up a remarkable conjunction of contemporary dramatists at a time when writing for the British theatre reached a zenith perhaps unmatched in the twentieth century. Harold Pinter, John Mortimer, N F Simpson, Shelagh Delaney, Brendan Behan, Joe Orton, John Arden, Henry Livings were all our authors, and I remember an editorial meeting when it was decided to let another rising star go to Jonathan Cape because it would look bad if Methuen had a total monopoly in the field of drama. John was married to a lively French wife and was wholly conversant with the French theatre too. Thus, Jean Anouilh, Jean Paul Sartre and Jean Giraudoux in translation were all on our list, and later, with help from the indefatigable John Willett, John Cullen started a whole industry relating to Bertolt Brecht and his contemporaries.

The last member of the leading triumvirate was my own particular friend, Tony Forster, who had brought me to Methuen's. He understudied Peter Wait with a rare ability but concerned himself also at that time with our books for schools.

He had, in fact, first joined the firm as a school traveller just after the war but had handed this work over to an exuberant character called Peter Woolf. Of Hungarian extraction, Peter stated even then that he would become a millionaire one day – and indeed he did, even though it took him quite a few years. Remarkably, he later built up a publishing house specialising in medical atlases, which towards the end of his life he sold at great profit. His boss, Methuen's sales director, was Halfdan Lynner, half Danish, half Norwegian, a man of great charm and high intelligence, he was an excellent salesman and brought the firm into close contact with a number of notable Scandinavian publishers, like Politikens, whose books were all beautifully illustrated with coloured drawings: then a rarity. However, Halfdan and I didn't always see eye to eye.

My first task, of course, was to change the structure of the production department so that it could produce the firm's books in the style I wanted. Unexpected events hastened along what I had to do. A senior staff member, with years of service behind her, was one Miss Berry, a charming, level-headed woman, who bought our paper: a vital job in book manufacturing. She suffered badly from arthritis and had difficulty in getting about. Within a short time of my arrival she was diagnosed as having severe cancer. It was my first encounter with the disease, and on visiting her in hospital, I was appalled at how speedily this cheerful soul became a Belsen-like skeleton with staring eyes, who had the greatest difficulty in speaking. My visit to her in hospital was one of those seminal moments in life that makes one grow up. She never had time to explain the details of how she worked but it became clear that she had been unwell for much longer than she admitted. The drawers of her desk were packed with an almighty mess of unpaid bills and orders for the paper for books in the pipeline which she had never sent off. It was a nightmare. But there was no one to whom I could turn for help. Sorting it out was an education. At Faber's, as I have said, all the paper ordering had been done by Dick de la Mare. Any errors could be very expensive, though in those days book papers cost only £120 a ton: the price in 1999 was well over £3,000. But it was an awesome sight in a printer's warehouse to see how a small slip of paper that constituted one's order form resulted in several huge containers of material.

Clearly we needed new staff, and the angels were on my side. Within a few days of each other I found two girls with great gifts, if little experience. Both stayed with the firm for many years and became essential linchpins in the publishing process. Janet Hampden was the daughter of a distinguished British Council officer and had some training at the Central School of Arts. She had a methodical mind with the wonderful eye for detail that one needs above all else in book production, and she was an outstanding typographical designer at the same time. She eventually became my Number Two. Carol Somerset looked after the vast number of reprints that

Methuen's put in hand each year, and she and Janet soon shared responsibility for paper buying.

Next I found the first of a long series of graphic designers to tackle the all-important jackets for our books. It is little appreciated that jackets are a publisher's principal marketing tool, because the firm's travellers show them to booksellers in order to drum up the subscription, that is the first orders, for any new title.

Two of them turned out to be particularly competent and innovative letterers. First there was Madeleine Dinkel, whose originality often startled our conventionally-minded sales staff. She came from a family with strong graphic links: her father was at that time Principal of the Edinburgh School of Art. Later, Michael Harvey also joined us. A few years earlier he had taken an interest in the work of Eric Gill and this so fired him with enthusiasm for letter design that he had apprenticed himself to that supreme master of wood engraving and lettering, Reynolds Stone. While he worked for us, Michael began to design alphabets especially for our jackets. These were so effective that we could print them on white paper and laminate them. Lamination was then a new process by which a thin film of transparent acetate could be used to cover the surface of a book jacket. Michael's all-white jackets stood out in any display of books but they would not get dirty because of the lamination. It was a brilliant sales gimmick at the time, in the very early 1960s, but it was soon copied by other publishers and we had to think of something else.

It is slow work bringing about a major shift in the appearance of a long-established publisher's books, but with the help of my now very competent but young staff, we were persuading our principal suppliers that we really knew, *and meant* what we were asking for, and we would not accept fudged compromises. In retrospect, we were not always right, but slowly the book trade, and eventually even the odd reviewer, began to notice that Methuen's books were looking different, and they liked them better for it.

Within a short time of my joining Methuen's a concatenation of events began to occur which no one had ever envisaged. Only a year after joining the firm I was made a director. This was unusually fast by publishing standards. The transition from being an ordinary mortal to being a director of a company was considered a huge upward step. I told my father the news. He had been very lukewarm about my move from Faber's to Methuen's and I expected him to be scathing about the appointment, but in fact he was amazingly pleased. I realised for the first time that there was more to this status business than I had thought. But I soon came to earth at the first board meeting that I attended. The accounts were presented by our company secretary, L A Youthed, one of Sir Algernon's original appointments. I did not understand a word. My fellow directors all nodded sagely but made no comment.

Director of Methuen's: newly-appointed.

The chairman of Methuen's at that time was Sir Nutcombe Hume, a well-padded man with something of a bullet head, a trim little moustache, rubicund cheeks and an incisive manner which was friendly but a mite patronising at the same time. He was widely referred to as 'Nut', and much revered. He had been an enormous success in the financial world, having been founder of a London financial company, Charterhouse Trust, with a worldwide reputation. It remained independent until fairly recently. An interesting side light on 'Nut' was that he and I had been to the same school, Westminster. At one Old Boys' function we met his charming, but devastatingly outspoken wife. Where, we wondered, was her husband. 'Oh, Nut', she responded, 'is, as usual, talking to some of his important friends'.

However, with some trepidation, at the end of the board meeting I confessed to Nut that I had not been able to follow the significance of Mr Youthed's analysis of Methuen's financial state (pretty sound at the time), and could this be put across in a more appropriate manner for non-accountants? My confusion acted as a catalyst: most of my fellow directors understood as little as I and welcomed a simpler approach to the presentation of our results.

It was not long afterwards, in May 1957, that there occurred what was for me a totally unexpected development. Methuen merged with another long-established general publisher called Eyre & Spottiswoode, and a small, technical offshoot called Spon. The majority shareholder was a Colonel Oliver Crosthwaite Eyre. His family – who, incidentally, were Roman Catholic – owned the right to publish the Church of England's Authorised Version of the Bible and the Prayer Book. The only other presses that were entitled to do this were the University Presses of Oxford and Cambridge. The Eyre & Spottiswoode accounts, which even I could understand, showed very clearly that the firm had made very small profits in the past, and losses in the previous two years. The man who ran the company, Douglas Jerrold, was well known throughout the trade as one of the grand old men of publishing, but also as being particularly tricky and difficult to get on with. The Methuen board had not been consulted in any way, and the outcome was presented to us as *fait accompli* on the occasion of meeting Colonel Crosthwaite Eyre, who was to succeed Nut as chairman. We were informed that collectively we were to be known as Associated Book Publishers in the future, unless someone could think of a better name – but no one did.

It gradually became clear that the reasoning behind the move was to save Eyre & Spottiswoode money by merging the work of production, accounting and distribution with Methuen's, thus saving staff and reducing overheads. This is transparently obvious today, but was a relatively novel idea at the time. Production was to be the first foray into collaboration. I began to attend the weekly E & S editorial meetings so that I could become familiar with what they published. The first such meetings were exciting because E & S had just published John Braine's *Room at the Top*. This had become a runaway bestseller overnight and reprints were called for every few days. These were now my responsibility. It was the sort of event that publishers dream of.

But thereafter things began to get prickly. Douglas Jerrold was just as difficult as people who knew him had said, and he kept asking for the impossible. One of my difficulties was that he had made special arrangements with one book printer during the war, under the terms of which that firm printed a large proportion of E & S's books. But as the firm's charges were higher than almost anyone else that I used, it made E & S's books more expensive. When I abandoned the printer in question there was all hell to pay. But soon after this the firm concerned was bought by another printing company and the new owner sacked all *seven* joint managing directors. I was not the only production manager who had had problems. The brighter side of things were the two young editor directors of E & S, Maurice Temple Smith and John Bright-Holmes, with whom my colleagues and I eventually got on very well.

This was also the period when my personal life underwent considerable changes. There was no doubt that our charming little flat in Bloomsbury Street was not the ideal place in which to bring up our first daughter, Camilla. We had always to leave the pram on the ground floor and carry her up to the third floor. The pram had then to be concealed behind a large black cloth, so that our landlady, Marjorie Towers, who seemed to object to children on principle, would not be able to see it. Also, our car, a little Ford Popular, which we had been parking in a side street opposite our flat for three years, suddenly could not be left there any more without incurring a fine. It was time to move.

Patricia and I had always felt that we wanted either to live in Central London or outside in a rural area. We started house hunting. Every weekend we set off with a bunch of estate agents' descriptions. We eventually looked at 115 houses. There was a near-miss in Surrey. It seemed charming until my father, an architect, inspected it for us and discovered it to be riddled with dry rot. There was another on the Hertfordshire/Essex borders. This was a 16th-century house (we were only interested in period houses), but the cost of converting it for modern living was prohibitive. One day we were sent the wrong Sunday newspaper and discovered in it a house in rural Essex, which seemed to offer everything we wanted. Essex was a county we had shunned because the train service to central London was poor at that time, and because our friends said – quite wrongly, as it turned out – that people in Essex were not welcoming. It is true that the relevant estate agent in Chelmsford proved obstreperous but we persevered and found the house of our dreams: a black-and-white timbered house of the late 16th century which had been sensitively modernised, with a large walled garden surrounding it. After we had been shown round the house by the owner's eleven year old daughter, I said to Patricia, 'That's the house we must buy'. 'Oh,' she responded, 'I never thought of it like that. I just felt how lucky those people were to live there.' We reckoned we could just afford the upkeep if there were no instant major repairs. My father inspected it for us, as before, but to his chagrin (he didn't want us to live so far away), could find nothing the matter with it. In fact, he felt bound to praise it. He even approved of

The house of our dreams: we had turned down 114 others before this one hove into view.

its siting, by dint of which we got as much sunlight as possible. They knew what they were doing in the 1570s!

The owner needed six months in which to complete a new bungalow he was building himself. We waited and moved in on April Fool's Day in 1958. We have been there ever since.

The commuting turned out not to be as hazardous as we had feared. The cost of an annual rail season ticket from Chelmsford to London Liverpool Street, inclusive of parking, was £42. Today it is something over £3,000.

Two little cottages opposite our gates housed two brother farmworkers. When I mentioned to one of them that I intended to go up to London *every day*, he looked at me in astonishment. He had only been to London once in his life – and he didn't like it. It is true that at that time there were not many of us who ventured on that daily journey.

*

It was a period when publishing began to boom. The decline that had occurred in book buying after the end of the war had gradually disappeared, and there was an urgent need for new books in the school and university world, and rapid developments in the scientific world also meant more publications. On the general side, Methuen's drama list began to take off and there was an increasing demand for books of entertainment. Television was not yet a major factor. The result was more and more new titles each year, and our small production team had to grow to keep up.

Then a new threat appeared on the horizon. There had been vast changes in the printing industry after the war. Ancient machinery was replaced, or improved; methodology improved. The trade unions, who had a tight grip on the industry, did not like it. Their pay had not kept pace with the increased profits of the printing companies. There were fierce, protracted public arguments about pay which rumbled on for eight or nine months. It was quite clear to me that these would result in total deadlock and probably a STRIKE. No one could actually remember a total cessation of work in the book printing industry for a very long time, but this time it seemed inevitable.

I geared up the production department to fever pitch. New titles went through at a vastly accelerated pace. Printing schedules were cut to ribbons. We ordered vast quantities of paper for vital reprints of text books, months in advance of the normal academic requirement dates. The usual working hours went by the board: we worked late every night. I had told Alan White my fear that the strike would take place and he backed absolutely my intention to speed up the normal production cycles. This was not only for Methuen's, but for all our associated companies – Eyre & Spottiswoode, whose best selling element was fiction; Chapman & Hall, who published not only Evelyn Waugh but also their high-powered science and technical list; and Spon, whose very existence depended on an annually revised builders' price book.

Book stocks soared; our warehouses were bulging with titles. But we had overlooked the simple fact that all this activity would cost a great deal of money – nobody had ever heard of cash flow projections in those days – and suddenly ABP was faced with a cash crisis of immense proportions, which worried the bank and which the management could not understand. The ABP board met in bewilderment. But nobody bothered to ask me, the mere production manager, who had brought it all about with the best of intentions.

We were saved by the strike when it came. Most publishers were caught unawares. We had every important title in stock. I had even managed to get delivery of an Eyre & Spotteswoode Book Society Choice, which meant 30,000 extra copies, by their then best-selling author Joy Packer (their other best-selling author was Frances Parkinson Keyes). Our sales shot up. The cash rolled in. The production manager, only recently thought of as a liability, became a hero.

The strike lasted six weeks, and there was literally a total standstill throughout the printing and binding industry. I used the time by working in the Charterhouse offices, learning about accounts under the aegis of a charming man who became a long-term friend. 'Nut' would look in very occasionally to see what progress I was making. It was a period of tuition that stood me in good stead all my life.

One of the lessons that the strike taught us was that in future we would have to plan the time allowed for each stage of the production process for every title. There was no difficulty in doing this at our end: the problem lay in getting printers and binders to adhere to such agreed schedules on the one hand, and to persuading our commissioning editors to convince their authors to turn round proofs with corrections, within the agreed time. This discipline gradually began to become effective, and in due course gave the production department great strength. When I mentioned to Dick de la Mare, my former boss at Faber's, that I had introduced this total planning concept, he could only shake his head in disbelief.

CHAPTER FOUR

The New Methuen's:
Merger Mania Sets In

Despite such progress, there was an increasing feeling of disgruntlement among the working directors of Methuen's in the early sixties. We felt we were drifting with no clear-cut objectives and profits remained at a level which we felt should be much higher. The problem was that our managing director, Alan White, seemed to have become virtually invisible within the firm after our merger with E & S. He had entered trade politics in a big way. Ultimately, he became President of the Publishers' Association and was an active member of a vast number of other official committees. I suppose it should really not have been a surprise to us. Alan had been at Methuen's more than 25 years. He had steered the firm through wartime difficulties and peace-time upheavals. By dint of clever delegation to his principal editors, like Peter Wait and John Cullen, and heads of department like Halfdan Lynner on sales (later taken over by Piers Raymond), and myself on production, he had to do relatively little practical work apart from keeping in touch with a few select major authors like H V Morton, Chiang Yee and the ageing Wyndham Lewis. The greater world called – and out there another distraction existed: his brother, Sir Dick White, ran the British Intelligence Service at MI6. This fact probably explained a story we never knew whether to believe that before the war, Methuen's continental traveller who went round bookshops in Europe taking orders for our books, had been one of the very few members of British Intelligence to find out what was happening in Nazi Germany. In fact, he was a spy.

A close friend of Alan's was Bob Lusty. Bob had recently left the dynamic little publishing firm started by Michael Joseph (our flat in Bloomsbury Street, it will be remembered, was Michael Joseph's *pied-à-terre* in London during the war). He had foresaken Michael Joseph after some sort of internal bust-up. He had then become managing director of Hutchinson and was busy knitting together the multitude of imprints that Walter Hutchinson had created in his heyday. Lusty was a very good publisher. He was also a brilliant publicist. He invented a bull as a group colophon which brought great *éclat*. Part of his contract with Hutchinson's owners stipulated that he should have a car and his own driver. So Lusty was driven around in a chauffeured Bentley. Seeing this, Alan persuaded Oliver Crosthwaite Eyre that he (Alan) too deserved a chauffeured Bentley, and what is more, he acquired a defensive secretary at the same time. Thus getting to see Alan was like making an appointment with the Archbishop of Canterbury. One ceased to try. So there was minimal communication at the top. Methuen board meetings, which had at least served as a useful platform for occasional discussions of policy, virtually ceased. At their request, I drafted a memorandum to Alan, on behalf of my fellow directors, to say that we had only had six such meetings in thirty months, and that there was a strong feeling among us that we were, in consequence, drifting along in a rudderless – and not very profitable – fashion. We put forward a number of practical proposals to rectify the situation.

The consequences, or perhaps the reasons for this state of affairs, were not what we expected. One of the things that had alarmed us was that there had been a sudden, unexpected bid in 1961 for the whole of the ABP share capital from Howard Samuel, a property developer. As a vehicle for his bid he used the tiny firm of publishers, MacGibbon & Kee, which he had bought for a song not long previously. I was a great deal more opposed to this development than my fellow directors. I remember when a snowstorm marooned my family and me in Essex, and I had to phone all of them to stiffen their sinews. At one stage Mr Samuel upped his bid by 20 per cent but even then not many shareholders were tempted to sell out and there was immense relief when he collapsed and died after a heart attack while bathing in the Mediterranean on the day when his offer closed.

Two years had passed since that sequence of events. Alan had not really stirred: hence our disgruntlement and hence our letter. We were now informed, squashed into his office, and long after it was all arranged bar the signing, that there was to be another merger. This time with a firm, larger and much stronger than us, whose publishing was in no way similar to our own. It was quite clear that we were going to be the junior partners. What he had not appreciated was that in contriving this, Alan was signing his own, metaphorical death warrant.

Our new partners were to be Sweet & Maxwell, a long established legal publishing house with many subsidiaries (a lot of them overseas). The principal shareholder was a member of the original family, Maurice Maxwell (no relation to the notorious Robert Maxwell). Why they felt it a good idea to be lumbered with ABP never really became clear to me.

In the early post-war period of publishing, book-keepers became accountants. Now in the sixties accountants were to become financial directors. In the past many great publishers had been owner/ entrepreneurs with considerable financial acumen. Algernon Methuen had been one such; Geoffrey Faber another; Jonathan Cape a third. We were now entering an era when most publishing firms were run by managers who needed strong support on the financial side. This too was not surprising. The various divisions of publishing – editorial, design and production, sales and publicity (not then called marketing), administration and distribution were all becoming more complex, particularly as firms grew in size and had to be very carefully controlled to remain profitable. All this could easily, and often did, stifle the creative part of the whole process. Curiously enough, it was the problem of keeping the creativity alive in this whole new group that eventually fell to me. But in the first instance we were now of such a size that my colleagues and I had to learn how to become corporate animals.

Sweet & Maxwell were ensconced on three floors of an anonymous, multi-storey office block in New Fetter Lane, and very soon it was decided that Methuen's from Essex Street and later Eyre & Spottiswoode, who were still in delightfully old-fashioned offices in Henrietta Street, near Covent Garden, would both have to move to New Fetter Lane. This was Methuen's first uprooting for nearly seventy years. Apart from the general disruption, it also involved the shedding of over ten tons of old editorial files. These included the correspondence with the authors of our books going back to the beginning of the century. Among them were all the titles that had appeared in the famous Methuen monographs series: Sir Edward Appleton and Einstein had been early authors; the Arden editions of Shakespeare's plays, which had had distinguished literary figures as editors, and many others. I was heartbroken at this wanton destruction of our history and searched feverishly for some archival institution that might accept this invaluable research material as a gift, but no one wanted it. Today it would be greatly valued by any number of academic libraries only too glad to own such material.

*

As luck would have it, the final day of the move coincided with an official enquiry into a local Essex matter in which Patricia and I took a very strong interest. This was the extraction of gravel from the farming land around us, which was taking place on an ever-increasing scale. Farmland sold for £250 an acre; gravel-bearing land could fetch up to £3,000. It was not surprising that the landowners would be tempted. We discovered, in consequence of rich mineral seams, that our own and the neighbouring parishes already had several gravel pits within their confines. Together with a neighbouring friend, Humphrey Spender, a renowned artist and photographer (and brother of Stephen Spender), we appeared as objectors to a planning application for a very large, new pit. It was the first time that I had taken part in such a tribunal. They were superbly chaired by official government inspectors. Any one with views on the subject could speak. My knowledge of presenting the facts and coping with cross-examination by barristers employed by the applicants came only from the watching of television programmes. But because we had done a lot of homework, we won our case, though we learned the hard way that it was simply the first round in a protracted legal battle that would go through many stages.

We had not been impressed at the hearing by the performance of the County Council solicitor or by the representative of a body supposedly speaking on behalf of rural parishes. Our own parish council, whose meetings Patricia now occasionally attended, had also seemed reluctant to get involved in what amounted to the damage the proliferation of gravel pits could do to rural living. So after that first enquiry had finished, some of us who had been involved founded a body we called the Chelmer Valley Society to keep a watchful eye on future gravel proposals and to fight them if necessary. The first step we took was to make the BBC aware of what happening and a programme on the subject was duly prepared by the well-known producer, René Cutforth. It caused quite a stir.

Patricia: my stalwart support in times of trouble, district councillor as well as magistrate for many years.

Two years later it was suggested, first to Patricia and then to me, that we should stand for election to the parish council when a vacancy arose. The then chairman, and his father before him, had been the only chairmen for nearly seventy years between them: that is, since the passing of the Local Government Act of 1894! The present one didn't want us to stand. It meant, he said, holding an election, and no election had been held in our parish for twenty-seven years. In fact, most people thought we just didn't have elections in our local parish. It would mean a farthing on the rates, he explained, a gross extravagance.

We went ahead nevertheless and were elected. In fact, we both came top of the poll. I remained a parish councillor for over thirty years. I retired at one stage, but was asked to come back. In Patricia's case, the parish council work led later to a long and highly successful career as an Independent, that is a non-party political, district councillor. I acted as Patricia's agent and enjoyed the periodic canvassing in the elections that took place every four years. When people asked us what we stood for we said 'better communications': better communications, that is, between authority and the populace, which at that time were largely non-existent.

*

Communication was also the name of the game as we got to know our new partners in ABP. From my own point of view the most important was the then managing director of Sweet & Maxwell, John Burke. He took upon himself the role of putting right what Alan White had so long neglected. John was a large man with a little bushy moustache, stooping slightly because of a war wound. He would arrive in the office wearing a bowler hat, a long, dark overcoat, spats, and carrying a furled umbrella. Though, in contrast, he owned a Jaguar which he was said to drive aggressively and at great speed. He was not that far off retirement and, as a former barrister, having led Sweet & Maxwell to great heights, he cannot have been over-pleased to become enmeshed in a new side of publishing that was quite strange to him. In a very hands-on manner, he came round and talked to each of us at length and listened to our pent-up feelings on what we felt needed to be done; and generally he empowered us to do it.

The enlarged company meant that the production department had to look after additional imprints. In the next couple of years we reached a peak when we were responsible for producing some 600 to 700 new titles and over 300 reprints a year. In consequence, my design and production staff had now risen to thirty.

In most publishers' production departments, design and administration are separated, but I had learned from Faber's how much more satisfactory it was if the man or woman who designed the book also saw it through the press. I therefore created the position of 'bookhandler', who undertook both sides of the work. It was not easy to find suitably talented people for the job and usually it involved a great deal of training, but in practice it was very effective.

On my side of ABP we had to invent management as we went along. It was a process of continuing refinement, but by this period it had begun to work very well, largely because of the degree of planning that went into our work. The only factor outside our control was human bloody-mindedness. My production department dealt with some twenty commissioning editors – that is, people who asked authors to write books where it was felt that there was a need for them. They were responsible for relations with those authors until their books were published. Only one editor refused to conform to the very flexible system we had evolved; he always knew better; he always wanted exceptional treatment, and rushed off to senior management to get his own way. Today I would probably be ruthless and get him sacked: in those days we were kind-hearted and tried always to be accommodating. Long after I left he caused the company a really major disaster and was sacked. There was some debate afterwards why this decision had been delayed so long.

But ABP was simply one of many publishing firms that were growing rapidly and the recruitment of trained staff became a universal problem. Some years earlier a number of production managers from all round the trade had formed a little group – under the umbrella of the Publishers' Association – and we met monthly to discuss common problems. This group decided that it would tackle the training problem itself, because we realised that no outside institution would know as well as we did what was wanted. We organised a course of lectures on different aspects of the work and found ourselves swamped with applicants who wanted to attend. It fell to me to devise the first ever – or so we thought – exam paper for a test at the end of the course, which would constitute an informal but useful qualification. I thoroughly enjoyed the task, and indeed the correction of the exam papers. I remember once more discussing this with Dick de la Mare; he expressed surprise that my generation felt that book production was a matter that could actually be taught, and not learned on the job.

I began to notice another lacuna. We simply could not find enough talented young book illustrators for the work we wanted to put out, particularly in the growing educational field. We discovered that the great majority of illustrated books were entrusted to a small nucleus of established artists, who were coming under such pressure of work that it caused frequent production delays. We had also found that the few young artists who tried to enter the field were not able to meet the standards of competence or imagination we required. On behalf of the Production Managers' Group I wrote to the heads of twenty-five art schools throughout the UK, suggesting that there was a market for such work and that a limited number of students should be trained for it. I ought to add that I was fairly familiar with the ways of art schools because I had been, for many years, an official 'visitor', first to the West of England College of Art in Bristol and later to the Brighton College of Art. The job of a visitor was to pay occasional visits to these colleges and to comment informally on the work and standards of teaching as evidenced by the students' work, from the point of view of a possible employer.

My letter aroused great interest and back came twenty-three replies. In general, they were extremely constructive. A common thread among them was that most students with suitable graphic abilities went straight into advertising because the agencies paid much better than publishers; another, that objective, representational drawing had almost died out in the face of the popularity of abstract art. One principal wrote 'I have discovered that most students have drawn a piece of bark, or a fragment of twisted root, but never drawn a tree. They have made rubbings of brick, stones and timber, but have rarely or never drawn a building.'

We decided that the best solution was to organise a seminar to survey all aspects of book illustration and to discover whether the recently introduced National Diploma of Art and Design course provided the right training for this type of work. Some eighty people attended the one-day meeting at the National Book League. They included lecturers and students from the art schools, artists' agents, representatives of H M School Inspectorate and a host of publishers, mostly children's book editors and production managers.

I kicked off for the publishers, accepting the blame for poor payment, but explaining the economics of publishing which left a limited amount for the artists' fees. But I vigorously attacked art school teachers for failing actually to teach; for so rarely criticising the students' work; in allowing what some termed 'liberalism gone mad'. Other speakers represented the art schools' point of view and the technical aspects of book illustration. As a result of the seminar, a lot of new talent came into the industry.

Within ABP's design and production department we cared passionately about standards, standards as they affected typographical design, type composition, machining, paper, binding and jackets. We were wildly self-critical. I kept hammering home to all and sundry that good book production was largely a matter of attention to detail. But such attention took time and ultimately cost money. Our books fared extremely well when it came to the annual selection of the best designed and produced books, at the exhibition held at the National Book League. They handled well and looked good and bookshops had soon begun to comment on this. Sweet & Maxwell books, in comparison, looked very much a second best. My first battle with John Burke was whether we should strive to maintain the high standards we had worked so hard to achieve. I do not think I argued my case very convincingly: it had never occurred to me that one should work to any standards that were not the highest that our restricted economics would allow. Maybe John Burke was just playing devil's advocate. He must have realised from my dogged opposition that I was not going to make any change. On several occasions I later heard him, when speaking in public, stress the importance of high standards in book production. The matter was never subsequently raised between us.

*

Ultimately a publisher's job is to find the right books to publish. Methuen's gave me the opportunity to do just that. At first I had to do so on the sly. Production managers were not supposed to get involved in editorial matters. My first such opportunity presented itself soon after I joined the firm.

The tiny but charming flat in Bloomsbury where my wife and I spent the first three years of our married life was enlivened by the

" HEEL ! "

Norman Thelwell's books and little girls on ponies became an important part of the social scene after we published *Angels on Horseback* in 1957.

weekly delivery of *Punch*, the subscription having been a Christmas present from my brother. A cartoonist we began to appreciate more than any other was Norman Thelwell. His theme, almost invariably, was little girls on ponies, and his background landscapes were in the best English watercolour tradition. We felt his work ought to be seen in a more permanent form than a weekly magazine.

Eventually, I summoned up the courage to write to Thelwell, asking whether he had ever thought of collecting his material into a book. Methuen's had a long tradition of links with *Punch* and with their authors and cartoonists; the most famous at the time was Fougasse, now largely forgotten. Thelwell wrote back saying that the idea had been suggested to him before, but he could not make it work. We agreed to meet. He came. We talked. I proposed a formula of contrasting themes on facing pages. I gave Thelwell a paper 'dummy' of blank pages in a suitable size.

Three weeks later he returned it with the cartoons neatly pasted inside and new captions. He thought, and I agreed with a great deal of pleasure, that the idea had worked perfectly. And thus was born *Angels on Horseback*. It appeared with a foreword I commissioned from the inimitable J B Boothroyd, editor of *Punch*, and it reprinted almost annually for years to come. The first book was followed by a series of others at annual intervals, probably the most famous being *A Leg at Each Corner*, one of Thelwell's most inspired titles.

But we took particular pride in *A Place of Your Own*. It came about in this way. Thelwell was looking for a house; so, as I have said earlier, were we. The Thelwell method was different. He found something basically suitable; photographed it; then decorated the photographic print with suitable paint and ink embellishments: a Georgian style porch; an attractive conservatory; pantiles instead of slates, and gave it to his architect to turn into plans, and then to build it.

We accumulated vast numbers of descriptions of houses from estate agents all over the home counties. We soon learned to know what such descriptions really meant. 'Transport close by', for example, meant in one instance: a main road in front of the house, and with it the noise of a incessant stream of traffic; a railway line behind, and, as it happened, a canal not far behind that. We gave our collection of blurbs to Thelwell and suggested that it would make a splendid theme for a book.

Not many weeks later we received another inspired dummy. He had utilised the estate agents' phrases to wonderful effect. The book sold well, not only to the public through book-shops but also to estate agents who bought it in bulk to give to their customers. As a profession they obviously had a sense of humour. One particular caption from that collection became a classic and was reproduced again and again. It showed a surveyor with a piece of wood in each hand, saying, 'No, no. *This* is wet rot and *that* is dry rot'. We had found plenty of both during our searches. Patricia and I kept the raw material for this title, which came out in 1960, in a cupboard for thirty years, and then gave it to the Essex Record Office. By that time the descriptions of the houses and the prices asked for them had become an interesting piece of social history.

By the time I left Methuen's, not only had Norman produced a long sequence of titles which an enthusiastic public waited for each year to give as Christmas presents, but we had dreamed up a whole string of new books for the future. Eventually Norman's work became

Norman Thelwell, at home.

so popular that he created a minor industry of Christmas cards, tea towels, models of little girls on ponies in plastic and porcelain based on his drawings, table mats and annual calendars. His work was held in the same high esteem all over Europe and America. Norman and I remained close friends for years and he recounted the beginning of our association in the same terms as I in his autobiography, *Wrestling with a Pencil* (1983).

*

A couple of years after joining the firm it was suggested that it would be useful if I attended the annual autumn pilgrimage to the Frankfurt Book Fair. It is fashionable to pour scorn on the event, but I loved it. For me it was genuinely a high point of each year. I found looking round to see what was reaching the bookshops in other parts of the world quite inspiring. The constant contacts with other publishers too proved very beneficial. It presented opportunities not only to see what they had on their stands, but also to find out what they would be publishing in the following year and to express an early interest in the British rights if the books suited our list. Conversely, one could whet appetites about one's own future books. After a few years I had established a network of friendly fellow publishers that proved invaluable.

It was at a Frankfurt Fair in the early 1960s, while looking round the stands of the publishers from the Netherlands, that I first spotted the work of Dick Bruna. Dick turned out to be the son of the owner of a large chain of railway station bookshops in Holland, the equivalent of W H Smith as it once was. They also published a thriving paperback series, for which Dick designed *all* the covers and jackets. It made them instantly recognisable as coming from the same publishing house. Dick had a wonderfully simple, colourful graphic style which appealed to me instantly. At that time it was totally original: now it is much imitated. Dick had produced a series of pocket-sized, virtually indestructable, children's books for the very youngest age group. It was just the thing I had always hoped to find for my children: books that they could look at and learn to love *before* they could read. The concept of what eventually became known in educational circles as 'pre-readers' was then almost unknown and I had the greatest difficulty in persuading some of our editorial team that it was commercially viable. They didn't have children. Eventually my enthusiasm won the day.

After long negotiations with Dick's charming colleagues in their attractive offices in Utrecht, Methuen's bought an edition of 5,000 of two of his titles. They were priced initially at 3s 6d, 17½ p in today's currency. They were so solidly produced that they could almost have passed for toys. But when we showed them to our travellers at Methuen's annual sales conference, they were sceptical. I had not then learned that travellers do not like what they do not know. The ideal outlet for Bruna books, I had thought, would be Heal's, who specialised in selling furniture and any number of other decorative

Bruna's Miffy.
Illustration Dick Bruna,
© copyright Mercis bv 1963

goods of a high standard of design. But it seemed that our salesmen were right when they came back with an order from Heal's for six copies of each title for the Christmas season. After a second shot at selling them the order went up slightly. But a couple of years later my faith in Bruna was justified. The public loved the books. We issued more titles each succeeding year and then we could not reprint them fast enough.

Heal's devoted a whole stand to them each Christmas and sold many hundreds. It was, as someone said with a degree of cynicism, 'The perfect modern design for grandmothers'.

Dick Bruna became a personal friend and would fly over to see us in Essex for the weekend, via nearby Southend, so that we could plan future titles, often with the help of our children. Twenty-five years after Bruna joined the Methuen's children's list, the firm gave a party to celebrate the unheard-of total sale of ten million copies of his books in the English language alone, and, just like Thelwell, Dick's designs were widely used for a whole range of commercial goods other than books.

Camilla, Lucilla, Paul and Piers in gum boots. The gum boots became an essential element in 25 years of photographic family Christmas cards.

It had not been usual for earlier Methuen production managers to attend regularly at the weekly editorial meetings, but I now did so and thoroughly enjoyed it. It was immensely useful to be aware of the feelings about a book by the editors concerned before it was taken on and contracted. One thing I soon learned was that an editor's enthusiasm was essential if a book was to thrive in publishing terms. Books taken on half-heartedly had a much smaller chance of real success. What I did not realise until a long time after I had left the firm was that I was regarded as something of a *Wunderkind* to have introduced two such immensely profitable series as Thelwell and Bruna, when officially it was not really part of my job.

At one of our weekly meetings in about 1964, Olive Jones, our children's editor, read out a letter from Penguin's asking if we would cede them the paperback rights of our famous four A A Milne titles: *When We Were Very Young*, *Winnie the Pooh*, *Now We Are Six* and *The House at Pooh Corner*. Publishing them as paperbacks had been discussed on many earlier occasions but always rejected because Alan White thought it would damage the very profitable hardback sales. On this occasion he was away on a trip to America. I jumped in to say that I thought we ought to publish the paperbacks ourselves. It had long been my ambition to do so. I offered to get out the necessary estimates to see whether we could do so profitably. These turned out fine and I got my way.

It was Ernest Shepard, of course, who had embellished Milne's immortal text with such brilliantly direct illustrations. I had been on friendly terms with him from the beginning of my time in Essex Street. It had come about quite unexpectedly. A letter arrived in our offices only three weeks after I had joined the firm, penned in an uncertain, childish hand. I remember that it had been roughly torn out of a pad of green ruled paper, with not a square edge to it. It pointed out that on page 31 of *Wind in the Willows*, one of Shepard's famous illustrations showed 'Ratty rowing the boat and Moley as a passenger when it ought to have been the other way round'. The little boy was absolutely right. Some sixty impressions of the classic had contained an incorrect illustration and no one had previously pointed it out. Regrettably for posterity, the observant young correspondent had forgotten to include his address on the letter, so we were never able to thank him.

I soon discovered that, by tradition, it was the production manager who handled such matters as commissioning art work. So I wrote off to Shepard and explained the situation. Almost by return of post I received a new drawing (the one with Toad Hall in the background), now correct in every detail and otherwise virtually a facsimile of the earlier one, in that every apparently careless line of his seemingly rather free style drawing was precisely where it had been in the first version. I did not know at that time that every few years Shepard held exhibitions in the top floor gallery of Foyle's Book Shop in Charing Cross Road, where he sold facsimile drawings of the illustrations for both *The Wind in the Willows* and the A A Milne books, priced at two guineas for the half page ones and five guineas for the full page ones. The only discernible difference I could find was that the later facsimiles were frequently signed with his initials. In recent years *all* Shepard drawings illustrating the work of Kenneth Grahame or Milne have fetched prices in many thousands of pounds when sold at auction by Sotheby's and Christies.

In any case, Shepard did not want a fee for the new drawing, but he did want to meet me and, again, by an apparently long-standing tradition we lunched up the road at Simpson's in the Strand, where he consumed steak-and-kidney pie, topped with an oyster. He preferred this to be washed down with champagne. It was the beginning of a long and very happy working relationship. He was known to his friends and intimates as 'Kipper', and it was thus that I addressed him for twenty years. With a little encouragement he soon produced, among other work, colour plates for *The World of Pooh*, *The World of Christopher Robin* and a special edition of *Wind in the Willows*. Now he brought in four charming jackets for the Milne paperback editions. They were issued early in 1965 at 2s 6d (12½p) each, with the four titles banded together with a bright yellow band (a new marketing idea then) proudly proclaiming 'THE WHOLE OF A A MILNE'S WORK FOR 10 SHILLINGS'.

The paperback launch was a success from the word go. It precipitated a great revival of interest in Pooh. I recall that many universities started Pooh clubs and we sold an amazing $2\frac{1}{4}$ million copies of the paperbacks in eighteen months. The hardback edition continued to sell at precisely the same rate as previously, of about 11,000 copies each year. In the following year we put out a paperback edition of *Wind in the Willows* with a new cover by Shepard. Alan White expressed himself very disappointed that it only sold 350,000 copies in the first twelve months, but then there were already a number of other editions of the book. The most delightful surprise in this realm of publishing had occurred when a translation of Pooh into Latin, *Winnie Ille Pooh*, reached us from a scholar living in Brazil. Even that sold in great numbers to an appreciative audience when it appeared.

When the excitement over the paperbacks had died down, I began to nag Shepard about producing colour versions of all the Milne illustrations, but he was well into his eighties by then, and his wife (his second) was very much opposed to the suggestion. But at another lunch at Simpson's I explained to Shepard how I would make it really easy for him to introduce the colour, and he became quite enthusiastic about the idea. I remember he gave me one of his puckish smiles and said, 'I'll do it, but it'll cost you!'.

So we selected the very best and least used of the many sets of the line blocks (electrotypes) of the illustrations we had at the printer. We proofed them up with the most careful inking, on very fine paper. We then made a new set of line blocks from these proofs *twice the original size* and pulled these up on the most expensive watercolour paper we could find. They were then hand-delivered by me to Shepard, with a suggestion on how he could colour them quite simply with watercolour washes. His wife was furious. 'The work will kill him', she said, 'and it will take him years.' Curtis Brown, the agents, had already told us that Shepard wanted the unheard of sum of £5,000 for the work, but everyone at Methuen's had agreed that it was worth it, and Shepard was dead keen to start. It took him less than six weeks to finish the work. Sadly, it was his wife who died soon afterwards. He survived her for many more years.

It took some time to translate the colour work into print. It also involved a massive new capital outlay, but these colour plate editions were reprinted innumerable times in many different forms, and have given pleasure to thousands of children, brought up to expect colour in books in an age when they see colour on television for hours each day. Shepard and I continued to correspond until shortly before his death. In his last long letter to me he answered a question I had put to him, how and where had he tackled the illustrations for *Wind in the Willows*. His letter ran to several pages and, sadly, it emerged that Kenneth Grahame did not see the finished drawings before his death.

Shepard wrote:

> You are quite right about where I found my inspiration for the drawings for 'The Willows'. It was Muller who took me to lunch with Grahame at his house in Pangbourne. It was a form of introduction of a new artist for this book . . . Later I took him some roughs for 'The Willows'. His first remark was "I'm glad you've made them real animals; all the other illustrators made them puppets". Then he told me to go along the river up past the Weir. He said, "If I weren't so infirm I'd come with you myself. It's a longish way and I am getting old".
>
> I had my sketchbook with me and I walked through the water meadows above the Weir and followed the course of the river. Then I explored the banks on the look-out for Ratty's house. And I almost thought I saw a tiny blue boat and, looking across the river, I imagined Mole scraping his way to welcome the morning sun. I looked further afield and there was 'Wild Wood'. I stayed till dusk making my sketches. A month later I took several drawings,

WOODMANCOTE
LODSWORTH
NR. PETWORTH

LODSWORTH 212

14 July/69

Dear Frank

You are quite right about where I found my inspiration for the drawings for "The Willows". It was Muller who took me to lunch with Grahame at his house in Pangbourne. It was a form of introduction of a new artists for this book and Grahame was very much on the defensive. However, he agreed to my making samples of my work for showing to him and this I did a few weeks later + I took him some roughs for the "Willows". His first remark was "I'm glad you've made them <u>real</u> animals,

The letter from Shepard that said it all.

some completed, to Pangbourne. When I showed them to Grahame he smiled and said "I'm glad you've made them real". He seemed satisfied and I felt confident to go ahead.

Another rescue operation among our children's books which I instituted proved rewarding. It was A A Milne who had suggested to Methuen's as far back as 1931 that they should publish translations from the French of Jean de Brunhoff's Babar books, about a lovable elephant family. Initially they appeared in a very large format, with the text set in a script type, simulating the hand-written French original. After the war the format was reduced, even for the further titles written by Jean's son, Laurent de Brunhoff, but the script remained. It began to be a deterrent to a new generation of book buyers, despite the brilliance of the translation. My children complained about it. Eventually our editors agreed that I should reset the text in a more conventional and readable type. The results were quite startling. Booksellers bought the whole series in much larger quantities; sales revived astonishingly and the life of the series was prolonged for years.

My editorial interests were by no means confined to children's books. I found our academic list just as fascinating. Occasionally I came across a new author myself, as when I got to know a near neighbour in Essex, Sir Eric Eastwood, who was research director for Marconi's and then the much larger group, G E C (now called Marconi once more). Eric was one of the world's experts on the development of radar, and he had applied its use to the study of his hobby, ornithology, and made astonishing discoveries in the field of bird migration. We published his book, *Radar Ornithology*, to great critical acclaim. Eric was made a Fellow of the Royal Society in the year of its publication.

But my real contribution to Methuen's academic list was a technical one, carried through in cooperation with my friend, Tony Forster. We both felt that the future lay in publishing books for university

As my editorial interests increased, I travelled frequently to overseas book fairs. The most important behind the Iron Curtain was in Warsaw. On my first visit there in 1962 - with Piers Raymond - Sir Bruce Ingram had asked me to photograph the city for his *Illustrated London News*. It turned out to be quite an adventure: I was constantly followed.

students in paperback form. The trick, we thought, was to produce a hardback edition for libraries and a paperback edition for students. We would bind up the same sheets in two different styles and generally publish them simultaneously. Again, it seems obvious now, but it had not often been attempted previously. One obstacle which conscientious publishers regarded as serious was that it might mean that the bibliographical information on the back of the title page would not be correct, as far as the date of publication was concerned, if hardback and paperback were *not* issued simultaneously, which occasionally occurred. The other difficulty was a technical one, of binding by glueing rather than by sewing. By dint of using new binding adhesives which had recently become available, we were able to overcome this difficulty. By the avoidance of sewing the sections and glueing the trimmed spine together instead (what is known, ironically, as 'perfect' binding in the book trade), we saved hugely on costs, which allowed us to charge a much reduced price for the paperback edition. In fact, the paperback bindings we produced in this way stood up so well to hard student use that they often acquired a second-hand value for the next generation of students. This had certainly not been our intention. But we did, at that stage, stop the use of paperback editions by libraries by including a note on the back of the title page, specifically prohibiting library use. The irony was that as the wording of this note became more and more legally complex, the use of paperbacks in libraries grew and grew.

University Paperbacks, as we called the series, did particularly well as exports. Our friend at Barnes & Noble – as it then was – John Mladinich, bought vast numbers of each title, which greatly increased the number of copies we were able to print. By 1975 University Paperbacks had reached its thousandth title and the series had become the backbone of Methuen's academic publishing.

Surprisingly, the most successful title with which I was involved during my thirteen years with ABP was a scientific one, which Eyre & Spottiswoode had published almost as if by accident just after the war. This was an extensive *Dictionary of Organic Compounds*. The one side of my generally abortive studies at Oxford which I had enjoyed was organic chemistry. I nagged and nagged that it was time for a new edition after the explosive growth of the subject, even though the initial cost would be prohibitive. Nobody much wanted to deal with it, so the project landed in my lap. First we had to build up a team of new editors, then each had to be allocated a section to revise. In the end, the new edition ran to five fat volumes. It contained line blocks of 33,000 structural formulae. Their correct identification alone by our printing compositors involved the introduction of new techniques. The production work was nearing completion after four years when John Burke arrived on the scene. The problem was at what price to publish it. Sweet & Maxwell were much more used to really expensive reference works for use by lawyers than we were. Hesitantly, I suggested to John that we should be bold and price the dictionary at £100 a set, then an almost unheard of figure. Maurice

After the photo-essay, I became a keen photographer and used my camera for many jackets and covers. Here the TSE photo, taken at Faber's, came in useful for one of the many University Paperback covers at Methuen.

Temple Smith sold a sizeable edition to the American branch of the Oxford University Press. They insisted that they should publish six weeks ahead of us so that no British bookseller could subvert the copyright restriction by selling the UK edition into the American market at a lower price than the American retail price. This was common practice among certain major British university bookshops. The delay in publishing at the British end caused a good many problems, but overall the sales were astonishing, and ABP made so much money out of the project that it did unusual things to the annual accounts for the year concerned.

It was very soon after the *Dictionary* came out in 1964 that Piers Raymond, who was Methuen's sales director, and I were appointed to the board of ABP. Piers and I became close friends, and he was generally regarded as particularly effective at his job. Together we battled hard to move the firm forward. There had been a surge of profitability between 1963 and 1964, the end of the Macmillan 'You've never had it so good' era, which cheered us all up. Much of it came from overseas sales. But Piers and I were also both characters who spoke our minds when it came to things that needed to be done, and our group board meetings became very lively. So much so that our chairman, Oliver Crosthwaite Eyre, warned of possible disagreements, began to attend them only rarely. Maurice Maxwell or John Burke, however, arbitrated skilfully in his absence, but the changes that Piers and I had thought about for so long now actually began to happen. We were fully launched on the corporate life.

By this time ABP had considerable stakes in various overseas companies, and these began to falter. John Burke felt it incumbent upon himself to go out to Australia, where the bulk of them was, to put things right. The production department was running very smoothly. Janet Hampden, my faithful No.2, left to get married, and Andrew Burrell took her place. He had come to us from Mullers (more about them later), and quickly settled in. John Burke felt that I had time on my hands. I was formally created Group Planning Director. If people asked me what that meant I would explain that he is the chap who pulls the towel-flow *before* he washes his hands, rather than afterwards. In practice, it gave me the authority to make changes in all aspects of our work if I thought it necessary. Probably more than any one else, I recognised it as a token of the trust John Burke had placed in me. Immediate objectives were to bring about a reduction in the vast stocks of our backlist which we were carrying; to improve our promotion of new titles as they came out; to sow the seeds of genuine marketing, and to preserve the loyalty of our individual imprints. The introduction of working in divisions had been chaotically counter-productive. I wanted to cut down the number of meetings which people had to attend, which often merely accentuated antagonisms; to stop the continual flow of memoranda and to persuade staff to talk to each other instead. But above all I wanted to encourage the publishing dynamic among the best of our editors so that they would use their enterprise and creativity to the full. This was often swamped by administration and committee work.

Maurice Maxwell, in Canada at the time, wrote to Piers Raymond, 'How is Frank getting along under his planning director's hat? It is a position of immense importance and, at the same time, difficult. It will not be easy for him to avoid treading on toes . . .'. I did the job for three years. In general, it worked well but it was a time of marked economic difficulties under the Labour government of Harold Wilson. The prosperity that encouraged book buying not only by the general public but by libraries, schools and universities, was being seriously eroded. All the more reason, I supposed, that as a group we should work efficiently. It was not always easy to discuss things with the two young Sweet & Maxwell directors, Peter Allsop and Dennis Alcock, whom John Burke had left in charge. What was very helpful was a continuing exchange of occasional long letters to John Burke. It gave me an opportunity to moan if I needed to, and his often wise responses provided encouragement.

In retrospect it is difficult to see how I coped with all this. We now had four young children and I never stopped work on the researches for a book on the history of collecting. It was also the period when my father decided that he wanted me to look after an overseas family property. But I was blessed with a wonderfully supportive wife at home, and an extremely hard working and efficient staff at New Fetter Lane.

If that load was not already sufficient, peteranddennis (as they were always known collectively), asked me, presumably with John Burke's consent, to become chairman of two component parts of ABP that were in trouble. The first was Methuen's old educational side, on which the firm had been founded, and the other was a number of bookshops which the group had assembled almost at random.

Our publishing for schools was definitely smitten by an excess of competition. Where there had been thirty or forty publishers concentrating on this area ten years earlier, there were now 165. It was a time when change was needed, but there was pedagogical and curricular uncertainty about what should take the place of the traditional teaching methods. This was not helped by the Labour Party's interference on political grounds. Research had brought about the so-called Nuffield and School Council's new approaches to teaching major subjects. Publishers had to compete for the right to publish these, which often meant that immediate profitability went out of the window in the expectation of future reprints. In my day, we were never awarded a Nuffield project but we had recently published very successfully new courses we had devised ourselves, and these kept us afloat. It was the future that looked bleak.

After so many years at it, my own analytical powers had reached a point where they were my most useful tool in management. I was shown a letter from peteranddennis to John Burke in which they told him that they had asked me to become responsible for the bookselling side 'because he is the one responsible person, who can approach the job with an open mind and no pre-conceived notions'. There were deeply engrained attitudes and little progress at first. Then we closed two of the retail sites, concentrated on selling books we produced ourselves in the legal and scientific areas, and helped it all along by much more intensive promotion. It was my first close contact with bookselling and it was to stand me in very good stead in the future.

All this extra work, it turned out, had been a sort of test. John Burke had swung the axe widely in Australia and now wanted to come home. **He wanted me to take over in Australia!** I had already been sent to Canada at one stage to suggest alterations in our printing department there. My proposals had been effective, so I presume that I passed my test. But I certainly did not want to go to Australia. Patricia and I did not have to discuss it long to reach a decision: there was no way we wanted to uproot ourselves, or our children now well advanced into education, from the home we had made for ourselves in Essex.

John Burke came back to New Fetter Lane. Someone else took over in Australia. I settled down to my many chores. Poor old Alan White sat in his office on the top floor and was rarely seen: a corporate outcast. Yet none of us within Methuen's would have got to the positions we now held without him. For decades he had upheld the uniquely venerable Methuen tradition. Now it was getting more and more difficult for us who were responsible to hang on to it.

Very suddenly in mid-1969 I parted from ABP. After asking Piers Raymond to take a round-the-world sales trip for six weeks with his

Piers Raymond: close friend and fellow campaigner at ABP.

wife, he was welcomed home on the day of his return by the senior Sweet & Maxwell directors with a hand-delivered letter telling him that he had been sacked and that he was never to return to his office. His belongings would be brought to him in due course.

I have rarely in my life been so incandescent with rage. If that was to be the way our efforts at building a new entity were to be rewarded, I did not want to be a part of it. I fumed in my exchanges with John Burke and peteranddennis. They explained meekly that they had handled Piers' dismissal in this manner after taking legal advice about it. No real reason for his abrupt removal was ever given. I threatened extremes if he was not allowed back into the office to say goodbye to his staff; if the terms of his severance were not vastly improved, and if the announcement of his departure was not totally reworded. It all happened, but the trust I had had in my colleagues had been terminally impaired. John Burke and I had a gloomy meeting to discuss my own departure. It was all pretty traumatic.

This sort of thing was beginning to happen all around us, and not only in the publishing industry. But be that as it may, a number of other senior members of staff who had worked closely with Piers also decided to go. The press comments, when the story broke, did ABP little good. It dawned on me that for a long time now I had simply been at the sharp end of 'merger mania'. It probably looked quite different seen from the point of view of the ultimate top management. What appalled me was that the culture and character of the individual firms that were being bundled together were never considered sufficiently seriously.

In publishing in the 1970s it was falling profits brought about by ever-increasing overheads and crippling taxation that took their toll. The competitive element which smote others, like the car manufacturers, the trade union dominated book printers in the face of overseas competition, even the run-of-the-mill small, mid-town grocers up against supermarkets, or later the insurance brokers, did not appear *directly* to affect us. Though in truth, our industry, in an effort to stave off the very thing that was destroying us, was producing far more titles than the public could absorb. The eventual destruction by merger of the old book publishing world by the mid-1990s had, in fact, been a mere ripple in the maelstrom of social history.

In 1987 it was ABP's own turn to be destroyed. On the way they had absorbed the sole New Zealand publisher of any size, A H and A W Reed; Routledge, Kegan Paul, who could trace their history back even further than Methuen's and were not unlike them; Croom Helm, principally an academic firm, founded in 1972, and – totally irrelevantly – Pitkin Pictorials, who published guide books to cathedrals and about the royal family. They had also bought large additional stakes in the overseas companies they already part-owned. The new buyer was the Thomson organisation. They were primarily interested in the profitable niche publishing for the legal world by Sweet & Maxwell. The name 'Methuen' survived only on the door of a single room in Paul Hamlyn's swollen empire, largely as a continuing vehicle for Milne, *Wind in the Willows*, Thelwell and Bruna.

Later on, Paul Hamlyn in turn sold out to the mammoth Reed Group, and Reed's own huge book side, as distinct from their magazine and newspaper publishing departments, was taken over by the English end of the American company, Random House. At the time the press reported that this involved the transfer of some 23,000 individual book contracts, 6,000 of which were said to be live. It is hard to imagine the labour and hopes that those 23,000 authors had invested in their books. At the end of 1999, *The Author* magazine reported that the minimum waiting time for an answer from Random House over any question relating to copyright was now six months. It was death by suffocation.

Even Random House was eventually bought by the giant German information conglomerate, Bertelsmann.

CHAPTER FIVE

All About The Giant Alexander

During my time at Methuen's one of the most delightful episodes of my life was the gradual transmogrification into being an author of children's books. Family life was the key. If one has four children, they demand a lot of entertainment, particularly when a working father returns home at the end of the day at going-to-bed-time. Love is sublimated into conversation (bitty), recounting experiences of the day (boring) or telling sagas (continually fascinating for both father and children). What is required is a vivid imagination and an ability to tell the most awful lies with a completely straight face. That is the bit the children like. 'Did he *really* eat three wheelbarrow loads of fried sausages?' 'Of course. He'd been working hard all day and was dead hungry.' This was about the Giant Alexander, of course – my great hero. Sixty feet tall – that is as tall as one telegraph pole on top of another. But we had better go back a bit to explain how all the story-telling started.

First we had Mrs Purplespots: a green pigeon with purple spots and a good head for figures. She had a large family, a lazy husband and made money by running a greengrocer's shop. In sagas intended to lull the children into bedtime willingness she was rather too fond of sententious moralising. 'Lots of children love spinach', to Lucilla, who would not touch it; 'The price of bananas was staggering', to Paul, who at one time would eat hardly anything else. Mrs Purplespots finished up with a *chain* of greengrocers' shops all over England, and management problems.

Along came Hortensia-Camelia, daughter of one of the highly skilled craftsmen who worked in terracotta and had come over from Italy to help build Layer Marney Tower in Tudor times. We were doing history now: a marvellous opportunity for details about life in olden times. (Layer Marney was chosen because it was a superb Tudor mansion not that far away from us in another part of Essex, and in a mad moment my wife and I had actually once considered buying it, but decided – though it was practically being given away – that our combined salaries would not pay for the annual roof repairs.) Eventually H-C, who could be sweet but had a vicious temper, degenerated into a twentieth-century person, acquired a bicycle and took to reading the *Daily Mirror* strips.

Then came the Giant Alexander. He was sixty feet tall; he was kind, willing, helpful – unusual beings need not be terrifying. There was continual scope for unusual adventures. Alexander went on and on. His fame spread. He was asked for at children's parties (not only our own), and by our children's teachers at their primary school.

What happened then is stranger than fiction. The *Manchester Guardian* (as it was in those days) had a feature about the problem of getting small children to sleep. I was moved to write suggesting saga-telling. My letter mentioned Mrs Purplespots, Hortensia-Camelia, the Giant Alexander, the advantages of adapting these to a family's own circumstances. Someone showed the printed letter to Olive Jones, our children's editor at Methuen's. 'Why don't you', she wrote to me on an office memo, 'turn the Giant Alexander into a children's story for publication?'

It was very hard work. There was a terrible definiteness about the written/typed/printed word. Narrative was so infinitely more flexible. Awkward verbal questions could be parried. The principal feature of the Giant Alexander was that he lived in a real place (Maldon, Essex) and that he read real newspapers (the *Daily Telegraph*) and that he was in every way linked with life as it was. So getting the stories down on paper was a combination of imagination linked with realism. I have always felt that this is one of the reasons why Alexander's appeal to children has been so long-lasting. But it gave publishers' editors – particularly in America – opportunity for argument and requests for change. I soon learned when to give in and when to remain obdurate, but Olive Jones was marvellous – her patience was combined with a lovely sense of humour, and I know that she was almost invariably right.

When the text was in final form we began to ponder about an illustrator. He was going to be so all-important. My close friend Thelwell had a first try, but his Alexander was rather gaunt. I then bethought myself of a children's book which had been one of my own favourites before the war, *The Football's Revolt* (Country Life, 1938). One of its illustrators, George Him, was still going strong. He had recently acquired fame through his 'Schweppeshire' advertisements, where Stephen Potter had written the text and George had drawn the pictures.

George needs to be briefly described. At twenty-five stone he was a remarkable and memorable character. He had a deep, rasping voice like a sawmill. He had been born in Russia and educated in Poland. He was a Doctor of Philosophy and had turned to illustration and design for his living when he came to England. He had been co-author of a famous series of children's books about a Little Red Engine. He had a brilliant mind and a wonderful vein of fun. His

George Him: illustrator of the Giant Alexander series and delightfully enthusiastic collaborator.

style of drawing was realistic, shot through with a strong sense of humour. He had achieved a very considerable reputation and was well known throughout the graphic world. We could not have been less alike but we got on like a house on fire. George's sample sketch of Alexander was exactly as I imagined him, and so was forged a partnership which gave us both unalloyed pleasure for fifteen years. George took infinite trouble over detail and getting it right. For example, Alexander used to drink out of a cup until George discovered that there was no kiln big enough to fire it, so the cup became a bucket. Children thought this much more sensible anyway. Earlier on I had had a delightful correspondence with a public relations officer at the Gas Board. He persuaded me gently, but firmly, that for very good technical reasons, old gas holders (*not* gasometers) would not make a suitable home for giants.

There were terrible problems over the production of the first book, largely over cost. I saw all the disadvantages of the author as his own sort-of publisher. But in the end Leslie Lonsdale-Cooper, Methuen's foreign rights manager, sold McGraw-Hill a seemingly enormous first edition. It was one of Methuen's first major co-edition ventures. We were off. Alexander truly hit the headlines. The reviews amazed me. They were all kind. *Punch* said 'the most charming children's book I have seen this season'. The *TLS* picked it out as 'a winner'. Peter Grosvenor splashed it all across his column in the *Daily Express*. My bank manager sent congratulations and said the Giant was 'absolutely fascinating'.

The financial side of authorship proved bewitching. When first faced with the Methuen/ABP contract *as an author* I suddenly saw loopholes and headaches I had never spotted before. Alexander catalysed a major revision of our standard contract. The drafting took many months. I also learned that, while advances may sound impressive, what really matters is the continuity of royalty statements and the delightful benefits of an increasing network of subsidiary rights. Alexander paid for my children's school fees for ten years. (The cost of private education was more modest in those days.) I was thrilled

when Alexander appeared on radio and television, though after the
first few instances it became aggravating that no one ever told me
when such events were going to happen, and it was only the children
who spotted them on television. Father was always at work. I was
appalled by what the BBC were prepared to pay in the way of fees.
Probably one of the greatest mistakes I made in the early days was
not to allow them to prepare a half-hour TV dramatisation. But when
after some correspondence (by Methuen's Rights Department, of
course), they insisted that twenty-five guineas (£26.25 in decimal currency) was the most they would pay, I decided that principles counted
for something too, and as a gesture towards my fellow authors I said
NO. I am afraid it made little impact on the BBC. And time is a good
healer. A BBC dramatisation appeared some years later.

Before long there was a reprint, but even more pleasurable was a
request for a second volume of Alexander's adventures. I still have a
copy of the relevant Minute from Methuen's editorial conference in
1965: 'Item 6117. Frank Herrmann. OJ said that good progress had

The Giant saga sold in large
quantities to primary schools. The
first jacket appeared on the cover of
the Methuen catalogue for schools.

been made with the Giant Alexander. She would now like to commission another children's book from FH. Agreed.' Eventually there were four books. They were mostly written while commuting between Essex and London. I found the journey from Hatfield Peverel to Liverpool Street conducive to authorship, particularly in the mornings when my mind was still fresh and uncluttered, and I knew exactly at what point the rails got too jumpy to continue writing.

McGraw-Hill took all four titles for the US market. Despite their initial misgivings, the Englishness of the Giant was something that American reviewers liked. Lavinia Russ, Helen Master and the *Library Journal* all thoroughly approved. There was a German educational edition. Later Puffin took the second, then the first book. Kaye Webb, head of Puffins and one of the most successful children's editors of her generation, had, incidentally, come out with some of the most perceptive comments when she reviewed the book on the BBC Light Programme years earlier, but Puffin's royalties were a disappointment. Although the numbers of copies sold were staggering, the result (which anyway I shared with George Him) was minute. I took my paperback publisher to lunch to celebrate the first royalty cheque. It didn't quite cover the cost.

But I have left the best bit till last: the contacts with children. These come in two kinds – letters, and talking to them in organised groups. The letters continue to come from all over the world. There is usually much evidence of rubbing out. I always reply, and occasionally the correspondence continues. A recent example is typical. 'Dear Mr Herrmann, I am so exsited to say something to you. How many metras is Alexander's garden? How old is he? Does he ever grow fat? I don't. I love your books. Love from Nicholas. PS I am six.'

Meeting children takes many forms. My first storytelling session was in a basement at Heal's. There have been many others in bookshops. Then there were prize-givings, opening fêtes, storytelling sessions at literature and arts festivals in libraries and, of course, in schools. At a local primary school fête in Maldon where I had to judge the best Giant's hat, the Fire Brigade had brought one of their

My first non-family audience (at Heal's).

appliances to show off on the sports field. I knew the team well. We had met five years earlier when one of our own chimneys had caught on fire. When the Brigade came, they had not got a ladder tall enough to reach our chimney. It exactly resembled an incident in *The Giant Alexander and the Circus*. When the fire had been quenched with water and the firemen's thirst with beer, I gave them a signed copy of the book. They felt it might help to get higher authority to grant them the necessary funds. But five years later they still had not got their ladder.

On many occasions George Him and I appeared as a duo act. He drew the pictures while I told the story. Later we preferred to separate the two. Obviously we were able to go to only a tiny proportion of the events to which we were invited. We discovered that the most rewarding places to visit by far were primary schools. I usually talked to groups of up to sixty children for half an hour. The ages ranged from six to ten. There was a lot of audience participation and a questions session afterwards. The most popular were almost invariably,

'How did you think of the Giant Alexander?' and 'How old are you'?
George and I could cope with up to three hundred children in two-
and-a-half hours. As often as not the schools had obtained copies of
the Puffin edition and there were long signing sessions afterwards:
my trade mark was to sign with a pink felt-tipped pen. I began to
learn from these sessions just what hard work teaching the young can
be: one must keep total concentration or attention wanders. I also
realised how many children in London schools do not speak English.

There was a renewed wave of interest when all the stories were
collected together in *All About the Giant Alexander*, and I added an
introduction which explained how Alexander had become a giant,
and listed some of the adventures which I had never developed into
stories. There were unending requests for this in the letters.

A Japanese edition of *All About* became something of a best-seller,
and for several royalty periods the gold poured in: George and I
were enchanted. When the first copy of the Japanese edition reached
him, George rang me up in consternation: 'They've put all the pictures in the wrong order', he growled, not realising at first that the
Japanese read from back to front.

Then the renowned German children's book publisher, Otto Maier,

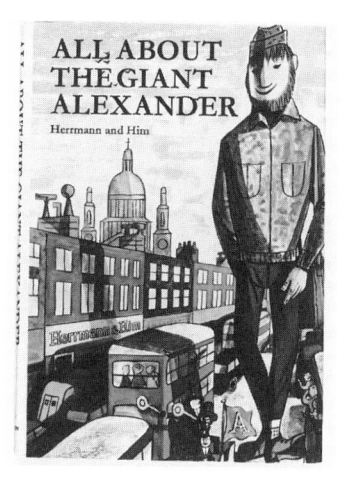

The collected edition was a
hit, particularly in Japan.

produced a paperback edition in German. As it happened, they already had a character called Alexander on their list, so they wanted to change *our* Alexander's name to something more Teutonic. Reluctantly, Alexander became Fridolin, but, unsurprisingly, this was not a success. In 1986 – twenty-two years after the Giant first came out – Piccolo (part of Pan Books) brought out a specially adapted paperback edition of *All About the Giant Alexander* with a vast printing number. To my delight it sold extremely well and received a new set of welcoming reviews. Sadly, George Him had not lived to see it: he had always hankered after a paperback edition of the whole saga with which he could shower his many fans.

But even that was not the end of the story. I was approached by an Essex music teacher with ambitions as a composer, asking whether I would allow him to compose a musical based on the stories. He did. I had agreed on condition that his songs were thoroughly melodic and could be easily sung by children. I have to confess that I was no lyricist but my secretary, Sheila Phillips, turned out to have a real gift for what was needed, and Bryan Barnes composed eight sparkling songs. Of course, it was Essex schools that took particular pleasure in performing the whole thing – often under Bryan's direction – and in the first few years it was put on as an end-of-term event for parents by a great many schools. Occasionally we heard of performances in distant places, such as South Africa, New Zealand, Singapore and the USA. And often a shower of drawings by the young participants flowed in after performances.

One Essex parent thought she would like to turn the musical into a video. This was no easy matter. We hired an aeroplane and photographed Alexander country from the air. To achieve the best musical version we staged a competition among local schools, and the winning version was used on the video. But we were ahead of our time in some respects. There were few distributors at that stage who were interested in marketing videos for children. That boom only came some years later.

There were a host of Alexander-related events. One of the most memorable was the Twelfth Annual Puffin Show, put on by Kaye Webb for the Puffin Club. The theme for the event that year was Giants, and the designer created a magnificent fifteen-foot model of Alexander, correct in every detail. On one day of the show I undertook to sign copies of the Puffin edition. I felt like a rock and roll star: signing my name and a message for excited children in an endless queue for two-and-a-half hours!

By the end of the 1980s there were over 600,000 Alexander books in print in the various editions, published in the UK, Europe and elsewhere; proving that books can still have a long life and that some characters *do* live long in the public mind. The early editions had been widely used as 'readers' in British primary schools. Nowadays, mothers and grandmothers who had learned reading from them write to me beseeching me for copies.

The highlight for an author is his continuing recognition. Once one of my sons, then aged seventeen, brought three six-year-olds from a Battersea primary school home to Essex for the day. They wanted to see the countryside. They were full of high spirits and not easy to control. After lunch I brought a copy of the Giant Alexander out onto the lawn to distract them. 'I know that book', one of them shouted. 'How amazing', I responded modestly. 'I wrote it.' 'You writ that book?' he said, incredulously. 'You writ that book! I never seen a real author.' And as I read it to the other two, he quietly recited all two thousand words. He knew the entire thing by heart. It was a tribute greater than any royalty cheque.

The English as Collectors

Sometime around 1960 I had embarked on a project that moved me into a new world. John Bright-Holmes, one of the two senior editors at Eyre & Spottiswoode, had started a series of highly readable anthologies which were selling well. We had taken a lot of trouble over their design and production and they made attractive packages. *The Cricketers Companion*, edited by Alan Ross, was followed by *The Footballers Companion*, edited by Brian Glanville. Cyril Ray's *Gourmet Companion* was followed by Brian Morgan's *Railway-Lovers Companion*. I thought it would be a good idea to ask my old friend, Frank Davis, to prepare a 'Collectors Companion'. Frank had for many years written on antique collecting for the *Illustrated London News* and had been a colleague of my brother's on that paper. Later he achieved a tremendous following for his weekly report on the art market in *Country Life*, which he continued to write well into his nineties. He and his charming French wife had visited us in our little Bloomsbury flat for dinner soon after Patricia and I were married. Somehow this had made a deep impression on him, for he continued to refer to it until shortly before his death in the mid-eighties.

I wrote to him with my suggestion. Back came the reply that he could not think of any books from which to extract the excerpts needed for such an anthology. I had long been interested in the history of collecting myself and sent him a list of a couple of dozen suitable titles, which I had picked up in second-hand bookshops. His instant rejoinder was that as I appeared to know the subject so well, I was the obvious editor for such a book. John Bright-Holmes agreed, and I started assembling the collecting literature in earnest. This brought me into touch with a most charming antiquarian bookseller in Cecil Court called Ernest Seligmann. He specialised in books on art history and art reference. The shop was lined from floor to ceiling on three sides with shelves containing every aspect of the literature. I began to call regularly. After a while I began to ask for specific titles. Mr Seligmann always had them, but it often involved his temporary disappearance into the basement where the more esoteric titles were kept. After a while he got to know my needs so well that there would always be a small pile of books he had got for me from his recent purchases. We even had an arrangement that if I ever wanted to part with any title, he would pay me the purchase price plus 15 per cent. I never returned a single book. Invariably I bought each pile that he kept for me in its entirety and I began to assemble a considerable library on collecting: more and more this turned out to consist of catalogues of actual collections. The prices by today's standards were incredibly low. Most of the books were scarce then. Today, even though I sit in the middle of the spider's web at Bloomsbury Book Auctions, they do not often pass through the rooms.

I began to realise that the nature of my interest was developing beyond the 'Companion' stage. It was becoming far too academic, and as I discussed the project with others, it became apparent that there really was a need for a serious scholarly but readable book on the history of art collecting in England. Clearly this was not right for Eyre & Spottiswoode's popular market. I looked around for another possible publisher. Chatto & Windus had recently published Francis Haskell's seminal *Patrons and Painters*, and this was much more the sort of book I had in mind. Chatto at that stage was run by one of the *eminences grises* of publishing, Ian Parsons. I had come across him because he had initiated a production company for a book cloth substitute, called Duralin, for which he had chosen particularly attractive colours. Because we bought vast quantities for the binding of our books at Associated Book Publishers, we had taken a small share in the company. I therefore met Ian regularly at the annual general meetings, which were sometimes quite lively occasions.

I wrote to Ian Parsons – with some trepidation – and sent him an outline of my projected book to ask whether Chattos would consider publishing it. The reply was prompt and positive. Yes. Would I like to come and discuss it over lunch at the Garrick Club, which was just round the corner from Chatto's then offices. It was the first time

MEMOIRS

OF

PAINTING,

WITH

A CHRONOLOGICAL HISTORY

OF

𝕿𝖍𝖊 𝕴𝖒𝖕𝖔𝖗𝖙𝖆𝖙𝖎𝖔𝖓

OF

𝕻𝖎𝖈𝖙𝖚𝖗𝖊𝖘 𝖇𝖞 𝖙𝖍𝖊 𝕲𝖗𝖊𝖆𝖙 𝕸𝖆𝖘𝖙𝖊𝖗𝖘

INTO

ENGLAND

SINCE THE FRENCH REVOLUTION.

BY W. BUCHANAN, ESQ.

" La chùte du tròne de Constantin porta dans l'Italie les debris de l'ancienne
Grèce ; la France s'enrichit à son tour de ces precieuses dépouilles."
J. J. ROUSSEAU.

VOL. I.

LONDON:
PRINTED FOR R. ACKERMANN, STRAND.
1824.

By 1896 one-third of the pictures in the National Gallery had, at one time or another, passed through Buchanan's hands. He figured prominently in *The English as Collectors*.

I had been into those hallowed portals and I enjoyed my lunch enormously. Ian at his best was wonderful company: a superb raconteur and a brilliant gossip. We dissected the trade.

Then I told him what I had in mind for the book. We agreed to meet again in Ian's office so that I could show him some of the early major works from which I would quote. It seemed to me to give readers a much more authentic picture of the history of collecting if one could quote from the most interesting examples of the earlier literature, and to annotate these excerpts rather than to paraphrase them. Another point in favour of this anthologising was that the most important works in the field were hard to find, and extremely expensive when one did so.

I felt that my book should concentrate on the collecting of painting and sculpture on the one hand, and the decorative arts on the other. The literature on book collecting was so immense that there seemed little need to include it. The era when the collecting of paintings reached a peak was the early part of the nineteenth century. The reason, in the main, was that Napoleon's impact on Europe was such that it dislodged works of art that had always seemed permanently

The uniquely knowledgeable
Dr Waagen.

attached, not only to princely and aristocratic families, but also to religious and other institutions, and these works could now be bought at prices that, in general, English collectors found reasonable. What was bought then – mostly with the help of professional connoisseurs – was often added to wonderful trophies acquired by earlier generations of the same families while they ambled through France, Germany, the Netherlands, Spain, but in particular, Italy, on what was generally known as 'the Grand Tour'. But there also existed in Britain a class of collector that did not exist elsewhere in Europe: the landed gentry, the yeomen of England. They farmed and hunted in the morning and devoted the afternoon to their libraries and collections of paintings.

The man who had made the most intensive, systematic study of the English collections thus garnered was a podgy little German art historian called Gustav Waagen, with a pin-sharp brain and a fantastic visual memory. At the time he first visited England, he was director of the Berlin Royal Gallery. In what purported to be a series of thirty detailed letters to his long-suffering wife, he described to her, item by item, the major collections that he had found. Before his journey to England he had undertaken an immense amount of initial research, followed by a voluminous correspondence to obtain introductions to the houses of the foremost collectors.

The eventual result of his labours was a three-volume work entitled *Works of Art and Artists in England*, published by John Murray in England in 1838[1]. The book made a formidable impact on the art loving community, and following further visits by Waagen during his many leaves-of-absence from his directorial duties in Berlin, it came out in a second, much enlarged edition, in 1854, now entitled *Treasures of Art in Great Britain: being an account of the chief collections of paintings, drawings, sculptures, illuminated manuscripts, etc., etc.* Even these three fat volumes were insufficient to encompass all that the diligent Waagen had seen and an extensive supplementary volume,

---

1 It had earlier come out in German

560 pages long, was published – still by Murray – in 1857. This then I felt was the ideal work on which to base my own researches.

There was a time in the sixties when I practically knew the whole of Waagen by heart, rather as in the days when I was a small schoolboy – as I recounted earlier – I (and most of my friends) knew the entire basic Stanley Gibbons stamp catalogue by heart. Waagen's work made clear that the English were unrivalled as collectors of art, and that by the time he wandered round the country, the number of outstanding pictures, antiquities and *objets d'arts* in England was probably exceeded by only one other European country – Italy. His work also pinpointed that this heyday of collecting in England had occurred roughly between 1770 and 1830.

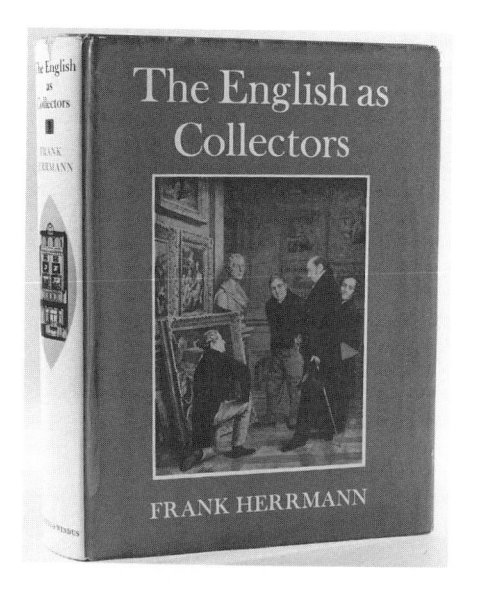

The first edition.

My researches into the history of collecting ultimately took me almost ten years. By the time I had completed my notes I had scrutinised, in one way or another, some 5,000 books, catalogues, papers and magazine articles. By 1971 I had made my choice of the most important pieces extracted from the literature; I had written long introductions to put each into its proper setting; I had a wonderful time writing explanatory footnotes; I had compiled a lengthy bibliography of the most useful books and catalogues (the first ever), and I had assembled a mass of photographs with which to illustrate the text. It is almost inconceivable to imagine today that all this was done mostly without photocopying. The process was then still something of a rarity.

John Burke of ABP had offered to prepare the index. It was a monumental undertaking, but I always thought not only that that sort of occupation appealed to his orderly legal mind, but also that he tackled my index as a sort of atonement for the way I had been treated before I left ABP. There were literally thousands of names which had to be listed and it kept him at work for many weeks (he had now retired). He made a superb job of it.

I was fortunate to have John Charlton as my editor to see the book through the press. John was one of the great unsung heroes of publishing – meticulous, self-effacing, tactful and wonderfully sane in his judgements. He had not long been a director of Chatto's and eventually became the firm's chairman. During the course of working on the collecting volume, and – later – the history of Sotheby's, we became close friends.

John – indeed Chatto's – were slightly taken aback by the size of my manuscript, but in due course the work appeared as a well-designed quarto book, priced, not as I had originally suggested to Ian Parsons at 42 shillings, but nearly five times that figure at the then enormous price of £10.

The whole venture had pitched me headlong into a new world of museum curators, art and antique dealers, auction houses, owners of stately homes, librarians and, above all, collectors. I loved it, and everywhere I received encouragement, because clearly the sort of book I wanted to create was needed.

This thought was strongly echoed by the reviewers when the work appeared. My publishers were as pleased as I that, in due course, it received no fewer than forty-two reviews in most of the major British newspapers and art historical journals. I was astonished that my amateur status as art historian had not been an impediment.

This was only the beginning. There followed a stream of queries from readers, which continued strongly for ten or twelve years and has never really ceased. The book was quoted as source material in numerous bibliographies in other people's books, and my terse, untrammelled notes on the 350 titles I had listed in my own bibliography were frequently quoted as authoritative statements in their catalogues by antiquarian booksellers. The most delightful consequence by far was a very good review by Sir Trenchard Cox, a former director of the Victoria & Albert Museum, in the *Journal* of the Society of Antiquaries. He even invited me for lunch and it was with his help, and that of our dynamic little Essex County Archivist, Derek Emmison, that I eventually became a Fellow of the Society of Antiquaries.

Later on, second-hand copies of *The English as Collectors* became expensive. There were occasional thoughts of a reprint but these did not become positive until 1996 (twenty-four years after the original publication of the book) when a New York bookseller mooted it. This gave me an opportunity to write a long, new introduction in which to outline the enormous changes that had occurred in the collecting world since the first publication in 1972. However, our New York bookseller friend never got the reprint off the ground until a thriving small publisher – who had also begun as a bookseller, but specialising in books about books and bibliography – took the plunge, and the Oak Knoll Press edition appeared in 1999. It was highly appropriate that John Murray published the UK edition, for it was they who, after all, had been the original publishers of Dr Gustav Waagen, Mrs Anna Jameson and Sir Charles and Lady Eastlake, and a host of other writers, in the first half of the nineteenth century whom I had quoted at length in *The English as Collectors*.

To my absolute delight the British new edition sold out in less than six months, this time with only two reviews.

CHAPTER SEVEN

The Quest for Solly

During my researches for material to be included in *The English as Collectors*, I came across a leading article in *The Times* of November 1905. It coincided with reports on the opening of a magnificent new museum complex in Berlin. This had absorbed Waagen's old museum and was called the Kaiser Friedrich Museum. It was the brain child of Wilhelm von Bode, probably Germany's most distinguished museum director of all time. The heading of the piece was 'Who Was Solly?' and read:

> It is surprising that in these days, when everything that bears upon the history of masterpieces and great collections is made the object of microscopic research, nobody seems to have written the life of a man who was evidently one of the most remarkable collectors that ever lived, and one of the most conspicuously in advance of his time.

What had happened was that, although the Solly collection was intermingled with many paintings of similar importance from other sources, critical English eyes realised for the first time what the nation had lost when Solly had decided that his vast collection should stay in Germany.

This was an exciting challenge: my book would not be complete without him. His collection was on a scale almost unparalleled in the whole of the nineteenth century. But initially wherever I turned for information about him, I drew a complete blank. It soon became apparent that, while Solly had settled in England after the 1830s, and no fewer than eight sales containing paintings he owned had taken place at Christie's and other auctioneers, the important part of his collecting period, between 1800 and 1821, had been spent first in Stockholm and then in Berlin. So it was to German archives that I had to turn for information. This was an occasion when being bilingual in German was again an enormous help.

Edward Solly turned out to have been one of five brothers who ran a highly successful timber-importing business from St Mary Axe in the City of London. They also traded in hemp, flax and cereals. Their father had foresaken his farming career near Sandwich in Kent to start the enterprise in London. He was a staunch non-conformist and had been the leading spirit in building a Presbyterian chapel near his home. The family he begot was energetic and intelligent beyond the ordinary. The eldest brother, Isaac, had lofty ideals of what a British merchant should be. As well as being head of the family business, he was chairman of the London Dock Company, a railway company and a shipping company. He was instrumental in starting the London Fire Brigade and a moving spirit in the foundation of London University. Another brother, Samuel, became a geologist and a member of the Royal Society. He took part in founding the British Institution. Edward, the second eldest, was something of a linguist who lived and worked on the Continent and looked after the purchasing side of the business. During the wars with France, the firm obtained immense contracts for supplying the British government dockyards with Polish and Prussian oak planking for shipbuilding. By 1800 it had its own large fleet of merchantmen. Edward, even more than his brothers, eventually became extremely wealthy.

About 1810 Edward became interested in the arts as a form of relaxation from his dynamic and enterprising life, and embarked on a study of pictures and the history of painting, particularly on his frequent travels round Europe. After a while he began to buy pictures himself, and only eleven years later, in 1821, he had assembled over three thousand. He had built extensive galleries around his fashionable residence in Berlin's Wilhelmstrasse to house them. His principal interest was in the paintings of the Italian schools. Seven large rooms were devoted to that part of his collection. He was one of the first to buy enthusiastically works of the Italian Primitives of the *Trecento* and *Quattrocento*. But he also had one or more examples of the works of the greatest masters of the Renaissance, such as Giotto, Taddeo Gaddi, Lippo Memmi, Botticelli, Fra Filippo and Filippino Lippi, Piero di Cosimo, Verrocchio, Giovanni and Gentile Bellini, Mantegna, Signorelli, Raphael and Titian. There were eight hundred paintings of the Madonna. All of these works came with unshakable provenances because they had only recently arrived from Italy at a time when an important decree had come into force – the so-called 'Secularisation of Religious Institutions' – which permitted the transfer of 'surplus' works of art out of the country, after they had been removed from monasteries, seminaries, churches and the like. But Solly also owned many works from the Netherlands, Germany and France. Visitors from all over the world came to look. It was probably the finest art collection in private, rather than in princely, hands.

But then disaster struck. First, the family business lost twenty of their vessels, which were captured and confiscated by the Danes, who were under Napoleon's control. This was because Solly had agreed to a secret *concordat* with the Prussian government that his ships could carry contraband goods between Germany and England. Then the Baltic timber trade between Prussia and England seriously declined. In order to restore the solvency of the business, Solly boldly decided in 1819 to offer *part* of his collection to the Prussian king, Frederick William III, who was known to be seeking paintings for the royal collection following his purchase of the Giustiani Collection from Paris four years earlier. But Solly was also moved by a desire to express his gratitude for the happy and successful years he had spent in Berlin. There were many people who enthusiastically welcomed the idea of keeping Solly's collection in Berlin. They realised that an opportunity for buying such prodigious, unmatched and probably unmatchable strength in the Italian schools would never be repeated.

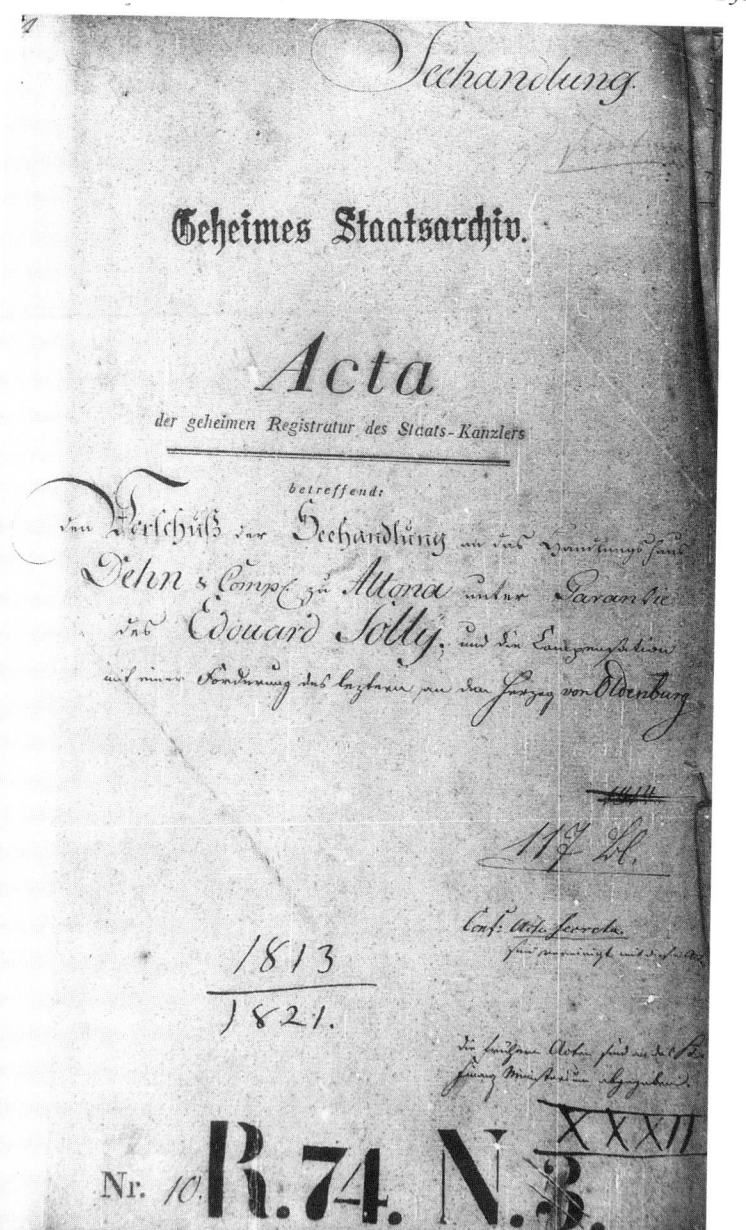

Solly's contract for compensation for the loss of his twenty merchantmen.

The negotiations between Solly and the State took an unconscionable time – more than two years – but with the help of several of the Prussian ministers of state, who were friends of Solly's, and no less a person than Goethe, the great German poet, on the one hand, and von Hardenberg, the Prime Minister, on the other, the sale was eventually agreed to. However, it was many years before Solly was actually paid for everything that was due to him. By that time he was in such dire straits that he had to sell his entire collection, not only the 880 paintings he had originally planned to part with.

The problem was the desperate shortage of Prussian national funds after the recent wars against Napoleon. Neither the state nor the king wanted to be seen spending the enormous sum Solly wanted, at a time when peasants were literally starving in some parts of the country.

It was fascinating for me to study history in the making among the documents in the German archive. The arguments in favour and against were clearly evident in this system of communication between the king and his ministers. It worked as follows: the king would pose a question in writing and accept written replies. These exchanges were contained in insetted 16-page sections of folio-sized parchment sheets creased vertically down the centre. The king's secretary would put the initial question on the right-hand side of page one. The first counsellor would write his answer on the right-hand half of page two. The king would make his annotations on the left-hand margin and pass it on to the next recipient, who would add *his* answer on page three, and so on. Messengers would carry the same folder from one correspondent to the next so that Hardenberg might give his views on the same matter three times on a single day, before it was finally resolved for action to everyone's satisfaction. The only snag in this otherwise delightfully simple means of communication was bad handwriting. Amenuenses had to make fair copies of some of the contributions – and this duplication produced filing problems.

A major tranche of paintings – 676 works – went immediately to the new Royal Berlin Gallery, of which Gustav Waagen became the first director; 538 further paintings were distributed among the numerous royal residences; the remainder, another 1,783 pictures, were put into storage in a reserve collection. Later, many of the last lot were moved into other German museums, and after further research and thorough restoration, many of the so-called geese thus left turned out to be swans. Overall it was something of an irony that the greatest collection on which many major German museums were based had been formed for the personal delectation of an eccentric Englishman.

Not a little chastened by his experiences during the inter-regnum between the actual sale and final payment, Solly returned to live in London – glad to be out of the timber business – and became a dealer in Old Masters. He gave evidence as such to a parliamentary committee which was investigating the purchasing policy of the London National Gallery where he stated that what fascinated him most were the 'different schools of the period of Raphael, which I consider the period of perfection'.

The problem of payment was solved by von Hardenberg by a most ingenious stratagem. Some years earlier, the king had made a large personal loan to the state during some desperate financial crisis. The interest due had never been paid. Von Hardenberg suggested that the Solly funds should be set against the unpaid interest, and this would not show in any officially published accounts. And so it was done.

This was the most intriguing aspect of the Solly saga – which explains why so little was known about it, and why it was only after sixty or seventy years that the first published description of the Solly collection began to appear.

However, I did not know any of this when I started my enquiries and sailed blithely into various German archives, such as the ominous-sounding Geheimes Staats Archiv in Berlin, to pore over ancient documents. To my surprise, I was eventually able to puzzle out not only precisely what Solly had assembled in the way of paintings, but also how they were acquired, and then later distributed among various German museums; also exactly what sums Solly was paid by the

Prussian state. At this stage I received much help from interested scholars in Berlin in deciphering the early German scripts. This transcription was an art in itself.

Much of the information I needed was in East Germany, the DDR: in particular, the detailed inventories associated with the entire transaction. But the East German authorities were the hardest nut to crack. It must be remembered that in the 1960s there was still a total lack of communication between East and West. The scholars in West Berlin were therefore exceedingly grateful on hearing there was an Englishman working on the subject who could – at least by telephone and post – elicit information for which they were themselves desperate and which they were totally unable to obtain.

After the relevant museum officials informed me on three separate occasions that the documentation on Solly had been entirely destroyed during the second world war, I found two elderly scholars in West Berlin who had seen the papers in question many years earlier in East Berlin on the one hand, and at Potsdam (part of the DDR) on the other. It was only when, by dint of this information, I was able to describe the actual shelf numbers, cupboards and their precise location in the relevant rooms that things began to happen. In one case, so substantial was the result of the search in some remote cellar in East Berlin, which I had instigated, that the authorities actually appointed a full-time archivist to sort it out, and proudly told me so. After two-and-a-half years of patiently persistent correspondence, I began to get the answers I needed. But I had to use a slightly unorthodox method to resolve the deadlock over obtaining the two vital and complete Solly inventories from the 'Commission for Parks and Palaces' in Potsdam.

On the scientific and technical side of Associated Book Publishers, we began to need short-run reprints of volumes that had gone out of print, but for which a limited commercial demand still existed. It was difficult to publish these small editions at an economic price, until we discovered that the official East Berlin export printing agency had built up a niche business in this very market. From time to time I was visited by a young lady from East Berlin – invariably accompanied by two burly minders – to negotiate such orders. The resulting price quotations were always set against a valuation in gold!

On one such visit, at a point when I was feeling particularly frustrated by the negative attitude of the Potsdam authorities over supplying me with copies of the vital inventories, the young lady in question looked slightly surprised when I took the dramatic step of telling her that I would place no further orders with her set-up until the papers I needed were in my hands. I gave her the precise details of what I required, and she went away, agreeing to see what she could do.

It turned out that the director of the Potsdam authority was aghast that someone in *England* was about to publish details of his beloved Solly collection, which he realised was virtually unknown. For he had rather hoped to surprise the world by doing so himself. The poor man was suddenly smitten with serious kidney trouble – and the only things he took with him to the Charité Hospital in East Berlin for a major operation were his pyjamas and the papers I wanted. My printing contact visited him in hospital, explained my need, and apparently just took the papers with her. I still have a telegram she sent to me: 'Fotokopies Solly Katalog heute abgeschickt' [Solly inventory photo copies despatched today], and indeed they arrived a few days later. Long, polite letters of explanation after the event – and after the poor man's recovery – helped to assuage his naturally ruffled feathers, and the flow of printing orders to East Berlin started afresh.

*

Soon after I started my researches into the history of collecting a kindly acquaintance, a retired dentist with similar interests to my own, had sold me a complete run of the magazine *Connoisseur*. It included every issue since its inception in September 1901. It was extremely useful as source material of what people had actually collected during the first half of this century, and the advertisement

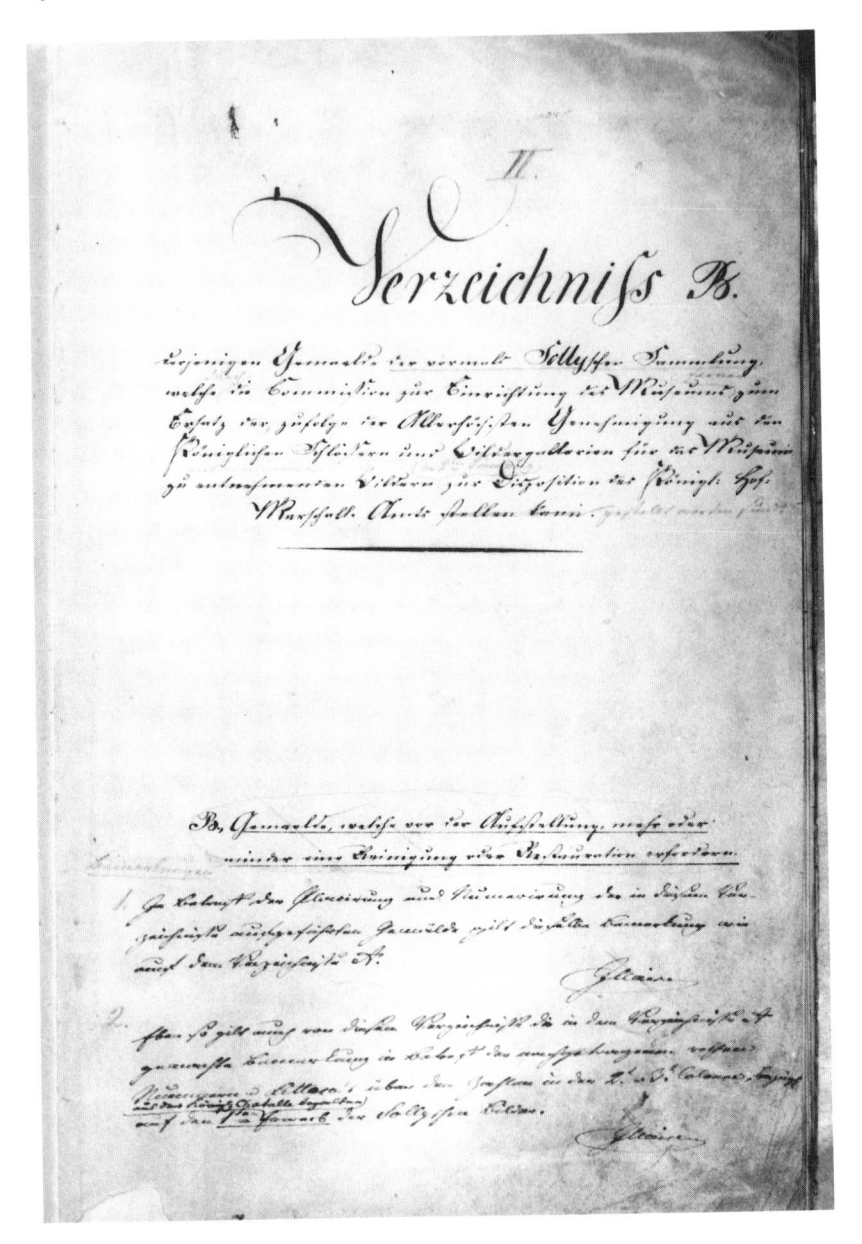

The vital Solly inventory: but it was difficult to read.

pages showed very clearly what collectors were being offered. The introduction to the first issue actually read: 'It is certainly a curious fact that until today . . . there has been no recognised and standard publication for the whole body of collectors'. I combed the many issues very carefully and noticed that there had hardly ever been any mention of what seemed to me the most important books about collecting in the early part of the nineteenth century. I therefore wrote to the editor suggesting a series about these collecting classics which I could write. To my delight a prompt reply came back saying 'Yes, please'.

Thus began a very happy friendship with Gwynne Ramsey, the editor, a talented, self-effacing and unperturbable man who ran the *Connoisseur* with a tiny staff. My series covered the work of Gustav Waagen of fame; Anna Jameson (a hugely popular author on the arts and moulder of taste in the middle of the nineteenth century); William Buchanan (the supreme art dealer of the Napoleanic era who had imported into England a large number of wonderful Old Masters, dislodged by the turbulence in Europe) and others. When Solly hove in view I discussed the project with Gwynne Ramsey. He wrote to me that he was extremely excited by the whole saga and begged me to let him publish it in a series of articles as I completed my researches. In fact, in a letter to me he once said: 'I am as excited as you are over your sensational Solly material. One should almost refer to the matter with a code word'.

The story eventually appeared in five lengthy, well illustrated articles in the *Connoisseur*, starting in April 1967. There was a gap of twelve months between the fourth and fifth articles because of the delay over the East German documents, but they solved the problems that had seemed intractable earlier. Re-reading them today they seem a little stiff, but at least the information they contained was brand new and totally unknown. And people liked them. The resultant interest in Solly was phenomenal. Almost everyone whose surname was Solly seemed to write to me to tell me that they had paintings that had formerly belonged to him, or had formerly had paintings that sadly no longer belonged to them, and would I answer the following queries. There was also massive interest from museums, art dealers, auction houses and collectors. For years I became known as the 'Solly Man'.

The material I had unearthed began to be quoted in the literature, sometimes with acknowledgement; sometimes without. I began to learn that certainly at that period an element of sophistry existed among professional art historians on the Continent. For example, I suppose I should have been honoured when the prestigious *Jahrbuch Preussischer Kulturbesitz* (Yearbook of Prussian Cultural Property) asked whether they could publish a condensed version, translated into German, of the six articles that eventually appeared in the *Connoisseur*. (The sixth related to the discovery of portraits of Solly and his wife.) But I was rather shaken when I found, while reading the proofs, that my text had been substantially altered to conceal the shabby treatment Solly had suffered over the payment for his collection. It was only when I threatened to refuse permission for publication that the text reverted to what I had found to be the true

Edward Solly, the
great collector.

story. I was even less pleased when another German museum official wrote a book on the foundation of the Berlin Museum for an English publisher, and quoted an entire chapter from my text without either permission or acknowledgement. When I took this up with him he explained that this was due to the fact that his publisher had not allowed him to include footnotes in the text!

I had said at the end of my articles that what I had presented was the raw material, but that it required a good deal of further study in the future. It was a real pleasure, therefore, to find that within a few years I had been consulted by six PhD students who were tackling theses on different aspects of the Solly saga. And, best of all, it was my own piece on Solly in *The English as Collectors* that seemed to excite reviewers the most.

My study of the history of collecting at this time gave me an opportunity to bring back to life personalities who had made a major contribution in their day but were now almost totally forgotten. What I had done for Waagen, I was able to do for Solly, and later, when it came to writing the history of Sotheby's, for a host of shadowy figures who had never been portrayed in any depth.

Another personality whom I began to admire enormously as I studied the subject of collecting in Germany, particularly in the museum world, was Wilhelm von Bode. This extraordinary, upright Prussian bureaucrat did more than anyone of his time to enrich the Berlin Museum, of which he eventually became director. He personified Charles Eastlake, John Pope-Hennessy, Kenneth Clarke and E H Gombrich all rolled into one, *and* he had the negotiating skills of a Lord Duveen. His frequent journeys to England, where he bought the most wonderful Old Masters from an impoverished aristocracy deserve close study in their own right, and indeed these forays are attracting scholarly attention at last. It seemed to me at the time that a biography of him was something that was needed. I felt very tempted to tackle the job myself. At first I was told that he had left no papers and that one would have to rely on his own two autobiographical works, *Mein Leben* (My Life), 1930, and *50 Jahre*

Museum Arbeit (50 Years in the Museum World), 1922.

Then it appeared – as is so often the case – that a vast amount of documentary material, some forty crates of it, had been found in a forgotten basement in East Berlin. I wrote to the lady in charge. After a while she responded. What her letter said was 'Will you be so kind as not to take this up. I really want to tackle the project myself'. I liked the directness of her refusal. But my interest in Bode has not decreased (though I have discovered that he could sometimes be more prickly than I had thought): after all, it was the opening of his dream museum in November 1905, the Kaiser Friedrich Museum, which led to *The Times* article that mentioned Solly which had started me on a singularly stimulating quest. For this I shall always be grateful to him.

CHAPTER EIGHT

A Necklace of Dead Albatrosses

After my final agonising weeks at ABP, it was good to know that I would not have to start job hunting. The offer of a job came about unexpectedly.

In 1969 my father, as President of a professional architectural body (the Institute of Registered Architects), was constantly being invited to social functions and celebratory dinners. On one such occasion he found himself sitting next to Gordon Brunton (now Sir Gordon), then managing director of the vast newspaper publishing group founded not so many years earlier by the Canadian, Lord Thomson. When, during the course of conversation, my father mentioned that he had a son in publishing, Gordon Brunton seemed to evince unusual interest and eventually asked my father that I should contact him. Thomson Newspapers already owned such book publishers as Hamish Hamilton and Michael Joseph, and the original packaging firm, Rainbird Maclean. Their first purchase in the book world had been Thomas Nelson in 1962, an old-established Edinburgh firm who had been moved to London some years earlier after their printing works had closed.

Brunton had a dynamic presence. He seemed a million miles away from peteranddennis. It was made clear to me that I was wanted, but as what was not so clear. At first it seemed I was destined for Hamish Hamilton, but Jimmy Hamilton was a man of enormous independence of mind. I had never moved within his golden circle. He was as hesitant about me as I felt about him. My initial enthusiasm began to ebb, but when the pointer moved to Thomas Nelson fate took a hand. I had for years been on friendly terms with Peter Hebdon, the sales director of Michael Joseph: a kindly, shrewd, genial man, always with a pipe in his mouth, whom I had known as a remote landlord ever since we had lived above Michael Joseph's trade counter at 1 Bloomsbury Street in the mid-fifties. Peter urged me to come to see him. He seemed almost to plead with me to take on the job of editorial director and deputy managing director at Nelson, which I had now been offered. I did not then know that beyond his role at Michael Joseph he was very much responsible for Thomson's book holdings. He said, 'Nelson is in a dreadful mess and you are one of the few people who could get them out of it. I will back you all the way'.

So Brunton guided me towards Jocelyn Baines, managing director of Nelson. Nelson had delightfully comfortable offices in Park Street in the heart of Mayfair. Jocelyn was known in the trade for saying outrageous things and getting away with it. He was at heart an intellectual who had strayed into management, and not found it easy. He had written the then standard biography of Joseph Conrad and was known to be very interested in antiquarian bookselling. By the time I met him he seemed nervous and highly strung: a worried man. Nelson had developed a strong educational side run by three stalwarts who knew their markets inside out and had profitable lists in various specialist fields. But it was Nelson's general trade side that had created excitement in the previous few years with huge blockbuster, full-colour coffee-table books, often published in association with *The Sunday Times*. James Mitchell and John Beasley, the two presiding geniuses on that side of Nelson, had recently departed to form a major packaging firm. It quickly soared to great heights, largely because James Mitchell was an enthusiastic salesman and persuaded publishers all over the world that the books he was packaging were second to none and would sell in vast numbers. Mitchell and Beasley took with them a considerable number of vital ancillary personnel from Nelson, including two very bright sparks: Christopher Dorling who ran the firm's cartographic department, and Peter Kindersley as art director. In fact, Dorling and Kindersley split off again not long afterwards and founded their own publishing firm, which rose to enormous heights over the years and has only recently been sold to

Pearsons for a multi-million pound sum. Mitchell Beasley itself was bought out by Paul Hamlyn after some years, but both James and John died young very soon thereafter.

The departure from Nelson of this group left Jocelyn with a man-sized hole in his area of responsibilities. I cheerfully accepted the responsibility for filling it, as it turned out, with far too little knowledge of what I was letting myself in for. Because it quickly became evident that, despite fulsome promises to the contrary, James Mitchell had left behind virtually nothing that could be published successfully beyond the immediate future.

Another disaster had befallen Nelson which nobody had warned me about. This was as a direct result of the firm's removal to London from Scotland. A hundred tons of sheet stock (the printed, flat sheets before they are bound up) had been transported totally un-systematically and dumped willy-nilly in a new warehouse. Nobody knew what there was or where it was. So that when it came to binding up more copies of a book which was running out of stock, there was complete uncertainty whether further sheets existed, or whether the book would have to be reprinted. Four men were employed in our warehouse in Sunbury, engaged on nothing but sorting this out.

In consequence of all this, profits were dwindling and the Thomson accountants were casting black looks at Jocelyn. It was not surprising that he seemed nervous.

I had a long meeting with Peter Hebdon just before he left for a trip to Australia. He, of course, was aware of the problems, though even he did not realise how bad things were. But he made encouraging noises and put forward useful suggestions, and we agreed to meet immediately after his return in order to discuss matters with Gordon Brunton. But that meeting was never to take place. Peter died of a heart attack twenty-four hours after landing in Australia.

So, to sum it up: here I was with dwindling sales of our backlist; practically no new books to publish in the future; few trained staff, particularly on the design and production side; floods of complex contractual queries about books which my predecessors had brought out, sometimes without even having a signed contract with the author; and, to top it all, a profit budget set before my arrival, which bore no resemblance to reality. I wrote to a friend at the time that I felt like a man with a necklace of dead albatrosses.

Soon I had to make it clear to my fellow directors that we should write off the remainder of 1969 and 1970 as a period of disaster; look to 1971 as a beginning of recovery when newly-commissioned books would come on stream, and 1972 as a return to normality. But clearly they did not like it. Nor did the Thomson management. Jocelyn looked increasingly despondent and one day, just as we were about to assemble for a Nelson board meeting, George Rainbird, of Rainbird Maclean – who had recently been put in charge of Thomson's publishing after Peter Hebdon's death – arrived with two main board directors and disappeared into Jocelyn's office. Forty minutes after his arrival on that day, George emerged to tell us that Jocelyn had been sacked and a new managing director was to be appointed in due course.

*

All this was the negative side of the balance sheet. On the positive side I found myself two extremely able personal assistants and, with their help, we were beginning to build up a new stable of authors. In many ways it presented a remarkable opportunity for which my duties as planning director at ABP had been a most useful training ground. In the last three years there it had been my responsibility to investigate every aspect of the book trade and to prepare reports of what I had found. These included detailed studies of the retail book trade both for academic and general books; of the UK public libraries; of various aspects of the American market for British books; of the use of text books and finding out what authors' attitudes were towards writing them; the idea of establishing a general paperback list; and every aspect of the market for educational books, including the formation of publishing consortia for major projects, which was very much in vogue.

My brief from Thomson had been to revive *all* aspects of the general list, and after six months I was able to present a paper on my plans for the future. Michael Joseph and Hamish Hamilton published fiction; Thomas Nelson had a wide-ranging general list excluding fiction. Jocelyn, too, had been most anxious that the new range of Nelson's books should be as wide as possible. For myself, I was determined that our new list was to be as market-orientated as possible and to publish books in areas where one knew of a strong public interest. As I had learned at Faber's, I wanted our books to make a genuine contribution in whatever subject they covered. Basically, publishers trade in ideas: the better they are, the more chance they have in a world congested with competing forms of communication. It was perhaps over-idealistic as an objective and not at all easy to stick to, when the pressures to create new turnover were so great.

I was asked also to revive the list of children's books. For the youngest group we found Pat Albeck who produced two series of charming, small format books that were to be our answer to Bruna. Pat achieved fame later as principal designer of goods, particularly textiles, for the National Trust shops. We found that her books sold not only through bookshops, but also to the expanding market for primary school libraries. We devised a book of stories about *Lions and Tigers and other Catlike Creatures,* to which I contributed an excursion away from the Giant Alexander called *The Lion who learned to Cook,* which, surprisingly, brought me a lot of correspondence. We followed this up with *A Book of Teddy Bears; Brown Bears, White Bears, Gruff Bears, Kind Bears, He-Bears, She-Bears* and *Very Little Furry Bears,* delightfully illustrated by Pat Albeck's husband, the designer Peter Rice. I found a number of charming, fully-illustrated children's books by distinguished artists on my trips to America, which gave us a form of 'instant publishing'. Arthur Ransome's widow, who was Russian, produced a fascinating book by him on their adventures in Russia.

I had learned at Methuen's the universal interest in any book that deals with horses. I had recently got to know well the editor of *Riding* magazine, Captain Elwyn Hartley Edwards. We devised a series on every aspect of equitation which we called *The Horsemaster* series. *Riding* had recently undertaken market research on who their readers were and what they most wanted to read about, so Elwyn proved to be a brilliant consultant and very quickly found a mass of competent authors for us. One book slipped into the series which we had not originally considered. It was on keeping donkeys. It proved to be by far the most successful, and later reprinted frequently.

I had also become fascinated by the great interest in die-cast model cars. We never achieved the hoped-for link up with Dinkie Toys because the company had internal problems, but a world authority on the subject, Cecil Gibson, produced two good texts for us very speedily and we illustrated them with what was then a novel idea, by posing the models collectively on stepped perspex shelves. This was technically difficult, but our photographer, Michael Langford, overcame all the problems. There were also two books on model railway engines. We thought the marketing element for the series most important and launched a readers' club, which we called the Troy Model Club, to arouse continuing interest. When I showed dummies of these little books to overseas publishers there was an unusually high level of interest. A Dutch publisher, for example, asked for prices on editions in Dutch of 40,000 and 60,000 copies. Nelson already had a series of motoring manuals, originating from the firm of Olyslager, which I planned to expand and they fitted well together with the Troy series. Sadly, the books appeared after I left Nelson, and the marketing was undertaken without any enthusiasm. Nelson soon remaindered the books, with the result that eventually they fetched enormous prices on the second-hand collectors' market.

All this is really to show that I was a firm believer in 'list' publishing: books on a particular theme which fitted well together, rather than the one-off blockbuster. My researches into the finances of such earlier Nelson titles showed that they were extremely costly to produce and only made a profit if vast numbers were sold to American publishers. They never sold outstandingly well in the UK. On the other hand, I was strongly urged to work as closely as possible with the features department of Thomson newspapers. Getting to see Harold Evans, the mercurial editor of *The Sunday Times*, had its problems. Secretaries would fix dates and times, but some crisis always intervened just as I arrived at his office, which totally absorbed his interest. However, it eventually emerged on one of the very few occasions when we coincided, that he had commissioned a very detailed study of the love life and sexual habits of the British public, a sort of response to Kinsey. The author was Geoffrey Gorer, an academic, well-known for his studies of social mores. Gorer was a charming but retiring man, and always slightly gloomy in outlook. I once asked him why he was so world-weary. The answer was amazing.

His father had been something of a collector, who frequently visited the seminal exhibitions held by the Phillips Brothers and Oliver Brown at their Leicester Gallery before the First World War.[1] They were among the first to show the work of the French Impressionists and Post-Impressionists. On one occasion they showed the work of a totally unknown Dutch artist called Vincent van Gogh. Gorer *père* was stunned by what he saw. There were four paintings of sunflowers at £100 each. Gorer *père* asked whether he might have all four of them at home for a weekend to see which he liked best. But his wife disliked them all intensely and refused to let him buy one. They all went back to the Leicester Galleries on the Monday morning. The Gorer family had never got over what they had missed.

We could not avoid occasional major disappointments. I remember hearing that Sir Fitzroy Maclean, author of *Eastern Approaches*, renowned for being parachuted into Yugoslavia as Churchill's personal representative and Commander of the British Mission with Tito's partisans throughout the last two years of the war, had spent months exploring those parts of Russia where tourists were virtually never allowed, and had taken masses of photographs which he wanted to publish under the title of *The Other Russias*. We met. He gave me

---

1 Anyone interested in the history of this extraordinarily influential gallery should read *Exhibition: the memoirs of Oliver Brown*, published in 1968.

the photographs and a draft text to work on, and agreed that Nelson should publish the book. We edited the text; we prepared the layout for the excellent photographs; we showed a dummy of the book at the Frankfurt Book Fair. It attracted much attention. We had strong co-publishing interests from America, France, Holland and Germany. When at this stage I sent Sir Fitzroy a contract he said he had always wanted a literary agent: could we recommend one. I put him in touch with London's most distinguished firm, for which he expressed gratitude. But I could not continue work on the project until a contract had been signed. We prodded the newly-appointed agent over and over again, because we were by now up against difficult deadlines if the publication was not to be postponed. At last I rang up in exasperation to explain this, only to be told curtly that 'Sir Fitzroy has decided to give the book to another publisher'. I felt betrayed. I wrote Maclean a letter saying that if authors generally started behaving like that, publishers would be in a poor state. There was never, of course, any reply. We got on with other things.

Several years later I joined a group of international publishers who were going on a prolonged tour of China to view the country after the fall of the rule of the notorious 'Gang of Four'. It was organised by a Yugoslav publisher. The Chinese and the Yugoslavs at that time embraced the same variety of communist outlook. We flew by Yugoslav Airlines and stopped for two days in Belgrade before going on to China. The climax of our Belgrade stay was the launch of a literary prize. Who should be the guest of honour but Maclean, a hero, of course, in Yugoslav eyes. When we were introduced I said, 'We already know each other'. Sir Fitzroy looked at me and responded. 'Oh my God. It's you', and walked off.

I felt that it was an interesting time to start a Nelson series on what one might call the social condition, largely as it affected women. We planned a book on pregnancy, by Faith Spicer: how it affected twelve women in very different circumstances; a book on divorce by Angela Reed (of the National Marriage Guidance Council), I decided to call it *Women on the Verge of Divorce* but it was a gross error to do so. Nobody wanted to be seen reading it, except in plain brown covers, though it received wonderful reviews. Angela Reed followed this up with another title for which there was a great need, called *Second Marriage*.

There were a good many books on other subjects of common interest, some a little more sensational, such as *All About Drugs* for which there was an instant demand; and, in particular, *The Truth About Breath Tests* by Dr Ronald Denny. These tests had only just been introduced and Dr Denny's acute examination of both the scientific aspect and the law turned into the best selling title I published at Nelson.

We commissioned books on business, finance and management – it was a time when broadsheet newspapers began to publish daily financial supplements to meet a growing public interest – on such subjects as mergers, management consultants, the difficulties of working with computers (the initial title was to be *The Confusion Industry!*), the Euro/Dollar, various aspects of marketing and – surprisingly – *The Return of the Entrepreneur to Management*. There were also books on Japanese industry (again crassly titled *The Plastic Pearl*), *The Diplomatic Apparatus* by a former senior Foreign Office official, a title on 'University Administration', then a much discussed topic on academic life after the foundation of a host of new British universities. We planned another on medical ethics.

I abandoned the initiation of trendy cookbooks, although two titles did come out in my time at Nelson's. They were *The Dictionary of Gastronomy* by André Simon and Robin Howe, and Margarete Costa's *Four Seasons Cookbook*.

As far as the world of arts was concerned, I discovered one title in the pipeline: this was based on the work by *The Times* saleroom correspondent, Geraldine Norman (then Keen). She had undertaken a study on the fluctuations of prices for different categories of works of art through what was called *The Times/Sotheby Index*. The manuscript had been speedily put together and needed editorial work done on it. It was then that I discovered that I had a highly distinguished member on my editorial staff, Nicolas Bentley, the celebrated illustrator and cartoonist, who was also, in fact, one of the founding directors of André Deutsch. He kept a very low profile in the office but loved the business of editing and was very good and painstaking about it. He helped to mould Geraldine's book which was, of course, on a subject near and dear to my heart, into a beautifully designed volume which we finally brought out as *The Sale of Works of Art*. Nick was a great standby in my early days. Although an extremely modest man, he had a strange ambition which was to have at least one published letter in the letter columns of *The Times* each month. He usually succeeded.

Another commission was *A History of the National Gallery* (which, curiously enough, had never been written), to coincide in 1974 with the one hundred and fiftieth anniversary of its foundation. A brilliant first chapter duly arrived, but this particular history was never completed. With the help of Gwynne Ramsey, editor of the *Connoisseur*, as adviser, we also initiated a series of books on the antiques of the first half of the nineteenth century: a period that had then been very little studied. Edward Joy produced a seminal work on furniture, but it was never published at Nelson. I published it later at Ward Lock.

I was also urged not to ignore titles aimed at university students. We simply did not have the manpower to commission textbooks (in non-scientific areas) so I made it easy for myself and began the republication of a series of well-known hardback titles in paperback form, not unlike Methuen's University Paperbacks. Here I could publish titles that had always appealed to me, if the rights were available, and I remember including John Steegman's almost forgotten book on *Victorian Taste*, and R W Ketton-Cremer's delightful study of Horace Walpole's life and work.

We did not ignore contemporary history. There was Richard Gott's monumental *Guerrilla Movements in Latin America* (I had been involved in publishing his equally fundamental *The Spanish Civil War*, while working for Eyre & Spottiswoode), and R Selucky's moving

Czechoslovakia: the Plan that Failed, about the general revolution initiated by Dubcek in the 1960s, which was so brutally put down by
Russia.

*

I could go on and on. With the help of my hard-working staff we
commissioned between seventy and eighty titles within eighteen
months. All were carefully assessed and there were many other possible books that fell by the wayside. So much depended on the skill
of the author: some did brilliantly; some never got beyond chapter
one, despite initially submitting detailed chapter synopses; some failed
completely. The man who had agreed to write the book on *Medical
Ethics*, for example – a really vital subject of great public interest, it
seemed to us – eventually decided that there was not enough to write
about!

*

A new set of problems faced us when the manuscripts that came in
had been edited because they were terribly slow to go into production. Nelson's new production staff turned out to be a disaster. While,
of course, it had awful problems of its own, it was so slow and books
were so delayed that I had to take over part of this element of our
work as well. When other directors, who suffered similar problems,
and I urged Jocelyn to sort this out, he had simply refused. After the
smooth running of the production department at ABP, I simply could
not understand how things could go so wrong.

But despite our hard work I gradually began to realise that the
senior management were not going to wait two or three years to get
things straight: for one thing, a vast amount of investment was required. No one could doubt any longer that the Mitchell and Beasley
clear-out had been terminal. It had already emerged during my first
few months at Nelson that most of their efforts in the period before
they left had been devoted to projects for their own new list. I could
never understand, for example, why I kept having to pass invoices for

the reproduction rights of photographs of the moon. The reason suddenly became crystal clear when Mitchell Beasley announced in the *Bookseller*, the trade paper, that they were about to publish a major atlas of the moon. One great contract they had left us. This was for Hugh Johnson's monumental *Wine Atlas*, over which I rejoiced. It was to sow the seeds for what became a whole new industry of commentaries on wine when it appeared. But when Jocelyn and I met James Mitchell at the Frankfurt Book Fair, he cheerfully told us that Hugh Johnson no longer wanted to be published by Nelson, that he proposed to cancel his contract with us and to transfer it to Mitchell Beasley. Alex Comfort was also still contracted to Nelson, but he too went over to James and John, and eventually wrote *The Joy of Sex* for them. It was these two books, by Hugh Johnson and Alex Comfort, that launched Mitchell Beasley into the publishing stratosphere for some years. For me, they were simply another pair of albatrosses.

However, from my own point of view there were also bits of luck. Nelson had an adviser whom I had inherited, who tended to drop in unannounced from time to time to make useful suggestions about possible books and authors. Dr Ken Watkins seemed to have amazing contacts, both within the publishing world and in the City where he acted as an adviser to financial companies. Ken was a lecturer in political history in the University of Sheffield. His political views were to the right of Genghis Khan. He made the most awful suggestions for books he wanted to write himself, but was very sound about other authors he put forward. He was extremely short-sighted and would peer at the papers he brought with him through pebble-like lenses to read out notes he had made. He was another constant pipe-smoker. His manner was always delightfully conspiratorial. He had known Jocelyn Baines for years and, after Jocelyn was sacked, was quite certain that my days at Nelson were also numbered. Long before matters came to a head, he had urged me to meet one of his financial contacts in the City who was interested in investing in publishing companies and needed someone to spearhead this for him. I tucked the thought away in my mind . . . just in case.

With the decline in new books to publish and the muddle over reprinting titles from the backlist, I managed to keep the cashflow strong by selling rights in forthcoming titles to overseas publishers, principally in New York, and by shedding elements from the old Nelson list for which we could see no future potential. There was, for example, a series of Biblical commentaries which originated from the firm's Edinburgh days. Four of the titles published, out of a projected list of forty, had sold three hundred copies each. With Ken's help, I was put in touch with a non-conformist, evangelical firm of religious publishers called Marshall, Morgan & Scott, and its head, one Peter Lardi, was delighted to buy the rights in the series from us for a very sizeable consideration. His firm had just been taken over by a financial institution, so suddenly he had generous funds. I was to see a good deal more of Peter in the next phase of my career. Another such series went to A & C Black.

One side of my Nelson inheritance I have not mentioned consisted of a number of vastly ambitious projects where little more than the title had been thought of, and yet huge advances had been pledged. They were the worst of my nightmares and I gradually managed to get Nelson released from taking them on. When I gave George Rainbird details he nearly had a fit. One result was that he began to take more interest in what I was doing and to make appreciative noises over my efforts during the previous eighteen months, which had probably saved Nelson's from bankruptcy. So life was a strange amalgam of the delights of building the new list on the one hand and the gloom of the management problems on the other, particularly during the long vacuum after Jocelyn had departed and his successor, whoever he was to be, had not yet arrived. As his supposed deputy, I applied for the job, but, unsurprisingly, was rejected.

Eventually, the new man arrived and after a few weeks I had a long chat with him. He was nice enough and I did not envy the task before him. He was reading from a prepared script and the message was clear. We do not want you to go on. Such a situation is always traumatic.

No one was more surprised, therefore, than George Rainbird when I wrote him a very polite letter – after taking advice from my wonderful lawyer, Sir Arthur Driver – that I was going to sue the firm for what was called constructive dismissal. I had all the promises that had been made and not fulfilled, in writing, and clearly he did not. He begged me to desist and undertook that there would be a wholly amicable settlement, which indeed materialised. I was even able to take with me many of the books I had commissioned, so that I could publish them myself under a different imprint at a later date. This led to cries of joy from many of the authors. Nelson did ask for the repayment of the advances against royalties I had paid, and some of the underlings involved in the transfer were a lot more obstreperous about it than George Rainbird had intended.

There were also two wholly unexpected sequels. The new managing director, who had come from Australia and who had sacked me, was himself sacked only a few weeks later, and moved into the museum world; and when the news of my departure broke, *The Times* Diary published a long paean of praise about my activities at Nelson and expressed the sadness of the many authors whom I had found. As *The Times* was the flagship of the Thomson Organisation, this was particularly surprising and I have always remained grateful to the then Diarist, who is still working on the paper thirty years later.

In the years that followed the great game of musical chairs continued. Thomson sold the Hamish Hamilton and Michael Joseph imprints to Penguin. Nelson shrank, concentrating purely on school books and was moved to Surrey. Rainbird as a company ceased to be soon after George retired. The newspaper management itself became more and more deeply embroiled in battles against intransigent trade unions and *The Times* and *Sunday Times* were sold to Rupert Murdoch. Jocelyn Baines took over the management of Bernard Quaritch, London's leading antiquarian bookseller, back to his old love. He wrote me a touching letter apologising for the mess he had handed over to me. But I shall always be grateful to him too for the fact that he had put me forward for membership of the Travellers'

Club in Pall Mall, which has continued through the years to give me great pleasure. It was one of life's ironies that I drafted all my prickly letters to George Rainbird in the Club's wonderful library. A few years after joining Quaritch, Jocelyn's personal problems got on top of him and he committed suicide. The Thomson Organisation continued to flourish. Some years later, as I have already said, they took over ABP but shed the bulk of it again later. Gordon Brunton rose to become one of the great captains of British industry and for a while even became chairman of Sotheby's as a sideline.

And me? I rejoiced in life at a slower tempo while it lasted. I was able to spend time at my writing work: *The English as Collectors* was nearing publication. In addition, Patricia and I founded a little company, the Plume Press, to absorb the titles we had taken over from Nelson and prepared for publication. Again it was a practical title that soared away to success. I had found it at a Frankfurt Book Fair, in German. We published it in translation as *The Beginner's Book of Sailing*. It sold 30,000 copies in no time at all. So we followed it up with *The Beginner's Book of Navigation*. The Plume Press continued in being for many years.

CHAPTER NINE

Embracing Mrs Beeton

When my departure from Nelson's was a certainty, Ken Watkins reminded me of our earlier conversation. He told me that he knew of a city financial firm who were most anxious to meet me. So it came about that I phoned to make an appointment to see Mr Pat Matthews of the First National Financial Corporation. To me this was a totally unknown quantity. Although the set-up sounded rather American, Ken assured me that it was not. To my friends who worked in the City, Matthews was apparently a figure of some mystery and great power who had made giant strides in the financial world in the previous five years.

When we met he was alone in his large office. He was polite but slightly distant; ill-at-ease, perhaps because I came from outside his magic circle of financial management. He was quite candid about the background and why I was needed. There had been an opportunity to buy a majority shareholding very reasonably in a small public company. It happened to be in publishing. The shares could be used for further expansion. The present management had not been a success. One or two other publishing houses might be acquired in the near future. It might be Ward Lock, or it might be Harrap, or it might even be Frederick Warne. At present he thought the first seemed the most likely. I asked him whether this build-up in publishing was a long-term objective. He seemed uncertain. 'More so than most of our other interests', he said. 'It's good for our image.'

He then outlined the terms. It was essential that I should be a substantial shareholder. If I could not provide the funds, his own bank, Cassell Arenz, would do so. And indeed they did. I had never borrowed money before (or since). But the whole situation seemed so dream-like and imbued with risk that I was quite prepared to go along with that part of it too. He assured me that, if appointed, I would be in charge, so any success we had would depend on me and would be well rewarded. My appointment would start if and when the further deal had been done. My tasks, he told me, were to restore Ward Lock, or whoever, to financial health and then to build up Marshall Morgan & Scott both by organic growth and by acquisition.

He then introduced me to Terry Maher, his colleague in charge of industrial acquisitions. But Mr Maher confessed that he was suffering from a man-sized hangover after some executive function on the previous night, and asked me to return a few days later.

Terry Maher and I spent a few weeks negotiating the terms of my contract. In view of my ignorance of the set-up, I felt it ought to be as foolproof as I could make it. My invaluable accountant, Henry Brandes, provided such expert advice, particularly over the taxation aspects on the proposed shareholding that it clearly took FNFC by surprise. Here, they thought, is a chap who seems to know all about taxation complexities. Later, after a pleasant lunch with Pat Matthews and his board, and further talks with Terry Maher, the contract was signed. All I had to do was to wait patiently while the vast cousinage of Ward Lock, a multitude of mini-shareholders, made up their minds to sell out. But I did not want to hang around in idleness. I felt it was a good moment to get more first-hand experience of the public's interest in general trade books. Where better to do so than as an assistant on the shop floor of a provincial bookshop? I had long known a particularly able and dynamic bookseller in Manchester, Hilary Patterson, at Willshaws. I approached her, took her into my confidence about my future and became a trainee assistant, there to help the public as they came into her extraordinarily busy shop. When I got there I was staggered. The sale of practical books on gardening, cookery, antiques, sports and general information was way beyond what I had imagined. The same went for children's books.

I was fully persuaded that here was a market the size of which I had seriously under-estimated with my far too intellectual and academic upbringing. Ward Lock, I thought, here I come. I have been at the sharp end and I now know what the public really wants.

My cover as a mere trainee was blown while I was actually still at Willshaws. A piece appeared in *The Bookseller* that I had been appointed joint managing director at Baker Street, the office of Ward Lock.

*

At the end of January 1971 Terry Maher took me to Ward Lock's offices to meet the assembled directors and staff. For some reason, rumour had led them to expect their new boss to be a rising politician named John Selwyn Gummer. I never found out why. So when they got me, there was a puzzled reaction. I outlined my publishing background, which relieved them. I stressed that inevitably there would be changes, but also that I wanted to get a very clear picture on how the whole company worked before embarking on them.

In the event it took me three months until my knowledge of the firm and its many components was such that I felt confident about undertaking them. Curiously enough, after only six weeks I was approached by a small deputation, led by Gerry Speck, the firm's editorial manager, complaining at the lack of change. He emphasized that changes were desperately necessary. I thanked the deputation for coming and asked them to be patient. When, after the stipulated three months, I began to change things really dramatically, no one complained.

Officially, I had been appointed as Ward Lock's joint managing director, jointly, that was, with Tony Shipton, formerly the managing director. Tony had a wonderful sense of humour and when asked about our relationship usually responded by saying, 'Oh, it's very simple: Frank is more joint than I am'. When he left Ward Lock some eighteen months later to start his own business, we were still on the best of terms. For some months Tony's aged father, the much revered Colonel Shipton, still came to the offices each day to read *The Times* and to telephone his friends. My sales and financial directors were the cousins, Peter and Christopher, both Locks and great-great-grandsons of one of the founders. Tony Shipton and they were cousins too.

Ward Lock had been founded in 1854 – the year of the Crimean War – by Ebenezer Ward and George Lock. The mainspring of its publishing business had been, and still was, the cookery and household books written by the young, brilliant and hyperactive Isabella Mary Beeton, before her early death at the age of twenty-eight in 1865. Ward Lock had acquired the rights in her books when they took over her unfortunate husband's publishing business. I found out that the two founders had insisted on doing their own travelling – instead of employing representatives as other publishers did – because they felt it kept them more closely in touch with what the public wanted. They also sought outlets for their books which their competitors did not bother about.

Apart from Mrs Beeton, the firm had published the works of many famous authors in its time, such as Conan Doyle (Sherlock Holmes, of course, 'lived' at 22b Baker Street), Rider Haggard, Edgar Wallace and Dornford Yates. The last was the author of the Berry books, star turns in the 1920s and '30s, which I intended to revive. After fifty years of association with the firm, Yates had written that 'After very few visits there I felt an atmosphere of honesty and goodwill, such as I had never before encountered upon business premises'.

Right from its beginnings, Ward Lock catered successfully for the demands of popular information and general education, but recent shifts in public taste and much greater competition had not been taken sufficiently into account and there had been increasingly grievous losses. In some panic, the firm had sold its own printing works, its bindery, a firm of paper merchants and various bits of property. Its branch in Australia too was losing money heavily and had to be sold. To replace lost trade it had been decided to diversify into all sorts of areas of publishing which the firm knew little about, and these had merely increased the haemorrhaging. The downward path was demonstrated very clearly by Ward Lock's budget for the year when I joined. A financial adviser had stressed to the old management the need for budgeting as an essential management tool. Thus, the first ever annual budget, fixed before my arrival, was for a *loss* of £70,000. This was the most important thing that I had to put right. In an early board meeting I re-christened this our 'negative surplus', and decreed that our principal priority should be to eliminate it.

There was another worrying matter. Ward Lock had, a few years earlier, been tempted into the educational market. Interesting books had been generated, particularly in the area of teacher training and the teaching of reading for the very young through a series of *Reading Workshops*, which were becoming popular as an alternative to class text books. The problem was that all this material was not selling in anything like acceptable numbers and we seemed to have vast stocks that barely seemed to move – and no cash.

It required drastic action if the educational company was to survive. I closed the offices for three weeks and sent the entire staff on the road to sell. And sell they did. Not only that, but they came into direct contact with schools and teachers who seemed impressed by such direct action and began to buy our material in healthy quantities. The story of this got out and about in the educational world and gave us quite a fillip.

*

I had been amazed to discover on working my way through each part of the firm that on the floor below my office there was a sort of editorial kitchen where books were prepared according to well-known recipes with scissors and paste from earlier publications, with a minimum of new input. Such books looked tired even before they got anywhere near production. Instead, we now commissioned authoritative books on practical subjects with a more attractive appeal in the fields that Ward Lock knew so well how to handle, such as crafts, cookery, particularly gardening and sports, antiques, militaria and travel guides. Ward Lock was famous for its guides. Most were for individual towns much frequented by holidaymakers. They were kept

Frank Herrmann by Frank Herrmann, and Frank Herrmann by Frank Herrmann. My namesake is a distinguished press photographer who had been sent along by *The Sunday Times* to see what I was doing at Ward Lock. We were often confused, not least on one occasion by the Inland Revenue. We *were* distantly related, but strangely on my mother's side.

up-to-date from edition to edition by a vast cohort of retired clergymen who corresponded regularly with the series editor. But something had come into play since the series started many years earlier which we called the 'mobility factor'. Many more people owned cars and did not just spend their time in a single location. We combined several such titles to cover a whole area, like South Devon or North Wales, and the sales soared up.

In the gardening field we had a magnificent prototype called Ward Lock's *Complete Book of Gardening* which reprinted regularly. We produced similar, all-embracing books on greenhouse culture, on sailing, horse riding and other subjects. These not only sold well in their own right, but could also be split up into smaller, individual subjects which we published as short full-colour paperbacks. They sold at 75p each in a series we called 'Concorde Books', after the now aged supersonic aircraft. These too reprinted at astonishingly short intervals. The bookshops and the public loved them. *Mrs Beeton's Cookery and Household Management* we dismembered and re-packaged in this way and such paperbacks were generally popular, particularly in Australia.

I remember being puzzled by the new domestic advance in deep freezing food. So we commissioned a paperback called *Preparing Food for your Freezer*. Other people must have been as ignorant as I. We sold 30,000 copies in a few weeks.

All this meant that the whole structure of the firm had to be changed. Thus we now needed two separate production units to cope with the very rapid expansion: one concentrating on new books and one on nursing along the back list. Our editorial department, too, completely changed. There was very close consultation with the sales department over fresh editorial ideas and often books were market tested in mock-up form before we put them in hand. Surprisingly this was a relatively novel idea, though it has to be said that sometimes I went ahead with a new project even if W H Smith, then by far our largest customer, had been less than enthusiastic.

While Ward Lock's sales department and team of travellers were highly efficient, we lacked an effective publicity apparatus – but we found it on our doorstep. Pat Matthews had introduced me to a young man who worked for him who was very anxious to get into publishing. After the initial re-organisation we called in the young man, Martin Dunitz, and he took on the job of marketing the sale of rights. He learned very quickly and turned out to be brilliant at it. His other great advantage from my point of view was that here was someone who had lived by the bottom line and knew how to get there. Eventually he had so much work that we had to find someone just to handle the publicity and press contacts. One of our brightest secretaries volunteered for the job. Ruth Tobin had an extraordinary gift for handling the press, and gradually the new Ward Lock books received a degree of press coverage that they never had before.

No one was more impressed than our travellers who revelled in this new-found attention to our books. Such exposure helped sales tremendously because people actually asked for the books in the bookshops after they had read about them in the press. It seemed so simple, but in publishing this was so hard to achieve. The publicity also helped us to find new sales outlets through books sponsored by major utilities, like the Gas Council, who ordered the books they backed in quantities we had never heard of before. It was a joy to see Martin at the Frankfurt Book Fair where every moment of his time was taken up with meetings with overseas publishers wanting to buy rights in our new and forthcoming titles.

There was one occasion when he and I were talking to an elderly American publisher, much given to smoking enormous cigars. He was anxious to buy our new *Complete Book of the Horse*, for which there was a lot of competition from other US publishers. We were deep in conversation when we suddenly noticed that the hustle and bustle around us had ceased. No one else was on our stand, or indeed on any of the stands around us. No one was rushing along the gangways in the usual way. There was an eerie silence in the whole Fair building. The Ward Lock stand that year happened to face the stand of the Israelis who, for obvious political reasons, always brought a lot of security personnel with them. They too had gone. But standing in front of their booth was a lone, unattended briefcase. Everyone had been cleared because the feeling was that it might contain a bomb. The cigar-smoking American, Martin and I beat a hasty retreat just as a brave, senior German policeman picked up the briefcase and took it outside. Later it was discovered to contain nothing more dangerous than a notebook, some sandwiches and an apple. But it showed the international tension at the time.

We asked, at the end of the Fair, that in the following year we should be moved to another area *not* facing the Israeli stand. The Fair authorities obviously had a sense of humour. They placed us facing the Egyptian stand, where the political tension was just as high.

Martin's greatest triumph was Ward Lock's first television tie-up. He heard of a book being written on Hatha Yoga. These are gentle physical yoga exercises, and the book was being written by Lyn Marshall, a former ballet dancer and model who ran such a yoga school of her own. She also happened to be extremely attractive.

The book came out just before the television series started. The early morning programmes soon became popular. The effect on the book sales was astonishing. *Wake Up to Yoga* reprinted eight times within a matter of weeks and sold 180,000 copies in its first year. There was, of course, a second television series and a second book. It somehow seemed absolutely right that yoga should become so important in the new Ward Lock persona. To the founders of the firm it would have been totally incomprehensible.

Occasionally, as things improved, we allowed ourselves the odd publicity bonanza. I had been persuaded that it was essential to metricate the recipes in Mrs Beeton, as metrication was now taught in schools and the rising generation would be more familiar with grams and centimetres than with ounces and inches. This was particularly important in the case of Mrs Beeton, because our luxury edition (there were many editions) was a standard wedding present which accounted for a large proportion of our sales.

The metrication was a complex and expensive business as all the recipes had apparently to be re-cooked to get the proportions right. When the new edition was ready, Tony Shipton and I decided to launch it in style. We hired Clement Freud, cookery authority, humorist and Liberal MP, to organise the event for us. It began with a lunch with him to discuss the arrangements. We met in what turned out to be London's most expensive restaurant. Tony literally went pale when he was presented with the bill. However, on the planned day we and a hundred guests all repaired to Paddington Station where the railway authorities had provided a stylish steam engine and three luxurious Pullman carriages for us. They must all have been at least seventy years old. We had invited a large press contingent and an even larger number of our most supportive booksellers and their wives. The moment they sat down, champagne and smoked salmon sandwiches were served. The press corps drank harder stuff at the bar in the first carriage in quantities which made Patricia and me wonder whether they would ever get to our destination upright, but obviously they were used to it. We had no casualties.

The train took us to the Cotswolds where Clement Freud had booked two complete hotels for our party, and laid on the most fabulous feast à la Mrs Beeton in a third. It was a hugely successful party. The food was beyond compare. The wines wonderful. I remember there were two sorts of salad dressing, one consisted of almost neat, chilled gin. Clement Freud entertained us with the speech of the century. When the train steamed back to Paddington next morning, after a memorable, substantial breakfast, straight out of Mrs Beeton, most people carried on sleeping. But there had been a brief excitement after breakfast involving Terry Maher's departure back to London. A number of large sheets appeared on the lawn in the garden. At precisely 9.30 a.m. a helicopter landed, took him on board and departed. This was not a method of travel the book trade normally adopted.

And the result? The press coverage consisted of one short tribute to Isabella in a remote journal. Probably no one could remember what had passed. But all the luminaries of the trade who had attended the party bought the new edition in very respectable quantities, so everyone was happy.

*

Such marketing efforts brought Martin and Ruth together, eventually in more senses than one. But I seem to remember that the path of true love did not always run smoothly and, because it seemed so right to combine such outstanding talents, many of us helped discreetly to bring it back onto an even course. The result was a riotous Jewish wedding, which Patricia and I enjoyed as much as any wedding we had ever attended. Later on, soon after I left the firm, Martin set up his own publishing firm specialising, surprisingly, in popular medical books, but after a while he moved to very specialist medical text books and did exceedingly well.

*

Ward Lock had been essentially a family firm. I felt it was important to keep this atmosphere as far as possible. Once the initial changes had been brought about and the staff knew exactly where we were going, there was a lively spirit about the place which resulted in superb team work: a startling contrast to the lugubrious atmosphere at Nelson's in Park Street.

Financially, progress was also helped by selling and distributing books for other companies as well as for ourselves. Ward Lock already had a strong link with an American publisher called Sterling, who specialised in craft books, shipped over to us under the imprint of 'Oak Tree Books'. This sort of agency helped to spread our selling overheads. Then we had a stroke of luck through a contact I had made at Nelson's. *The Times* asked us to sell and distribute the new edition of their magnificent *World Atlas* which had recently been totally revised, as well as the other atlases and books they published. This generated a great deal of turnover and gave our representatives two bites at the cherry and entry to a lot of outlets on which they had not previously called. Even more surprising, both *The Times* and *The Sunday Times* asked us to put forward ideas for joint venture projects. This, of course, is what should have happened at Nelson's but never did.

Ward Lock's past kept helping us too. I found that we still had rights in one Conan Doyle title, probably one of the most popular, *A Study in Scarlet*. John Murray published all his other works. They were happy to buy the rights in *A Study in Scarlet* from us for £5,000.

Mrs Beeton kept coming to our rescue. A food manufacturer asked whether, for a substantial fee, they could use the name for a series of sauces and pickles. We thought that seeing the name around would help to remind people of the book. We said yes.

*

The net result of all this effort was that in my first year at Baker Street we eliminated the 'negative surplus' and made a profit of £40,000. In the second year this went up by 50 per cent, and by the fifth year – despite the world financial débâcle of 1974 – our budgeted profit was £130,000. Such progress enabled me to find a really good editorial director for Ward Lock, Michael Raeburn, so that I could begin concentrating on the other parts of the briefing from Pat Matthews.

CHAPTER TEN

Growth by Acquisition

I had not forgotten about growth by acquisition. For one thing Terry Maher was always there to remind me about it. As we got to know each other we spent many hours discussing how things were done in the world of investment banking and the best ways of tackling mergers and acquisitions, although he himself had only been at it for some three years. He was an able tutor and I enjoyed learning about the practical aspects of that arcane world. Terry Maher, at that time, had a Beatle-like haircut (he was very fond of the Beatles) and wore thick horn-rimmed spectacles. He came from an impoverished Liverpool Irish Catholic background. His education had been badly interrupted by a triple dose of tuberculosis, but it had given him the opportunity for almost uninterrupted reading of books for many, many months. He started his working life in the office of an accountant, took his professional exams and moved to the UK side of the giant American Carborundum Company, where he had risen into the top management. Pat Matthews had head-hunted him from there to become financial controller at FNFC. From that position he had been transferred to begin building up an investment portfolio of small companies that could be expanded. Marshall Morgan & Scott had been one of his purchases; a second was Austin Hall, a company making garden buildings.

I was now truly on the other side of the merger mania fence, but I hoped to go about it more humanely than had been the case in my days at New Fetter Lane, now long ago. Of course I had been keeping my ear close to the ground for companies that might be coming up for sale. I began to hear rumours about a Manchester-based firm called World Distributors. All that that name had meant to me formerly was a small display window opposite Hamish Hamilton in Great Russell Street. For years I had been puzzled by its proud name-plate bearing the simple legend, 'John Pemberton, Publisher'.

Now I rapidly found out that World Distributors specialised in publishing mass-market books for children and that they were currently owned by the *News of the World*, actually News International, Rupert Murdoch's then much smaller newspaper empire. Surprisingly, Paul Hamlyn of fame (in the publishing world anyway) was Murdoch's deputy. He had recently foresaken the first publishing company he had built up at IPC (then owners of the *Daily Mirror*). I had never met him before but a head-hunter had once tried to tempt me to become his production manager. (I had turned the job down and recommended a friend.) Paul confirmed that World Distributors was indeed for sale. We talked sagely about balance sheets and a possible price. Terry and I came back with a possible offer figure. A few days later I met John Pemberton in Paul's office. Judiciously, Paul had withdrawn and left the two of us to it. Unsurprisingly John looked at me coldly with a great deal of suspicion, but when he began to realise that I was a publisher and not a financier the iciness gradually thawed. I could guess exactly what was going through his mind. For years he had been his own man in Manchester and he did not relish the idea of being beholden to anyone else. Terry and I went to Manchester and were impressed by all that we saw. We discovered that as well as the publishing side, there was also a substantial wholesaling establishment dealing in books, paperbacks, stationery and toys – a veritable Aladdin's cave at first sight for any publishing father with young children; then there was a further unique organisation largely concerned with remaindering paperbacks. The publishing office was in a freehold property close to the very centre of Manchester, and was owned by the company, while its distribution was carried out from one of the immense former textile mills in which Manchester abounded.

The business had been started by John's father in 1919 and latterly run by John's two older half-brothers, both of whom had recently died. Since taking over five years earlier, he had dramatically strengthened the business and made it extremely profitable. The core of the publishing side was a group of some fifty 'annuals', based on the most popular licensed characters from film, radio and television, such as Star Trek, Dr Who, Blue Peter, various Disney characters, and later, the Wombles. So there were strong links with America, in particular with the Western Publishing Company, at the time by far the largest and most powerful children's book publisher in America. Indeed, they had earlier attempted to buy World Distributors but the deal had fallen through. I was impressed by the sheer professionalism of the team John had built up around him and became extremely enthusiastic that we should buy the business.

We had recently divided the original Marshall Morgan & Scott company into two parts: the publishing side and a holding company, so we were able to acquire World Distributors for newly issued shares which the market seemed more than willing to absorb. With tact and diplomacy, the offer of more money, and the skills of our accountants, Touche Ross, and our lawyers, Clifford-Turner, the takeover went through very smoothly and quickly.

I now paid regular and frequent visits to Manchester. I had not earlier appreciated the very different ethos pertaining in the North of England. It was brasher, speech was more direct, but it was also a more trusting world. I liked it. I also liked my new colleagues. John Pemberton was very much in the astute North Country mould. He worked immensely hard but also knew how to enjoy the good things in life. He was on supremely good terms with his American licence-holders who would visit Manchester to meet what they regarded as this swashbuckling but civilised Englishman, so different from the urbane publishers they met in London.

A few months after World joined Marshall Morgan & Scott, the financial background changed radically. Terry Maher and Pat Matthews fell out and decided to part company. Terry borrowed a lot of money in order to buy from First National Finance Corporation most of their shares in Austin Hall and the Marshall Morgan &

Scott Holding Company. That company then bought Ward Lock from FNFC, so we were now on our own. FNFC was to rise to great heights a little later but then crashed spectacularly following the great upheaval in the property world after 1974. I had one experience while Pat Matthews was still our chairman which demonstrated what a grisly fermenting firmament the world of city operations could be. We had heard of an educational wholesaling company and library supplier called Thomas Hope and Sankey & Hudson who were anxious to talk to us. Terry Maher and I went off to look round the company in the Midlands. We had been persuaded to buy a shareholding in it, even before we looked at it. While waiting to change trains on the way there, Terry had to phone his office for some reason. He came back looking extremely flustered. He had received a message from another so-called investment banker. The message simply said: 'Keep off the grass, or you will regret it'. The wholesaling company did not suit my idea of what we wanted anyway. It was also felt we had better heed the warning. Our rivals bought it to combine it with a large employment agency. The shares soared impressively. We sold out at a substantial profit.

*

Then an infinitely more tempting opportunity arose. Peter Lock was on very good terms with the Hudson family who ran one of the best book retailing companies in England. Their principal shop was situated in the very heart of Birmingham, Britain's second largest city, and there were two smaller but very profitable outlets in the university campuses of Edgbaston and Aston.

My short stay with Hilary Patterson at Willshaw's had given me an appetite for bookselling and I felt that our group would benefit enormously if we became involved with retailing as well as publishing. Hudson was a dynamic family firm run by the brothers John and Barry and their sister Pat, who was chairman. Publishers loved dealing with them because they were supremely efficient and always paid their bills on time. Because their shop was so central, and very close to the principal railway station, they could and did shift enormous quantities of books. They carried a vast range of titles; they had a specialist department dealing in medical books; they acted as library suppliers in the educational field and through their two university outlets were deeply involved in academic bookselling.

Terry was reluctant at first to consider the idea of including retailing in our group. Strange really, when eventually he abandoned publishing and most of his other activities to concentrate entirely on bookselling. But a visit to Birmingham convinced him too that Hudson's was a superb business, a veritable jewel, which we could not afford to miss. The family trio was very impressive.

I admired the Hudsons for putting their faith in us, but apparently they had possible death duty problems, which the sale of the business, at that stage, resolved. Our takeover team of Touche Ross and Clifford-Turner were now getting used to the Frank Herrmann/MM&S methodology and we made the purchase in a very relaxed manner, half in MM&S shares and half in cash. The ultimate price was dependent on the profits for the first year. The management easily reached the required target.

I became chairman of Hudson's. On looking through the minutes of earlier board meetings, it emerged that the siblings had hardly ever reached a unanimous decision: one or other of them had always been against it. So an outside chairman was obviously a welcome catalyst. In general in my time, the family directors were cooperative, but sometimes my proposals for change were not met with great fervour. For example, I suggested that we should have a small section in the shop in which we should sell 'remainders'. These are publishers' overstocks which retail at much reduced prices, but the profit margins on them can be very high. The family felt that this was not only slightly demeaning to the image of Hudson's they liked to present, but, more importantly, that it might inhibit customers from buying books at full prices. However, we started the experiment on a small scale. Six months later the profits were seen to be enormous and the labour input much lower than anywhere else in the shop. I then had to dampen down enthusiasm and restrict remainders to no more than a small percentage of our total turnover.

On a similar tack, I felt that our very rewarding medical department was in too prominent a position within the shop for the limited, but moneyed, clientele it served. We moved it nearer the back of the shop and started a separate, much enlarged, children's book department with its own specialist staff. This received enthusiastic local press coverage – ours was the first such department in Birmingham – and it too proved a valuable experiment. The medical department grew unexpectedly by leaps and bounds and not much later we had to invest in a special new shop for it.

One of the Hudson's strengths lay in taking great trouble over the training of staff, of whom there were more than two hundred. This was Pat's particular interest and it gave us a useful lead over our competitors. Our shop assistants really knew about the books they were selling, precisely where they could be found on the shelves, other titles the same authors had written and how they could be ordered if books were not in stock. (With over 100,000 titles in stock, they usually were.) It has to be remembered that this was decades before the introduction of computers which now make all this sort of information available at the press of a button. The family had also trained up a young, future management team and they soon joined our board. I found being chairman of Hudson's an enormously stimulating environment and it was certainly one of the most enjoyable parts of my increasingly complex job.

Just as the annual Frankfurt Book Fair was the most important event for publishers on the export calendar and for the sale of rights, the principal meeting place between booksellers and publishers within the UK was the annual so-called Booksellers' Conference, which moved to a different city each year. Its most important component was a series of talks by prominent figures on either side of the trade about current problems, and the debates and discussions that followed. I now attended these conferences with a foot on both sides of the great divide. This was not only particularly exhilarating but, I felt, also something of a privilege. At times, however, it could also mean getting the stick from either side.

I particularly remember attending the first such conference since my Hudson involvement, seated in the hall with Barry, John and Pat. The speaker was Robert Maxwell. It was not that long since he had run the trade's favourite, old-established wholesaler, Simpkin Marshall, into the ground, bankrupting it in a very short time by mismanagement. But Maxwell had since then built up Pergamon Press to prominence as publishers of scientific books and journals, initially with the help of the German publisher, Springer. Maxwell also had strong links with communist bloc countries in Eastern Europe, where he placed much of his printing.

On this occasion, with his well-known bravura, he was to address the conference on the subject of backing him to launch a new book wholesaling firm. Such an establishment was indeed needed, so what he proposed was not frivolous, but it was larded with almost embarrassing arrogance. When he finished speaking, Barry Hudson, who had been quietly fuming beside me, shot up and, addressing Maxwell and the entire conference in a loud voice, gave one of the most withering speeches I have ever heard. He impugned Maxwell as a cheat and a liar with the most blood-curdling invective and warned the audience to have nothing to do with the ex-Captain. Maxwell visibly shrank as Barry continued his lambasting to huge applause from the audience, who were obviously delighted that someone had scuppered the project at birth. Maxwell slunk out of the conference hall, departed at once for Oxford and the subject was never raised again.

*

While Hudson's established us in a new sphere, we had, in fact, taken over another business slightly earlier which we thought would give additional strength to World Distributors. This was Whitman (UK) Limited, the British subsidiary of the giant Western Publishing Company based in Racine, which I have mentioned earlier. The British company concentrated largely on the production and sale of jigsaw puzzles, but had not flourished. It was offered to us at a very low price. We bought it because the jigsaw sales would be an admirable addition to our World Distributors representatives' repertoire – not only for the Christmas season, but all the year round. It also gave us a chance to negotiate arrangements with Western by which a proportion of rights in their publications could come to us automatically. This was an important factor in publishing related to licensed characters, and it gave us a stake in some of their most rewarding series.

Whitman was the first instance of a private management theory that I had begun to formulate, that we could usefully add smaller businesses to our core activities, like World Distributors, which could be managed by them rather than at the centre of our operations. Whitman proved a very useful acquisition and we tripled its sales in a relatively short time.

*

I have said very little about Marshall Morgan & Scott itself, the begetter of our entire enterprise. Its history went back a long way. The bare facts may not be epoch-making but they are interesting in that they show how the company had developed through amalgamations and a good many changes of ownership.

It began in 1859 when R C Morgan, then a publisher's assistant, left Paternoster Row to enter into partnership with a fellow Welshman, Samuel Chase, as printers and publishers devoted to the 'Furtherance of the Gospel through the Press'. Ten years later they were joined by a Glasgow merchant, Robert Scott, and the firm became known as Morgan, Chase & Scott. Chase died a year later, but the firm continued strongly on its course as a religious, moral and evangelical publisher. By the 1920s it found itself competing more and more often – and more and more successfully – with its old rivals, Marshall Brothers. The origin of that firm went back to Simpkin and Marshall, where the brothers Herbert and Edwin started work in the 1860s and set up their own, independent firm in 1870. Each company owned one of the major religious papers of the time: Morgan & Scott *The Christian* and Marshall *The Life of Faith* (more about the latter later).

The rivalry between Morgan & Scott and Marshall Brothers led to a great deal of acrimony, and although they were much the weaker of the two, the initiative came from Marshall Brothers to amalgamate with Morgan & Scott by purchase of that company's shares. The merger took place in 1928 under the guidance and chairmanship of Sir Leon Levison, a distinguished financier and founder and head of the Christian Hebrew Alliance. Thus, Marshall Morgan & Scott came into being as a public company with a new capital structure, new management and a good many wounds to heal. But things settled down under a succession of managing directors, and in 1945 the firm acquired Oliphant's, an old-established Edinburgh publisher. In 1961, Wilfred Harvey of Purnells, long one of MM&S's principal printers and binders, bought a considerable holding in the company. This was enlarged in 1965 when Clifford Gibbs, whom I had known from my Faber days as Purnell's super-persuasive representative, had become chairman. His father had been founder of a prominent mission. Then when Purnell and the major printing firm of Hazell, Watson & Viney with Sun Printers, merged to become the British Printing Corporation, the evangelical list of MM&S did not fit easily into the complex framework of BPC in the troubled days of the late 1960s. It must, therefore, have seemed a pleasant surprise to the shareholders when in June 1969 an offer was made at nearly twice the market price for the publicly quoted shares of MM&S. The buyer was, of course, Terry Maher, acting on behalf of Pat Matthews and FNFC. As it happens, BPC was later bought by Robert Maxwell. Publishing can be a curious mix of cross-currents.

By the time I arrived on the scene, the first management put in by FNFC had gone, but with a great deal of huffing and puffing a 'record' annual profit of £24,000 on a turnover of just over £300,000 had been achieved. A particularly competent younger director, Peter Lardi, had been put in charge, assisted by the somewhat older Stanley Grant.

The third member of the management team was the company secretary and accountant, Tom Nicholas, a tiny, bottle-nosed man who was what the Germans would call an 'unicum', a 'one-off', a character never likely to appear on the world stage again. Repressed by earlier management for years, he was a brilliant accountant and blossomed in the new environment in which we placed him. MM&S was housed in a small, brand new office block in a side street near Grays Inn and there Tom performed his minor financial miracles for Peter Lardi and Stanley Grant. It was really only when we moved the religious publishing side to join Ward Lock in Baker Street that I began to understand how their publishing worked. When I did, I soon decided that its values were not ones with which I was in the least familiar and that I would watch and comment from the sidelines. In fact, after we had hived off the religious publishing side (which we now called Marshall Morgan & Scott Publications) from the holding company, I was also to become its chairman. It had been Peter Lardi who had purchased that series of Bible commentaries from me at Nelson, which I considered as useless and which he regarded as a life saver. MM&S Publications published a good many other Biblical commentaries, a huge list of religious and theological paperbacks, hymn books, greetings cards and calendars (collectively known as 'Art'), and records and tapes, all with a strongly evangelical bias.

In addition, we still published that weekly newspaper, *The Life of Faith*, under its long-term editor, the Reverend H F Stephenson. As it was losing money quite heavily I asked him to come and talk to me. I explained that we really ought to try to improve the financial situation. 'Oh. You mean we ought to make a profit?' He said it as if the thought had never occurred to him. He inquired whether I had any ideas how this could be brought about. I suggested selling more copies to increase the circulation and getting more advertising. He looked at me in puzzlement as if my suggestions were quite childish, but instead he said, 'That's easy', obviously relieved that I had not suggested cutting his tiny salary. And he did increase the circulation *and* the advertising, which, of course, became simpler to sell in consequence. After a year we were making a useful profit, for the first time – as I later found out – in the twentieth century.

In 1974 the paper celebrated its centenary. MM&S took part each year in a week of religious celebration in the Lake District town of Keswick. This was known as the Keswick Convention. Keswick's main street was closed. Publishers and religious societies put up their booths along it and great multitudes of fervent evangelicals came to see what was on offer and for a week's holiday. What claimed to be the biggest tent in Europe was erected each year for services in the morning and evening. It seated five thousand people and was nearly always full. Keswick we felt was the place to celebrate the centenary of *The Life of Faith*. We hired a leading hotel for a tea party. I insisted on a huge supply of cucumber sandwiches as well as cakes and pastries. We invited well over a hundred clergymen and their wives, all present at the convention, to attend the party. They were due to arrive at four o'clock. They did. All of them. By ten past four there was not a morsel of food left. It could easily have been a case of the loaves and the fishes.

As MM&S's chairman I had to make a speech of welcome. My language at the time tended to be rather 'blue', because, I suppose, of the increasing stress as our group grew. After the most anxious solicitation by Peter and Stanley to keep my speech devoid of any word or phrase the assembled clergy might find objectionable, I entertained them with a few carefully garnered funny stories about the misadventures that could occur in publishing. I think they all went home entirely happy, with their free copy of *The Life of Faith*, of course.

CHAPTER ELEVEN

Management: Joys and Sorrows

It was no good just sitting in the office and hoping. If I wanted people in our group to invigorate their publishing and other activities I had to be among them and give guidance, and to initiate and manage their creativity. Above all, I had to understand what they had done in the past before I could make suggestions about what they should do in the future.

In the fourteen months since I had taken on the job at MM&S, between February 1971 and April 1972, our turnover had multiplied by nearly fifteen times and our market capitalisation a good deal more than that. By the end of the financial year our profits in 1972 had risen from the earlier figure of £24,000 to £470,000. MM&S had absorbed Ward Lock and its educational subsidiary, World Distributors and its associated companies, Hudsons and Whitmans. The nature of the original company had changed completely and we now covered a vast spectrum of the book trade. Our shareholders were happy too: their dividends had tripled and they seemed keen that we should go on expanding. The question most frequently asked was about management. Well, management was now my primary occupation.

I was blessed with four extremely able financial directors to keep the score. In particular, Bob Harris, who had come to us from a large tobacco company in Bristol to look after the group's finances, was a tower of strength and a strong bond of empathy grew up between us. I bounced most of my thoughts on how to manage MM&S off him. The two most important factors were planning and communication. It was back to my earlier days in production at ABP where planning proved so vital, except that now the whole thing was on a much bigger scale. What should each unit's objectives be?

What was attainable? If an editorial department commissioned more books, could the production department cope? If it could, could the marketing and sales department do what was expected of them? The Achilles heel of publishers and the bugbear of the book trade was always the speed and efficiency with which publishers got their books into the shops. Ward Lock in particular had a lot of catching up to do on this score. In this respect, having Hudsons among us was extremely useful. They reported any tardiness or deficiencies.

Did we have enough financial resources to achieve what we planned? It was heady stuff. I travelled constantly between our London offices, Birmingham and Manchester, kept on schedule by a wonderfully competent sequence of secretaries. When the first one left in 1974, she typed out ten pages of what the job involved for her successor. I must have been a pernickety employer.

While Terry Maher employed a PR consultant, and figured frequently in the financial columns of the press, (usually described as a bright young man, recently out of the FNFC stable), I felt it was important that I should explain to the book trade who we now were and what we were up to. A long, candid article in *The Bookseller* set the scene. I explained that we had a tiny headquarters staff and that from there we initiated regular and detailed financial reporting procedures, objectives, targets and budgets, but all only after the most searching discussions with those who had to provide them, so that they felt confident that they could produce what was expected of them. I stressed that for us, people were more important than systems and that talent was the asset we needed to nurture more than any other. We were actually one of the few publishing companies that had introduced our own executive share incentive scheme, soon after I started. I explained the importance I attached to planning *and* flexibility. The article cleared up any mystery that might have existed about our intentions, and the publishing world looked at us with increasing interest. I received a number of letters from people who wanted to work for us in consequence, which, in fact, helped to fill vacancies for a considerable time.

The surge forward continued in 1973, '74 and '75, sometimes in the face of extreme obstacles brought about by the general economic turmoil following the first global oil crisis, after the Yom Kippur War. The annual turnover in the years 1971 to 1974 rose from £2,700,000 to £5.6 million to £8.3 million and, finally, to £11.6 million. Terry Maher looked on in astonishment and sometimes, I thought, in envy. Through a number of ingenious deals he had by now shed the initial bank debt he incurred when he started his own business after leaving FNFC. After re-naming his company Pentos, he began to make his mark in the financial world and embarked on a continuous shopping spree for companies. He would revitalise and sell, or re-finance and sell, or sometimes just keep them. Sometimes he was lucky; sometimes less so. He had also adopted the Alan White syndrome and moved around in a chauffeur-driven Bentley. Fortunately, all this activity meant that my stewardship of MM&S was relatively uninterrupted. I kept in close touch with my opposite number at Austin Hall, the other company into which Terry had bought when he left FNFC, who made garden buildings. Maurice Grimoldby was a delightful man with a splendid sense of humour. Though he really had a harder row to hoe than I, the problems we experienced were not dissimilar and we attended each other's management meetings, where possible solutions were discussed at length. It helped.

During 1973 we acquired a second religious publisher, a company called Samuel Baxter, which fitted in well with MM&S Publications. It came with its own printing company, Hollen Street Press, in Slough, and a charming small distribution centre in Thrapston. Rather against my better judgement we acquired Baxter for cash instead of shares. Later on this brought about problems we could have avoided. In July 1973, Sandle Brothers also joined the group. Like World Distributors, they published a low-priced range of children's books and also acted as wholesalers, so this fitted in neatly with World Distributors and we were able to house them within our existing premises in Manchester. A little later, in a burst of exuberance, we started a series of toy shops called Playgroup in the Northern cities, which were largely fed from our expanded wholesalers.

The tail end of 1974 and the spring of 1975 was a period one would rather forget about. As oil prices soared, inflation began to rise alarmingly. Bank rate went up from 5 per cent to 13 per cent. Commercial property prices, which had risen dramatically in previous years, almost halved, and financial institutions who owned the properties and were dependent on borrowed money, collapsed in unheard of numbers. We did not escape the desperate cash shortage. At one moment our Manchester financial director had to call personally on a huge mail order house to collect £1,000 in cash just to keep the publishing office going. The firm concerned owed us £25,000 at the time. Bank managers sat in their offices and cowered. Anything new that involved the slightest risk was *out*. At the time the London *Evening Standard* carried a headline: 'Will National Westminster Bank survive?'. Nat West were our bankers.

In August of 1974 they caused a crisis. At what was for us the worst possible moment, when we were owed vast sums of money by bookshops everywhere, a young, newly-appointed manager of Nat West in Manchester suddenly demanded the return of a loan which had been negotiated on a long-term basis; in fact, to pay, in part, for the acquisition of Samuel Baxter. Arguments seemed to cut no ice with him because he really did not know anything about World Distributors, one of his larger and certainly most outstanding customers. The senior management of MM&S got really alarmed. We bethought ourselves of County Bank, a London investment bank recently formed by National Westminster, and a bright young man from County, named Jonathan Cohen, helped us to find a solution. The relief was almost palpable.

The supply of money was not our only problem. The oil crisis had done terrible things to paper production all over the world. There was suddenly a global paper shortage and prices shot up. So much so that they seriously affected the prices of the books we were publishing and our customers had to be persuaded to pay substantially more for them. Even then we were delighted if we could find what paper was needed for our much enlarged publishing programme. It was to be many years before there was movement the other way and the price of paper decreased.

By and large, we were spared the troubles with intransigent British trade unions which did, however, seriously affect all our UK printers and binders (so much so that increasingly our books were produced in Spain, Italy and Holland, and later on in Hong Kong and Singapore). But Baxters did bring such troubles with it. Hollen Street Press had a small staff of only about forty people. It was managed outstandingly by its own MD, Mike Ballands. But even in so small a firm, he had four separate trade unions to deal with. By tradition, the lithographers were one of the most difficult. There was a moment when the Labour government, having prohibited wage increases of any substance for a long period, graciously permitted an increase of £6 per week for all workers. We were happy to award this to all at Hollen Street Press, but the lithographers refused to accept it on orders from senior union management. In fact, perversely, they threatened us with strike action if we proceeded to give it to them. However, we felt that management was there to manage, and we went ahead so that they would not be out of kilter with the other trade unions. Somehow sense prevailed: we did not have a stoppage.

I mentioned earlier that Baxters had a wonderfully cosy and extremely efficient little distribution centre in the small Midland town of Thrapston. It was entirely run by local ladies working part-time. In fact, it was so good that we moved Marshall Morgan & Scott Publications' 'Art' side there from the Ward Lock warehouse in Edmonton where we had had great problems with it. For two years we never had a hitch at Thrapston and I really enjoyed my occasional visits there. Then, as the business grew, we had to find additional staff. Among them was a lady whose husband was a local trade union organiser. She persuaded or cajoled the entire staff there to join the relevant local union. Soon the highly competent boss lady resigned. Output deteriorated sharply and one of my saddest duties at

MM&S was to close the place down and move all the work elsewhere.

One of the success stories of our growth was the extent to which our export sales grew. Our most important markets were Australia, New Zealand and South Africa, and both Ward Lock and World Distributors had strong links with Australian publishers and wholesale houses. Ward Lock also had its own sales distribution company in Melbourne. Almost every year, in the early spring, Peter Lock flew off to South Africa and the Antipodes to see how things were going and to sell new product. I decided to go with him. We always flew to Johannesburg and called on our major customers there, and a few days later embarked on one of the longest flights in the world, from Johannesburg to Perth in Australia. The usual half-way stop was Mauritius where I was constantly astonished by the beauty of what little I saw of the island and the female element of the airport staff. This last was a well-known fact with seasoned travellers. I remember Peter once saying in the airport lounge, 'I really must come back here and bring my wife'. Another traveller heard the comment, and leaning over to Peter said, 'Come back by all means, but don't bring your wife'! Having landed at Perth and been thoroughly sprayed by the Immigration Authorities to destroy any insect pests we might be harbouring inadvertently, we would go to our hotel and sleep for the best part of twenty-four hours to recover from the journey.

On such trips we carried with us an extensive collection of 'dummies' of the books we proposed to publish in the autumn season for Christmas sales. The texts would have been written and set up in type and a small part of this would be pasted into blank books with proofs of the relevant illustrations – mostly in colour – and a virtually finished jacket. All the estimates and costings would have been carefully prepared, so that we could quote prices for finished copies, depending on the quantities ordered. If an Australian publisher bought the local rights, we would not, of course 'subscribe', i.e. pre-sell, the book to local wholesalers, but only in the case of about one book in five would there be a separate Australian edition.

Our normal route across Australia would be Perth, Adelaide, Melbourne, Sydney and Brisbane. Back in Sydney we would launch off on a three-day excursion to New Zealand, calling on customers in Christchurch, Wellington and Auckland. Everywhere, it must be said, we would be met with the warmest of welcomes, even if the orders were sometimes quite small, for Peter was a particularly welcome visitor from London. Everybody would be looking forward to hearing his famous and truly raucous laugh.

After a few more days in Sydney we would fly in different years either to Singapore or Hong Kong, where we would place orders for the printing and binding of the books we had previously shown to our customers. It required very precise planning and discipline to organise it all. The most complex part of the whole process was in the hands of a tiny Japanese shipping expert who would plan drop shipments to the various parts of Australia and eventually to Britain. As our business of this kind grew, we had to send a member of our staff to Singapore to assist with the day-to-day production process in order to be able to take decisions on the spot. When it worked it was wonderful and highly profitable, but later on things became so complex that the procedure we had crammed into one year had to be spread over two.

On one such journey we were met with a particularly enthusiastic welcome because the current best seller in Australia, on which a television series had been based, was *Seven Little Australians*, a book which Ward Lock had first published in 1894, and it was, of course, still in print. After the last of such exhausting three-week trips, during which we changed flights sixteen times, Peter and I came home jubilant with firm orders for over £400,000, a huge sum twenty-five years ago. However, when a senior member of the Pentos board, on hearing how many books we had sold, said to me 'Is that all you could manage?', it really was a whiplash blow. I began to think that perhaps we had reached a peak and it might be time for me to find other pastures for employment

*

In the autumn of 1975 I set off to the Frankfurt Book Fair with a large contingent of colleagues. It was extraordinarily stimulating because in each of our many diverse spheres, the new and forthcoming books had really caught on and were much in demand by foreign publishers. On my return to the office towards the end of October, our new finance director looked distinctly anxious. Had I, he asked, spoken to Terry Maher? I hadn't. I went to see him two days later. He too looked drawn and seemed nervous. How would I react, he asked eventually, to Pentos making an offer for the Marshall, Morgan & Scott shares it did not already own?

I knew that figure precisely. It was 73 per cent. I had been half expecting such a move for some time, but had hoped it would not happen. There was a tacit – it may even have been written – agreement that Pentos would not attempt to take us over, particularly as Terry was our chairman. We were much the bigger company and I doubted whether Pentos had the resources to pay for the 73 per cent of the shares, if they were valued at a true price. I replied that I was less than enthusiastic about the idea. We were doing extremely well on our own, but while I supposed that it had a certain degree of inevitability about it, I was not convinced that MM&S fitted into an industrial holding company, which was how Pentos was now describing itself. There had been earlier precedents where publishers had become part of such conglomorates, and they had not been a long-term success. To reassure me, Terry gave me an undertaking that I would continue to be free to run the company exactly as I had for the previous five years.

But the die was cast. Obviously Marshall, Morgan & Scott needed a professional team of its own to represent them in any negotiations, because we shared so many advisers with Pentos and they themselves were supposedly the financial advisers on whom we would call if we had had such an approach from another quarter. My first priority was to find a merchant bank to act on our behalf. We had slight links with Barings. But they dithered and, after keeping us waiting for forty-eight hours, said no. Then we remembered Jonathan Cohen of

County Bank, who had saved the day for us when we had our spot of bother with Nat West in Manchester. We turned to County Bank and, bless them, after only the briefest hesitation, they said yes, they would act for us.

A few days later Terry Maher made his offer for us public. Under the terms of the takeover rules, he was not then supposed to talk to our four directors any more regarding any aspect of the offer. Of course, the fact that he was our chairman complicated the matter. For one thing, it left me in charge.

There then followed a wild series of phone calls and meetings. We found a new lawyer, a stockbroker, accountants, and rapidly built up the complete team who were to act for us. I did not much care for the Pentos offer. It seemed to value our shares well below their true worth and it would not, I thought, be fair to our shareholders to accept it. County Bank agreed with us. And so began a month of pure trauma, which must happen hundreds of times a year, when people who have been friends and with whom one has worked closely, suddenly take on an adversarial role. It was extremely disturbing.

Another major obstacle was that apparently the company making the offer for shares ought to make public a forecast of its profits for the current financial year if it was well under way, so that the shareholders could have some idea of what sort of animal was aiming to take over their company. Pentos was ten months into their full financial year, but flatly refused to do so. One could only assume that they must have a good reason for not revealing this.

So it looked like fireworks. The two young men who were advising us, Jonathan Cohen and David Reed, were marvellously patient and supportive, and their boss, John Padovan, who ran County Bank, was a man I began to admire more and more. There were only four of us on the MM&S board. John Pemberton and myself, an outside non-executive director who had been on the board since before the days when FNFC had become involved, and our relatively new financial director.

County Bank wrote us an eight-page letter to summarise the situation. What it said very clearly was that the Pentos offer as first made was unacceptable. Our lawyer, our stock brokers, our acting accountants, all said the same thing. The stockbroker, Laing and Cruickshank, added that the market very much preferred MM&S shares to Pentos shares. John Pemberton in particular found the situation intolerable. He regarded Terry as a firm friend and close ally, and kept saying that he could not understand the position in which the takeover idea placed us. But, noble man, he was prepared to back me to the hilt.

The Pentos approach was described by them all the way through the discussions as a merger and not a takeover, which put the two companies on an equal footing. Another adviser insisted that if the deal went through, I should be deputy chairman of Pentos. I was by no means sure whether that was something I wanted. Our outside director refused for a single moment to countenance accepting the offer as it was first made. Regrettably, our financial director could not decide which side his bread was buttered on, switched sides and disappeared.

So a letter went from County Bank to Pentos stating that we wanted a higher offer for the shares (100p instead of 80p) and a profit forecast. Bit by bit Terry Maher yielded. We got the forecast: it did not look very exciting. It was clear that Pentos needed MM&S more than MM&S needed Pentos. The offer for the shares went up, but not enough. He asked for a meeting of all concerned at County Bank.

It was held in their huge, slightly gloomy, panelled board room with our three directors and our advisers at one end of a long table, and Terry with two or three of his colleagues at the other. It was a macabre scene, etched on my mind for ever more. The Pentos team seemed visibly to shrink as the meeting progressed. Jonathan Cohen acted as our spokesman. When tempers became heated, as they did, John Padovan calmed the contestants in a quietly effective, magisterial manner. The Pentos terms again moved very slightly in the right direction, but not far enough. It was becoming clear to me that our advisers' valuations of the shares involved a greater amount of money than was readily available. In fact, Terry had said at one point that his fellow directors would not allow him to go up to the level being demanded. So his own position was not without problems. The meeting broke up with nothing finally agreed.

I kept a diary of the phone calls and meetings among ourselves which followed. In retrospect I seem to have remained very calm and objective, considering the pressures involved. The situation now seemed clear: would we opt for independence or would we wait for Pentos to squeeze their resources and meet our demands? We lowered them very slightly in order to reach a non-contested resolution which everyone, but Pentos most of all, seemed desperately anxious to achieve. During the days which followed, Pentos, in fact, raised the ante by offering Convertible Unsecured Loan Stock, known in financial circles simply as CULS, as well as a cash alternative. This meant that not all the money had to be paid out at once; but most important, it meant that our shareholders were getting a reasonable deal.

On that basis the deal was concluded, but this was by no means the end of the matter.

*

It took time for the wounds to heal. Inevitably, the fierce struggle of the takeover – it certainly was not a merger – and, particularly, the additional sum that Pentos had had to find for the MM&S shareholders, left a bitter taste. At first a sort of harmony prevailed. This was followed by mere pin pricks to which I reacted strongly. These gradually grew into Napoleonic directives which made it quite clear that a new philosophy was abroad. And it was not one that appealed to me: in fact, it looked like evolving into the very sort of didactic management control I had struggled so hard to avoid: it generated fear, not confidence. The relative freedom of action I had given to local management seemed in danger of erosion, though I could see that there was a tremendous temptation to interfere and to exercise the control that went with hundred per cent ownership.

When I was offered a new contract, I talked the matter over with Patricia at great length. We were educating four children at the time. Departure might mean financial problems for us. But she was adamant that I should give up. The pressure-cooker lifestyle was fine if it brought happiness. It could be hell if one was miserable with it. As it happened, the matter that finally made the worm turn came from an unexpected quarter. My earnings now consisted of a basic salary, plus a bonus based on our profits; and our profits were a mighty £1,250,000. When I received the bonus it turned out to be laughable. I had overlooked the fact that I was being taxed on it at 96 per cent by our Labour Chancellor. So even the inducement of high earnings had gone.

When I delivered my resignation it did not bring about the relief at Pentos I expected: in fact, it brought fury. Maverick I might have been – people told me – but the results had been successful totally beyond expectations. Disentanglement takes time. There are pension rights and other contractual obligations to sort out. For another thing, there is also the matter of goodbyes and God-speeds.

I received shoals of letters of regret at my parting, mostly from the people with whom I had worked so closely who were genuinely upset at my departure. Two stick in my memory: the first was from Pat Hudson, the former bookshop chairman whom I had succeeded. She wrote:

> . . . I am just writing to say how very much we appreciated your leadership during the the past four years. Your kindness and goodwill and common sense have done so much to bring about a happy and successful takeover, and we all realise that this was largely due to your consideration for people, however odd they might be.

The second letter came from John Harris, our Home Trade Manager and senior traveller at Ward Lock. He said:

> . . . I think every member of the staff at Baker Street feels a deep sense of loss. I would like to thank you for five

glorious years of leadership, understanding and friendship, the most exciting and rewarding of all my years in publishing. You gave us a sense of urgency and achievement which has never been bettered anywhere . . .

Both were proof of the fact that the gentler, understanding approach to growth by acquisition had worked.

But business is transient. Pentos soon turned almost exclusively to bookselling. Terry Maher built up a huge chain of outlets in constant competition with Tim Waterstone. Between them they transformed the business of British bookselling. The Pentos publishing businesses were disposed of: World Distributors to a Danish firm; Ward Lock to Cassels, who not long after was itself absorbed by Orion (once Weidenfeld & Nicholson), and they, in turn, were bought by the French publisher Hachette. MM&S joined up with yet another religious publishing house. Terry Maher was eventually ejected from Pentos by his own non-executive directors who thereafter announced that the firm had lost seventy million pounds. On the way he had, almost single-handedly, brought about the abolition of the net-book agreement whereby publishers could fix the prices at which their books were to be sold in the shops. Whether the book trade has genuinely benefited is still an open question. The abolition certainly killed off many of the small, independent booksellers that abounded.

*

But despite the downbeat ending, it had been a wonderful five years: one of those periods – rare in life – when everything comes together in the right way. The obvious truth is that creative talent is what matters in publishing, but that talent needs fostering and support from all the other elements in the process that get the book to the reader.

And me? I was a free man at last, at the ripe old age of forty-nine, determined that I would retain my independence from now on. I had exercised my rights to buy all the Pentos shares to which I was entitled, and this helped when eventually I sold them at the highest point they ever reached.

CHAPTER TWELVE

Sotheby Days

When *The English as Collectors* was approaching its publication date, John Charlton and I took another decision which was to have far-reaching consequences. That was to hold an exhibition of all the books mentioned in my extensive bibliography. This was certainly the first annotated listing ever published of volumes on the history of collecting. The obvious venue for such a show was the National Book League, then still in its magnificent headquarters at 7 Albemarle Street: the site found for it just after the war, and the institution where Patricia had toiled at her first job as assistant to its then director, John Hadfield, before joining Faber's production department where we had met. I had never organised an exhibition before but the staff member of the NBL who had been deputised to work on it with me, Cynthia Sanford, was helpfulness personified. It gave me enormous pleasure to arrange the display of all the books, prints and photographs which I had so painstakingly assembled over the years. In order to raise funds for the NBL exhibition, publishers were asked to submit current publications of their own on any aspect of collecting, and to pay for the privilege of having them included, not only as a special part of the exhibition, but also to have them listed in the printed catalogue.

Peter Wilson, the celebrated Chairman of Sotheby's, whom the world associated with the surge of interest that had taken place in the collecting of antiques and the rise of the art market in the previous twenty years, was asked to open the exhibition, and agreed. But as the day of the opening approached it became clear that, as he was in the States on some vital business, he was unlikely to return in time. It was proposed that John Carter should take his place. John was a well-known bibliophile, at first Sotheby's representative in the United States, now a member of the firm's book department, but above all, author of *Taste and Technique in Book Collecting* and the *ABC of Book Collecting*. His initial renown stemmed from his joint authorship with Graham Pollard of the innocuous sounding *An Enquiry into the Nature of Certain Nineteenth Century Pamphlets*, the book which had toppled Thomas J Wise from his position of bibliographical pre-eminence.

John had just written an immensely detailed and rather laudatory review of *The English as Collectors* for *Books and Bookmen* and I was

The author with Martyn Goff (left), then Director of the National Book League and for many years organiser of the Booker Prize, and John Carter, bibliographer extraordinary, at the exhibition to launch *The English as Collectors*. It was on this occasion that the idea of the Sotheby history came into being.

longing to meet him. I did so in order to show him round the exhibition, so that he knew what he was opening. We got on well. I
teased him about the fact that there were four works on the history
of Christie's, and none on Sotheby's. He confessed that he was supposedly at work on just such a project, but finding it rather difficult.
I countered by saying that if he ever needed assistance, I would be
happy to provide it. To my astonishment he soon responded in a
letter asking me to outline how I would elicit the necessary information from the existing literature, as he had discovered to his horror
that Sotheby's had virtually no archive to speak of. What, of course,
he did not realise – and I certainly did not know at the time – was
that there was a perfectly understandable reason for this: a huge fire
in 1865 had destroyed the firm's premises and all its records, and none
of the partners subsequently had ever had the heart, or the time, to
re-establish a proper archive in the following century. Looking back-
wards was almost regarded as a nugatory occupation: it was the
present and, above all, the future that counted in the world of the
auctioneer.

I replied to John that I would cull Lugt's three monumental volumes entitled *Repertoire des catalogues de Ventes Publiques*, of 1938,
1953 and 1964, in order to establish what the important sales had
been, then look at the relevant catalogues which were in the British
Library, mile after mile after mile of them. After that I would check
the relevant newspapers of the day to see what the saleroom correspondents had said of the sales. In retrospect, it was a crazy idea – it
would have taken several lifetimes – but clearly it intrigued John and
he invited me to lunch. The outcome of the lunch was that he asked
me to take over the writing of the history of Sotheby's.

Thus began a decade in which I devoted a very substantial part of
my activities to Sotheby's. Throughout I was in the unusual position
of an outsider who had learned more about the firm than the great
majority of the insiders, and this was eventually to become my
strength as adviser, consultant and later active principal in the management of the auction house. Even later on, during the two or three

years when I was a paid employee of the firm, I knew that I was my own master. Nevertheless, when my departure drew nigh, it was more abrupt than I could have wished.

The firm had begun in 1744 so there was sure to be a lot of history, but nobody knew what it was or where to find it. John Carter himself was already the fifth putative author to have attempted to tackle such a book. The Sotheby board had agreed with him that I was now the person to make a go of it. I felt deeply tickled, and said yes. Fortunately I also said at once that it would probably take me seven years to complete the job. I was, after all, running a very large publishing enterprise at the same time. John, in turn, explained that Sotheby's was not as rich as everybody thought. They could offer me £750 for each of the first two years of the research it would entail. Apart from that, it was up to me to make the best deal I could with

Tim Munby, my distinguished mentor on the history of the book trade.

my two publishers, Chatto & Windus in London and W W Norton in New York. 'And, oh yes', he said as an afterthought, 'you can call upon two research assistants if you want them. One is myself; the other is Tim Munby, Librarian of Kings College, Cambridge.' Tim was the chronicler of a host of bibliographical personalities and the author of much historical research on the antiquarian book trade. I had a lot to report to Patricia that day when I got back home.

None of the books I had written so far fitted into a typecast category, which, of course, made them more difficult to publish and, indeed, more difficult to sell. For a company history covering nearly two hundred and fifty years, which concerned itself primarily with events, I decided early on that I would stand the thing on its head and concentrate on the personalities behind the events. Initially, therefore, I made it my business to list the major sales the firm had held and then to find out more about the collectors, the dealers, the men and women who had directed the firm (there proved to be only one woman who had been a director and an auctioneer), the cataloguers and any other personalities who had had a major role to play. It was slow work and there were many disappointments. But in the end I interviewed almost one hunded and fifty people. This was fun, and it gave me a superb insight into the workings of the art market. They not only had information of their own, but often had source material which they had hoarded away and which, on many occasions, they were pleased to be able to give me.[1]

When I came to question former members of the staff – or, indeed, the trade – about specific sales, there was a huge disparity in the detail of what people remembered. I frequently felt like some military intelligence officer trying to piece together a true picture of a major conflict. This was where the supreme importance of documentation became evident. I tracked down files in hidden corners of

[1] The most difficult people to get hold of were members of Sotheby's own staff. In the end I was given official help by a senior administrator in the firm in order to arrange the appointments. But even so, usually more than half of them were broken the first time round. History was not a priority.

the building, or material that had been sold and passed through many hands, and a multitude of old letters, where the unvarnished truth finally lay in my hands, if only I could read it. Old handwritings were often very difficult to read. I also rapidly learned how anecdotal memory is among the old. The pointed stories had stayed in the mind but the surrounding framework had completely disappeared.

This was certainly not true of Jim Kiddell, one of the most important Sotheby stalwarts of an older generation. He had joined the firm in 1922 as 'Works Manager'. That is, to look after the porter staff (eighteen enormous ex-Guardsmen), the mounting of sales, the fabric of the building and occasionally to act as relief auctioneer. Jim had had an unusual career in the army during the First World War as an adjutant, cooperating for a long period with the little known mutiny-breaking staff, and as five of his former commanding officers reported when asked by Sotheby's for a reference, he had been renowned for his tact and success in this difficult and demanding task. By the time I began to share an office with him in 1977 – for some three years, while I was at work on the firm's history – he had had fifty-five years of unremitting hard work at Bond Street behind him.

For many people Jim Kiddell personified Sotheby's. His was the tall, friendly, immaculately dressed figure that greeted them at viewings and sales. He was adored alike by dealers and collectors. He was always about in the rooms (even at eighty-six) peering benignly over the half lenses of his glasses. He had the alert, quizzical look of the scholar who has strayed into a non-academic scene, though he was more the senior schoolmaster than the absent-minded professor, for he exuded benevolent discipline, competence and a sense of order. If things had gone wrong he would at once concentrate on putting them right: as a sort of clients' guardian angel.

It was astonishing that such a small head could contain so many facts, figures and such an extraordinary memory for faces and recollections of personalities; and that one mind could have such total recall in the realms of pottery, porcelain, glass, oriental art in particular, furniture, carpets and even the intricacies and pitfalls of ancient antiquities of all kinds. The 'relief auctioneer' had turned into one of the most remarkably knowledgeable all-rounders for works of art that Sotheby's had ever had. He became a cataloguer of glass almost immediately after joining the firm because the specialist who usually did such work had had an emergency operation. Jim never gave it up, published much original research on the subject of glass and became vice-president of the Glass Circle. He had been president of the prestigious English Ceramic Circle for seventeen years when I first met him.

Tim Wilder (left); Jim Kiddell (right), in 1978. Tim had joined Sotheby's in 1911; Jim in 1921. The Sotheby history benefited greatly from their superb collective memories.

For me, Jim Kiddell was the richest vein of historic information. In fact, I was disturbed that his vast knowledge of collectors and the remarkable dealing fraternities of the years between the wars could well be completely forgotten if Jim did not write down what he knew about them. Patiently, if slightly unwillingly, he jotted down for me pen portraits of the principal personalities involved. When the writing became too difficult for him, he dictated the relevant facts to my secretary. All this information turned out to be a unique source of material for subsequent research.

One other Kiddell characteristic was of supreme importance to the firm. Jim first looked at every major piece that came his way to see if it was genuine, in whole or in part. His early training at the hands of dealers in furniture, silver, porcelain and carpets who had admired his charm and his total integrity had taught him that this was essential. The number of fakes about even then was substantial. In his room he accumulated a collection of objects that looked right, but weren't. This was called his 'Black Museum'. He showed me every piece so that I too, like a multitude of cataloguers before me, learned from him. He left this collection to Sotheby's after his death. Jim had an unusual hobby: he was the world authority on fighting cocks. Lovable character that he was, I dedicated my Sotheby history to him. Later I was privileged to sell his lifetime's assembly of working papers on pottery and porcelain at Bloomsbury Book Auctions: the catalogue we produced became a minor work of reference.

PCW, as Peter Wilson was known inside the firm, had the most enormous affection for 'Cuddles' (as Jim Kiddell was usually known) and had been trained by him before the war, but no two men could have been less alike. I have had to write about Wilson many times in the past. He was a hard man to pin down, but because he was undoubtedly the mainspring of Sotheby's growth, I made it my business to get to know him well and to formulate a clear understanding of how his remarkable and agile mind worked. So much so that, without asking many questions, I could soon work out how he had handled past problems and what his reaction would be to present – and sometimes future – ones. Eventually he trusted me to the extent of asking me to write documents for him which – if his time had allowed – he should have written himself. Even after he had checked them, the pieces remained virtually uncorrected. While he encouraged me to get on with the history, I was not able to see him as often as I would have liked. He was perpetually under the greatest pressure. His loyal secretary, Katherine McLean, had had to perfect the art of defending him in order to allow him to get on with what he regarded as most important for the firm.

It cannot often be the case that a major commercial enterprise has at its head a man so completely devoted to that business and so totally convinced that the future can only hold prospects of ever greater triumphs; and PCW had been right in predicting them for over twenty years. Two abilities in particular had helped him: one was to think big and always to opt for the more ambitious of any two alternatives; and the second was to give his undivided attention to anyone with whom he was in conversation, to a degree so convincing that the other person was left with a firm impression that to Peter Wilson he or she was the most important person in the world.

Throughout the years Wilson had demonstrated a truly remarkable eye for quality. He cared passionately about great art, but equally it would be fair to say that he cared passionately about great artists as creators of outstanding objects which he could sell, if at all possible to someone who would really appreciate them. He was already fully aware in the mid-fifties that Sotheby's future lay in the sale of the works of the Impressionist painters. It was this dual appreciation of real worth in the artistic sense, and value in the financial sense, that had helped to create an environment where great works of art could be bought or sold at will. It is easy to forget today how much simpler this process has become in the last thirty or forty years, as the auction houses have developed into great power houses.

Wilson was at his best in the rostrum, some twenty minutes into a major sale when the ever-present anxieties of a sticky beginning were behind him. He was a past master of the pregnant gesture, the momentary pause, the head tilted left and come-on smile, the raised eyebrow, the deprecatory look that said 'you really should have made another bid'. His facial expressions conveyed concern, humour, encouragement and a special form of instant communication with a hesitant bidder that generated confidence. The tempo could be agonisingly slow or move at the speed of lightning. Wilson was always firmly in control. That was why, until his retirement as Chairman, he was Sotheby's ultimate weapon when it came to persuading a hesitant client to sell a great painting or a great work of art through Sotheby's and not through some other rival.

His training as an auctioneer had given him an ability to think at enormous speed and, if need be, to take instant decisions. He was one of the few people who would always say 'let us decide it now', rather than 'let us think about it tomorrow'. Inevitably he had had to learn the skills of a diplomat, resilience in the face of public controversy, a ready charm, a certain sense of guile, a diffusion of bluntness, but he had few equals in being devastatingly direct in analysis when the occasion permitted – or demanded – it. With an iconoclastic wit went a puckish sense of humour, a saving grace in the constant crises that the management faced as a matter of routine. He also had a finely developed sense of showmanship and one of his strengths was that his tall, distinguished, urbane and rather conventional appearance masked a distinctive, unconventional and very agile mind. The one medium in which he was perfectly hopeless under pressure was on television. Camera close-ups always seemed to give away that he was thinking one thing and saying another, and thus he lacked conviction.

Although we got on so well during the seven years in which I was writing the history – I do not think he approved later on of my becoming a director of Sotheby's, let alone head of overseas operations. This was some time after his retirement to the South of France. Perhaps he feared that I had got to know him too well. The general belief was that he had named his cousin, Lord Westmorland, as his successor so that he, Peter, could continue to influence, if not control, matters in Bond Street from his villa, Clavary, near Grasse. And indeed there were telephone conversations which occupied Lord Westmorland and his deputy, Graham Llewellyn, head of Sotheby's jewellery department, for long periods almost every morning.

Sotheby's had started a Monte Carlo office in January 1975 at a time when Britain's economy was very slowly recovering from a state of disarray unequalled since the depression of 1930. The first sale there had been a highly theatrical occasion when some of the property of Baron Guy de Rothschild, and his close friend Baron de Redé, had been dispersed. The results had been spectacular, and the standard of Monte Carlo's sales which took place with increasing frequency thereafter, rarely dropped. Such sales, in common with all others in Europe, were ultimately my responsibility after I became director of overseas operations, even though PCW regarded those in Monte Carlo as his personal fiefdom. I had intended to be at one such sale of some importance and to arrive two or three days before it took place. However, a row of such cataclysmic proportions occurred in London when a senior director, who also happened to be a particularly close friend of PCW's, resigned in a huff, that I was delayed by interminable meetings on the subject. PCW was furious because the London management had done nothing to impede the man's departure, and even more furious with me for arriving late, not that I would have had much of a role in arranging the material to be viewed for the sale. I was certainly not prepared for the cascade of vituperation to which I was subjected, initially in a state of slight stupefaction. This increased by leaps and bounds when it turned out that PCW was expecting me in future to play a leading managerial role in Sotheby affairs generally in London and New York. Such thoughts had certainly never entered my head. I very much enjoyed the limited role of looking after the overseas offices, principally in Europe, but I was clearly not cut out for such responsibilities and in no way ambitious enough to undertake them. The torrent of abuse and criticism, however, continued. I had rarely – if ever – seen a man so wild with fury. In the end I could take it no longer and my temper too began to give way. I do not believe PCW had ever been told so bluntly, simply to shut up, and to have explained to him in words of one syllable that if he didn't like the current London management, that was entirely his own fault. As Chairman for twenty-one years he had had ample opportunity to arrange for a successor of his liking and if things were not running smoothly, it was principally because he had opted out and departed from the firm without giving anyone more than the shortest of short notices. I had attended the highly charged staff meeting where he announced that he was leaving London, not next week, next month or next year, but NOW, at once. The entire staff was stunned. The dramatic effect was heightened by an enormous thunderstorm occurring at the same time. The gods clearly didn't like what they were hearing!

I explained to him, without mincing my words, that the turbulence and problems that had arisen in consequence were enormous and entirely of his making. God knows what murderous thoughts were passing through his mind as I spoke. He froze; then, po-faced, slowly began to apologise. Our exchange had certainly taken up one of the most memorable and traumatic hours of my life, and I was left limp for several days afterwards. Although we came face to face from time to time, we never really spoke again at any length.

I did not know until much later that he was suffering from an acute form of diabetes and that this could lead to irritability and occasional irrational behaviour. It probably prompted his outburst. But he had played a considerable role in my life and, despite what had passed, I continue to regard him as a great man and a towering figure in the world of art and antiques.

He died in 1984 of leukaemia, some four years after he had gone to live in France. Four years after that I was asked to write the entry on him in the *Dictionary of National Biography*, as I had done for John Carter some years earlier. It was an intriguing moral challenge. I gave him all the credit that was his due, but didn't duck his homosexuality or his difficult final years. Later, because it was known that I had accumulated a great deal of information about PCW, various other authors approached me about supplying text for a full biography, but so far no one has completed the job.

*

During the years 1976, 1977 and 1978 I attended three many-sessioned sales, because it seemed to me that they would be of extraordinary significance in completing the history of Sotheby's.

The first took place in New York and consisted of the estate of Mrs Geraldine Marcellus Hartley Dodge, the daughter of William Rockefeller, the President of Standard Oil. When she had married Mr Dodge in 1907, she and her husband were referred to as 'the richest young couple in the world'.

It became the most outstanding American house sale ever held with some eight complete sales sessions, in which nearly 8,000 lots were sold. But what amazed Sotheby's American management was the ease with which the various houses owned by Mrs Dodge were sold by a prominent estate agent, in contrast to the sale of their contents. Such work seemed infinitely less labour-intensive: a stark contrast to the auctioneer's weary toil over many months – and it was much more profitable. It was, indeed, the sale of the Dodge town house at a vast price that led directly to the decision to form a Sotheby property company specialising in expensive dream houses. The consequence of that decision to go into the real estate business was something that no one at that stage could have imagined, as we shall see later.

*

In May of the following year, 1977, Sotheby's in England undertook a house sale of even greater proportions, certainly the largest the firm had ever undertaken. I was much involved as participating observer.

Mentmore was a huge, strangely winsome pile erected in the rolling Buckinghamshire countryside in the 1850s. It had been designed by Sir Joseph Paxton in a 'Jacobethan' style, flanked by four formidable towers, at the behest of Baron Mayer Amshel de Rothschild who, as the youngest of four sons, was much more active as a connoisseur, collector and lover of the turf than he was in the traditional family banking business. The style and richness of the interior of his new residence became something of a prototype for housing the great

Rothschild art collections of the nineteenth century elsewhere in England and in France. But after 120 years, Mentmore had spent itself. It had been designed for a lifestyle that was almost totally extinct in Britain and by 1977 the house had become a majestic white elephant. Yet in its death throes Mentmore became a *cause célèbre* which epitomised the conflict between conservation and dispersal during a period when the State had taken over almost every form of patronage.

When the government decided, in January of 1977, that it would not make an offer for Mentmore and its contents, Lord Rosebery's mother, the eighty-two year old Dowager Countess, helped to conduct parties of journalists (including me) round the house, and long articles on Mentmore, its contents and the forthcoming dispersal by Sotheby's, planned for May 1977, were featured prominently in leading newspapers and journals. I began to accumulate what turned out to be a huge volume of press cuttings.

Ultimately, despite a host of further nerve-racking rumours to the contrary, it was decided that the sale of Mentmore was on.

In the superbly beautiful setting of the Vale of Aylesbury in a late, seemingly reluctant spring, the ten days of actual auction, after the months of frenzied organisation and preparation, were like a long outing into a forgotten world. There was a tremendous disparity between the portent-laden brouhaha preceding the sale and the reality of the occasion itself. The preview of the thousands of lots that were to come under the hammer demonstrated to many the difficulties of turning Mentmore into a permanent public showcase. Years of neglect were visible everywhere, and such neglect in the long term was simply a sentence of death. It became obvious that the sale would re-circulate a lot of magnificent objects that might otherwise have just rotted away.

Sotheby's had given Mentmore a festive dress for the occasion of its end as a Rothschild/Rosebery preserve. There were marquees outside the house for refreshment, for the despatch of goods and an enormous striped, draped and decorated affair for the sale itself which could seat two thousand and house also a great battery of reporters, photographers and TV crews from all over the world. Entrance was by ticket only. The catalogues had a special magnificence about them, and although 11,000 sets of the five volumes were printed, and sold at £30 a set, they had gone out of print three weeks before the sale started and sets were said to be changing hands at up to £300. A special paperback edition – devoid of colour – had to be rushed through the press.

Lord Rosebery and his family were in attendance throughout. His Lordship himself, an enthusiastic expert on stage lighting and sound reproduction since his days at Oxford, came to the rescue when, just as the first sale was about to start, it was found that the principal microphone was not working.

When I saw Peter Wilson strolling around behind the scenes half an hour before the opening furniture sale was about to begin on that sunny May morning, it was not surprising that I found him tense and nervous. The firm had never had a build-up of such proportions before any sale. The very antagonism of the conservationists had made Mentmore a household name. The eyes of the world were focused on the sale and most British morning newspapers gave it front page treatment. The delay over the microphone lasted twenty-five agonising minutes and added enormously to the pre-sale tension. But when the bidding began at last, it became clear within minutes that the occasion was going to be a success. Prices were much higher than the estimates and the bidding was vigorous and widespread. With forethought typical of the whole undertaking, Sotheby's had brought a number of New York staff over for the occasion who acted as additional bid callers (a normal feature at Madison Avenue), because the auctioneer could not see every deliberate movement in the vast sea of faces in front of him.

The most amusing part of the proceedings was the sale of the household goods, pedestrian perhaps by Victorian standards, but historically fascinating as well as being quaintly useful in the 1970s. There was enormous competition for the old but elegant wooden coat-hangers and towel rails, the brass and copper hot water jugs and laundry baskets, and fire irons and coal-scuttles (catalogued as Purdoniums), the kitchen china and the maids' plain chests of drawers. All had been displayed in the long stables behind the house, among busts of ancestors and famous politians and live chickens pecking away at ancient ears of wheat.

The total sum raised by the eighteen sale sessions came to £6,390,000 – the highest ever figure by far for any house sale. For Marcus Linell, then managing director, and John Cann, organiser *extraordinaire*, who had been responsible for the organisation, and those who had toiled with them, it had been the most enormous job of work, at times in dreadfully dispiriting conditions because of the initial uncertainties and political overtones. Their greatest achievement was that an event that might have been funereal or merely unprepossessing had, in fact, been imbued with an enormous sense of fun and style and was crowned with great success.

But Mentmore was merely the high point in the most active summer season that anyone at Sotheby's could ever remember. It stretched the staff in all departments to extremes. It was a good time to see the great auction apparatus at work. Within the 1976/77 auction season the firm had staged well over 1,000 separate sales, not only in London and New York, but also in Amsterdam, Monte Carlo, Zurich, Florence, Hong Kong and Johannesburg. The question that began to pass through my mind was how much longer there would be enough material to keep the engine going. Certainly the scale of operations could not be kept up for many more years. With hindsight one could see that this was the moment when prices were going to rise, and rise very steeply.

*

As the Mentmore sale reached its end, Patricia and I decided that we needed a brief holiday. Each of us in our respective roles was thoroughly exhausted by the constant calls on our time. We booked rooms in what seemed a wonderful country hotel in Oxfordshire and told our daughter Lucilla not to tell anyone where we were, unless it was a matter of life or death. While we were changing for dinner soon after our arrival, the telephone rang. It was Peregrine Pollen, deputy chairman of Sotheby's. 'How on earth did you find us?' I asked. 'We told our daughter not to tell anyone where we were unless it was a matter of life or death.' Peregrine explained that he thought his reason for phoning was just that; but he would not tell me what the reason was. He was insistent that I should attend a vital meeting at the offices of Slaughter & May, a famous firm of city solicitors in Basinghall Street, at 9.00 a.m. the following morning. I resolutely refused, but Peregrine is a persuasive fellow, and after some three quarters of an hour on the phone, I reluctantly agreed, still in ignorance of what it was all about.

Next morning, instead of the hoped-for long lie-in, we had to get up at the crack of dawn. Patricia dropped me at Slaughter & May's offices and I was ushered into a large meeting room. Sitting round a circular table were Peregrine Pollen and Peter Spira, the latter having not long before joined Sotheby's as finance director, and eight or more other men in serious suits who were completely unknown to me. Peregrine explained that the meeting had been called to find out from me the bones of Sotheby's history. So began the most amazing cross-examination in which I was asked to talk about Samuel Baker, George Leigh, the three members of the Sotheby family, John Wilkinson, the Hodges – father and son, Barlow, Hobson and Warre, and Vere Pilkington; the offices they occupied; the sales they had held; the staff they had employed. Frankly, I was astonished how much I knew. I had had no inkling about this inquisition; I had no notes or reference books on hand of any kind. But all these shadows from Sotheby's past had become familiar friends and I enjoyed talking about them. After three hours, I asked for a break and I was told in a kindly manner to get some fresh air, and to come back in half an hour.

When I returned I asked for an explanation. In fact, I seem to remember saying that I was not prepared to go on unless it was explained to me what this was all about. After a lengthy adjuration and

the strictest insistence upon secrecy, I was told that it was planned to
turn Sotheby's into a public company, and the long cross-examination about the firm's history had been to establish if I was capable of
writing the necessary section of the relevant offer document. In view
of the fact that Sotheby's had been established as long ago as 1744,
the financiers felt that the history should be its most promiment part.
After my five years at Marshall, Morgan & Scott, dealing with a string
of mergers and takeovers, this sort of corporate challenge was meat
and drink to me. I had spent endless agonising periods in the offices
of Clifford-Turner, our solicitors, checking documents by impossible deadlines. It took me no time at all to agree to undertake the job.

There followed several weeks of mayhem. I became just as thoroughly involved with the financial implications as with detailing the
historical facts. I was summoned to drafting meetings when I would
be asked to think up alternative wordings. The question always was:
should they be bland, definite, incisive, aggressive. All such variants
were called for and they were well mixed in the final document.

This share offer was to be the first since the great Stock Exchange
meltdown in February 1974 when the FT Index had plunged to 140
(as I write, it is well over 5000) and a really wealthy Middle-Eastern
oil potentate could have bought the bulk of Britain's industry without seriously feeling the pinch. But in the event Sotheby was pipped
at the post: BP came in with a sudden share offer, and everything
had to be put on hold until that was out of the way. When eventually
the Sotheby share offer was announced, it was over-subscribed by
twenty-seven times by the closing date. Our advisers were jubilant
and I received a host of graceful compliments; not only that, but
from Rothschild's – one of our three merchant bankers (the other
two were Kleinwort Benson and S G Warburg) – a transparent, plastic cube containing a miniaturised offer document, as a keepsake. I
had not been allowed to buy any shares, but it was generally agreed
that the history had played an important role in attracting shareholders. The worst part of the job for me, which nobody had warned
me about at the beginning, was that I had to produce written proof

of evidence for every statement I had made in my six long pages of text: this alone took another four weeks.

The question I then had to ask myself was what was I going to charge Sotheby's for several months of incredibly hard work that had gone on at all hours and over weekends, and had put a stop to all my other activities. I consulted my accountant, the redoubtable Henry Brandes, who said: 'Whatever invoice you send them, it isn't high enough unless you feel embarrassed about submitting it!'. Clearly I interpreted him correctly, because Sotheby's were taken aback by the size of my bill. It was agreed they would pay 80 per cent and suggested that I should prepare – that is, write and design – the layout and text of their first annual accounts as a public company, *and* if we won the prize for the best-produced accounts of the year, they would triple the missing bit. I had no idea that there were 3,000 applicants for such a competition, but in any case we won.

I looked after the following three annual accounts as well and in each case was asked to draft the chairman's statement. By this time I was so familiar with what was going on that I didn't even get a briefing.

It turned out to be a marvellous first year of my independent existence financially. It also established a wonderfully close rapport with senior members of the Sotheby management, which helped considerably with the compilation of the firm's history. People were much more willing to unburden themselves now that they had got to know me, particularly when I wanted to have answers to difficult questions.

*

However, in the short term, another momentous sale began to occupy the firm. The circumstances surrounding it could not have been more different than Mentmore. It was the well-loved private collection of Robert von Hirsch, formed in one very old man's lifetime, mostly during a period when what particularly interested him was not widely sought after. It had been assembled in Germany, moved to Switzerland and was now to be dispersed in London. Although the collection ranged widely over paintings and drawings from the fifteenth to the twentieth century, and included furniture, silver, porcelain and decorative works of art of many kinds, it was the contents of a single glass display cabinet that stirred the acquisitive imagination of scholarly collectors and curators all over the world, and which was to have a monumental impact on the entire art market. It contained medieval antiquities of a quality and rarity that had rarely been sold at auction before. Peter Wilson had known von Hirsch for many years and the sale represented the zenith of Wilson's career. It achieved many record prices and raised a total of over £18,000,000.

*

It was to be two more years before the Sotheby history was published. I was disappointed by its initial reception. Reviewers used the opportunity to air their own feelings about what they considered the firm's shortcomings: few actually read the book. I was repeatedly accused of vital omissions when the subjects referred to were clearly listed in the index and certainly covered at length within the text. I had thought that, ultimately, there would be more interest in the recent history and less in the firm's early days when it concerned itself primarily with books, and I said so in my introduction. But I was wrong. There had been few other efforts to cover the early days of book collecting, or library building, in relation to the activities of the contemporary antiquarian book trade. This seemed to fascinate a substantial readership and it led to voluminous correspondence with readers. Later on, the history of Sotheby's became an unrivalled source book for other people writing on the art market or the collecting world. I know of six or seven books that quarried my text extensively: only three did so with my permission. As a publisher, I felt that I had written a book for a wider understanding of the subject and the better to inform the people who were interested in it. But as an author I hated it when others used my work without any acknowledgement (and received large advances of royalties for doing so). However, in publishing terms the book was a success.

The 10,000 copies we had printed sold out within eighteen months, on both sides of the Atlantic. Eighteen years later, I still get a steady stream of correspondence about it. At the time when the firm celebrated its 250th anniversary, I had over a hundred requests for information, many of them from within Sotheby's itself.

If I had thought that the publication of the book would be the end of my relationship with the firm, I was proved wrong. There was a lot more to come. I had rejected a number of tentative suggestions that I should work for Sotheby's. My very strong feeling was that if I did so before the book about the firm came out, I could

The book appeared in 1980: 10,000 copies sold within eighteen months. The text has been plagiarized continuously ever since. The illustration shows Peter Wilson in the rostrum.

indeed be accused of doing a whitewash job. (In fact, it was part of my contractual agreement that I had the untrammelled right to say what I wanted.)

So that when soon after I had handed the manuscript over to my publisher, Chatto, Marcus Linell, managing director of Sotheby UK, asked me if I would consider helping to reorganise the book

department, I agreed without hesitation. The twin objectives were
to combine its two parts, housed separately in Bond Street and at
the old Hodgson's Rooms in Chancery Lane, and to move the whole
into entirely different premises that were being prepared for it in the
reconstructed former Aeolian Hall which Sotheby's had recently acquired to deal with its increasing space problem. In rough terms,
Bond Street dealt with books published before 1830; Chancery Lane
with books that had appeared later. The second objective was to speed
up the time it took to bring books to the point of sale: the volume
passing through the firm was so great at the time that it took fourteen months between the time when someone brought in a book to
sell, and the moment when it came under the hammer. Clients were
complaining bitterly about this delay. After what had happened over
the offer document, Marcus and I fixed a fee for the job at the outset: the time it was to take was dictated by the impending move which,
of course, also involved the closure of the Chancery Lane building
after more than a hundred years as a saleroom – a matter of great
regret to many.

   Reorganisation appealed to my analytical mind. It is what I had
to tackle when I came to Methuen's as production manager, and as
managing director when I took on Ward Lock and the growing world
of M M & S. Subsequently, it had become necessary in other places
to catch up with a rapidly changing world. But this was reorganisation on an altogether different scale. I had greatly to change an
intricate system which had evolved over 240 years: one that seemed
as firmly entrenched as constitutional law. What is more, the Sotheby
management wanted the number of book sales increased from thirty-
five a year to fifty.

   My first move was to get to know all the people involved and to
find out precisely what they did and how they did it. The staff of the
book department numbered in excess of thirty people and there were
legions more in ancillary departments who oiled the wheels of the
auction apparatus. The most important person by far was Lord John
Kerr, the head of the book department, as relaxed a man as one might

ever hope to meet with a charming sense of humour; a brilliant auctioneer with a manner all his own and a bookman with the wisdom
of years of accumulated experience behind him. But he knew that he
needed help from somebody not involved with the daily hurly-burly
inside the department. After a few discussions and a written outline
plan of what needed to be done, he gave me his absolute backing. In
a letter to Marcus Linell, sketching out my approach, I wrote, 'While
it may be necessary to formulate a grand plan, I think it would be
much more satisfactory in human terms to decide on change one step
at a time and thus to fulfil our objectives with a minimum of upset
and resentment'. The grand plan did, of course, exist: the three areas
that needed a radical shake-up were managerial (there was no hierarchy); the organisation (the administration creaked and nobody, let
alone Lord John, knew what books there were in the building), and
the commercial (few people had any real knowledge of the financial
considerations or the level of profits being made).

I formed a departmental committee of six who met once a week
to consider not only the day-to-day running of the department –
and what was going wrong – but made it clear before each meeting
what the reorganisation should achieve to put things right. I hardly
ever attended these meetings myself: it was important that the staff
should convince themselves of what was necessary. As the months
progressed, increased efficiency and speed of action began to become
a norm.

Altogether I was surprised that Sotheby's allowed an outsider as
much freedom to do what was necessary as the firm allowed me at
the time. For this reason alone I regarded it essential that at all
times the entire staff involved should know what changes we were
planning and why and how these affected them. It worked. But it
only worked because most members of the committee wanted it to
work.

I invented a completely new concept, 'Fast Sales'. The first of these
took place on 21 May 1981. Sotheby's had publicised it widely. The
blurb stated that 'Although the catalogue descriptions will be brief,

there will be no lowering of standards . . . Books will be within the budget of the young collectors, with average prices within the region of £100 to £200'.

The key points were that such sales would take place very frequently; that books would come up at auction within four to six weeks after being brought in, and that payment would be made one week from completion of each sale. It was this last that really attracted the trade. We made one or two other auction innovations. The uniform 10 per cent commission rate included insurance cover, and we introduced late viewing up to 7.30 in the evening on Mondays (the sales took place on Tuesdays). Although new property began to pour in, the fast sales cleared our backlog wonderfully.

Changing the systems was one thing, but I also had to organise the moves from the old Bond Street book department and Hodgson's Rooms in Chancery Lane. There were endless meetings with the architects and administrators on how Bloomsbury Place, the former Aeolian Hall, should be fitted out. There were constant changes of mind because costs looked like exceeding budgets, but more so because experts are by nature temperamental. To add to our problems, the book department at Sotheby's in New York was in serious trouble and this syphoned off some of our managerial strength. I had begun work on all this during the summer of 1979: the department started operating from Bloomsbury Place in May 1981, as planned.

What I had thought was a final ingenious ploy at the time, boomeranged on me later. When the lease for Hodgson's Rooms, which were now obviously redundant, was sold, we inserted a clause that it could not in future be used as an auction room. But of course, when we started Bloomsbury Book Auctions, that is exactly where we would have liked to have gone!

The jewellery and coin department shared the new building. It is difficult to believe today that I had been asked to plan for twenty-six two-day book sales, two one-day illuminated manuscript sales, three or four sales of oriental material, six to eight sales of autograph material, fourteen one-day jewellery sales and eighteen coin and medal sales, *plus* forty-one of our new one-day fast book sales. Where on earth did the management think that that much property would come from? But my arguments on this point were brushed aside. Euphoria was in the air: the unspoken comment seemed to be that FH had not been in the auction business long enough to understand these things.

*

My life at the beginning of the 1980 decade was pretty crazy. Apart from the work at the book department, I was correcting the final proofs of the Sotheby history and planning the marketing of the book. I was acting as principal editorial adviser to the publishing house of Frederick Muller, recently bought by Harlech Television (HTV) to whom I was publishing consultant. I was much involved with the publishing activities in the art historical field of Philip Wilson Publishers, where I was a substantial shareholder. That year, for example, I travelled to Lugano, with our senior editor to devise a plan for publication in many volumes of the Thyssen-Bornemisza collection. At Philip Wilson we published all the books that came out under the Sotheby Publication imprint. Quite separately, I was a major shareholder of Sweeten's Bookshops in and around Preston where we not only owned five bookshops but were also developing a computer company which created software for bookshops and publishing. I was on the committee of various bibliographical organisations, and to top it all, I started to drain out the pond outside our house, a job which took me just over a year!

Apart from all this, I was hard at work on the most difficult writing assignment of my life: the catalogue of the Norton Simon Museum in Pasadena. It had required three trips to California and we went through eighteen stages of proofing. It finished with litigation of such ferocity that Philip Wilson and I – we were publishing the book – thought it would be curtains for both of us. But we won through. I will revert to Norton Simon later.

But if I thought the early part of 1980 was busy, I was to get a completely new set of surprises by the autumn.

In the meantime, the book department plans were maturing and I was less involved on a day-to-day basis. Patricia and I took our youngest child, Piers, to Sweden and Norway on a long holiday: we crossed on a brand new car ferry and took our Volvo. It turned out to be one long series of adventures. Then I took my aged mother to our German property in Pretzfeld, a trip which she particularly enjoyed. And then, suddenly, there was a new development which looked as if it was going to put all my previous involvements with the auction world in the shade.

Patricia and I met at the Festival Hall one sunny evening in September 1980, to dine there and then to listen to an inspired concert given by the English Chamber Orchestra. We both burst out with a simultaneous, 'I've got a lot to tell you!' Patricia had been asked if she would be prepared to stand for the chairmanship of our local District Council in the following year. She had been an independent councillor for our own area for many years, and had become particularly expert on planning and on mineral extraction: both subjects that were of constant concern to our parishes. She was quite uncertain whether she would be acceptable as chairman of a largely Conservative council. But if elected, chairmanship would mean attendance at many more meetings and participation in an unending round of civic celebration. She would be away from home a good deal. Did I mind?

'Not at all', said I, 'particularly if you listen to what has happened to me.' I was still seeing a good deal of the Sotheby management and earlier in the week, Marcus Linell, the managing director of Sotheby's UK, had asked me to see him. He explained that he realised I was coming to the end of my work on the book department and wondered whether I would be interested in taking on another Sotheby assignment.

This turned out to be nothing less than becoming head of all Sotheby's Overseas Operations outside the UK and the US. Basically it involved the supervision of the twenty-something offices in Europe and others further afield. I don't now remember my reaction, but in retrospect I am still amazed. I must have said yes in principle, although I reacted at once by saying that because of my other commitments I could probably only devote three days a week to the job, and that I did not want a long-term, permanent post. The salary Marcus suggested shook me to the core. He also felt it important that I should become a director of Sotheby's main London board, as well as a member of its executive committee. Patricia was as delighted by this opportunity for me as I was for hers. In each case it would be a crowning event after years of apprenticeship. We enjoyed the concert, went home and started planning.

In my case it meant countless meetings with the top brass at Sotheby's, in order to make all the necessary arrangements and to brief me. I spent a lot of time with David Westmorland, the chairman; Graham Llewellyn (generally known as GDL), his deputy and the director ultimately responsible for activities outside the UK; Marcus Linell; Peregrine Pollen; and Peter Spira, the financial director. Peter Wilson telephoned frequently from Clavery in the South of France to offer his mite of wisdom: I was, after all, suddenly to be in charge of territory he very much regarded as his own.

To me the whole thing was an awesome challenge. But I was not blinkered about the difficulties. I had sensed and seen some of them while at work on the history.

In my first few days I spent a long time talking, in particular, to Graham Llewellyn. He was very tall, urbane, wonderful with clients, supremely knowledgeable about jewellery and an excellent and considerate auctioneer. He had started life in the jewellery department at Harrod's before coming to Sotheby's. He was the personification of everything English. It was typical of Sotheby's that he had been put in charge of the expansion of the overseas offices: most of the overseas representatives found it extremely difficult to communicate with him. In David Westmorland's days as chairman, GDL became the managerial 'repair man'; an excellent tactician, but, in total contrast to PCW, no strategist. Nominally he was my boss, but he said right at the outset of my employment that he proposed to leave me strictly alone as he had more than enough problems in other areas, more often than not in pacifying warring individuals inside the firm.

We began our collaboration in the usual quirky way. I had been in the office only a couple of days when a sudden, important meeting of all London directors (there were forty-eight of them in those days) and senior staff was called. There must have been about seventy of us at least, crowded into one of the big salerooms. GDL addressed us. Customs and Excise had lodged a severe complaint with Sotheby's (and, as it turned out, with Christie's too) that most members of staff took little action about declaring goods they brought into the country, nor did they prepare the necessary paperwork to do so. Two or three had been caught recently and the firm was threatened with death and damnation if this matter, which amounted to smuggling, was not put right. Staff could face prison sentences: it applied equally to the export of goods over a certain value.

We all went back to our offices chastened. It was, of course, to be my concern more than anyone elses. GDL asked if I could come and see him: an underlining, I thought, of what had just been said: but not at all. 'I think you're going to Geneva tomorrow, Frank,' he said. 'Could you just slip this into your pocket and give it to Nicholas Rayner?' (our jewellery expert in Switzerland). 'This' was a diamond necklace, valued even then at over £100,000. I wanted to remain a director of Sotheby's for more than two days. I refused. In a funny way GDL never forgave me.

I started travelling abroad at once to meet the many Sotheby representatives in their local offices. I went to see and to listen. I had quickly learned about the problems voiced by the London end of the business. Now I wanted to hear what the other end had to say.

One has to remember that these overseas outposts had been started on a random basis over a period of about fifteen years, and had never been properly coordinated. There was no conformity of organisation; each office had its own way of doing things and a stream of often contradictory memos from London had not done much to help. I had under me an exceedingly competent financial director, Julian

Harrison. He had taken the trouble to visit all the offices and got them to work on a common financial reporting system, but that was as far as it went. What I had to achieve was better liaison between the London expert departments and the overseas representatives and, above all, to encourage them to get more property.

The London experts were constantly undertaking journeys to the continent to inspect the merits of property that had been brought into the offices in, say, Brussels, Paris, Hamburg, Rome or Stockholm, but if these offices didn't have plenty of warning of such impending visits, they often didn't have sufficient property to merit the cost of the journeys. Similarly, poor photographs of Old Masters, carpets, jewellery or pieces of arms and armour, as they winged their way to London, needed to be accompanied by detailed condition reports so that the expert could respond with a reasonably accurate estimate of what the client could expect to receive from their sales.

There were a few instant problems which needed tactful resolution. For example, what Sotheby's had not told me until my appointment was almost clinched, was that they had already appointed another person to do my work, whom they now regarded as too gentle for the task. 'You sort it out', they said, 'if you can.' I did. After a while the poor man decided to go elsewhere. In Portugal, Sotheby's had half-appointed two competing official representatives, which led to constant strife. I was splendidly wooed by both when I went there: in one instance a whole mothballed palace was opened to entertain me, the servants in livery and powdered wigs. It was fabulous, but I had to be very careful what I said.

I only learned after I left the firm that the London management had expected me to sack most of the existing representatives, but in general I found them to be both competent and extremely hard working. The majority cooperated magnificently once they understood what I wanted them to do. The results were astonishing. The turnover of the goods sent to London from the European offices in my first year went up by £19 million, and the percentage of what was sold in London emanating from European clients reached a record 51 per cent of the turnover. On top of this, our increasingly good sales in Zurich, Geneva, Amsterdam, Florence and Monte Carlo yielded substantial profits.

It has to be said, however, that not many London directors appreciated this success. The in-fighting and bickering at the weekly executive meetings I attended, over what seemed to me trivia, was truly astonishing. There was constant friction over how to run the smaller provincial auction houses Sotheby's had recently acquired; over the way the firm should publicise itself; over the fact that the London management – and they, after all, were supposed to run the whole global operation – seemed totally out of touch and completely out of control of the crazy surge of expansion in New York; over the importance of the trade as compared to the private buyer at a time when the firm was threatened with legal action by the trade associations about the introduction of the much resented premium, the charge made to the buyer on top of the hammer price. As I have written elsewhere, it really seemed to me that of the eleven members of the executive committee, only two didn't want to be chairman: one was the existing chairman, Lord Westmorland, and the other was me.

However, my attendance at these meetings did give me the opportunity to explain the difficulties faced by my overseas colleagues, and to point out the simple fact that people in Rome didn't think like people in Amsterdam, or Frankfurt, or Madrid. Nor did their clients. The overseas network needed flexibility of understanding.

The other thing that amazed me was the dislike of one foreign office for another. The Belgians had it in for Mak van Waay, the long-established Amsterdam auction house bought by Peter Wilson some years previously; the Italians found it difficult to get on with Monte Carlo; there was certainly no love lost between Oslo and Stockholm, and the Swiss looked askance at the Germans. In fact, Switzerland and Germany were the two most profitable offices. Jurg Wille in Zurich, scion of a famous Swiss military family, was one of those rare men who are brilliant on the wider strategy of what needed to be done, as well as being a perfectionist on detail. Sotheby's held sales in Zurich and Geneva, and these were almost always a success. The jewellery sale in my first year of action in 1981 was a sensation. The jewellery on show was so fabulous that Jurg Wille constantly roamed around with a revolver in his pocket. As it happened, this precaution was insufficient to stop an ingenious piece of chicanery. Two men took wax impressions of the two most expensive diamonds on view on day one; and came back later with excellent plastic reproductions which they substituted on day two. The swap was, of course, quickly discovered. But the culprits were only caught some eighteen months later.

No man could have been more different from Jurg Wille than Ernst Behrens, head of the three German offices. He was based in a superb office in the Odeonsplatz in Munich, also run with tremendous efficiency. Ernst had been head of the Goethe Institutes in Germany before he came to Sotheby's and was something of an intellectual, as well as a brilliant publicist: the one thing that seemed quite certain, however, was that whatever he did, it always upset London. Even though he produced far more property than any other European office – and valuable property too – I spent a lot of my time in London defending him and his staff. The Teutonic outlook on life – at any rate at that time – was very different from the British. But Ernst and I became very good friends. I owe it to his enthusiasm for my grandfather's work as a painter, that we staged the first of the recent run of Curt Herrmann exhibitions. It took place in Sotheby's gallery in Munich. It was its colossal success there, both in terms of the number of visitors and good reviews that really led to the renewal of interest in Curt Herrmann as a painter within the last twenty years.

Ultimately, Ernst found the excessively materialistic world of the auction business too much for him, and he became a monk. Patricia and I visited him some years later in the Benedictine cloister of Kremsmünster. He was in charge of the fish tanks and the wonderful collection of cabinets of curiosities. He may have exchanged his dark blue suit for a monk's habit and a shorn head, but he still displayed the same delightfully cynical sense of humour with which he had regarded the London management while at Sotheby's. Sadly, he died of the most cruel form of cancer in 1997 without completing the many tasks he had set himself. His number two, Graf Peter von Elst, another black sheep in London's eyes, later left Sotheby's and helped to found and run the Berlin auction house, Villa Grisebach, which became extremely successful.

*

In order to give *all* the heads of our overseas offices the opportunity to meet and to discuss common problems with their London opposite numbers, I organised a conference for just that purpose, over three days in Stockholm, a city that hardly anyone among them knew.

Since their entry into Europe, Sotheby's – and indeed Christie's – had regarded it as important to appoint titled aristocrats to help in their business-getting activities. I had a round dozen counts, barons and princesses working under me. Nowhere was this more in evidence than in Sotheby's three Italian offices in Milan, Florence and Rome. These worked under the benevolent eye of Count Alvise di Robilant, a seemingly gentle, retiring, North Italian but with a streak of steel hidden deep inside him, with whom I got on particularly well. There were grave doubts about Alvise in London, but it was common knowledge that the Italian art world was such an extraordinary maze of deviance and intrigue that Alvise was the ideal man to be in charge, because he was universally respected. He was something of a demon driver and had written off two large Fiats in the previous year, without any damage to himself. The fact that Italian law prohibited the export of virtually all Italian antiques or works of art of any quality meant that regular sales had to be held in Florence and, occasionally, Milan. Alvise, with the help of a cohort of beautiful young women, seemed to organise these very efficiently. Payment by the buyers, however, was another matter! Sadly, Alvise was murdered in mysterious circumstances in 1997, long after his retirement.

Our Swedish representative, Rolf Larsen, was occasionally assisted by two able aristocrats, Count Gustav Trollé-Bunde and Countess Marianne Bernadotte. She was, I believe, an aunt of the present King of Sweden, and when she heard that I intended to pitch one of our much vaunted international meetings in Stockholm, I received a message from her asking whether I would like her to organise a lunch for the Sotheby management with the King and Queen of Sweden. Who would have said no? From that moment on, all the London top brass, who had been rather reluctant to attend the meeting, decided to come.

The lunch was a splendid and memorable occasion. We were seated round a long, long table, beautifully decorated with flowers and silver in a narrow, low, yellow dining room. At the end of the lunch, the double doors at one end of the room suddenly opened and in came a small, five-year-old girl, who made her way round the table, very formally shaking everybody's hand. It was Princess Victoria, the eldest child of the royal couple. The Swedish parliament had just decided that in future the royal succession would go to the first-born child, whether girl or boy, and it was explained to us that this was the first public duty for the young Princess as heir to the throne.

After the lunch we all retired to a drawing room for coffee. Peter Wilson and Graham Llewellyn were chatting informally with the King and Queen. The little princess reverted to being a five-year-old. She pushed around a little horse on wheels, and when she saw the serious backs of Peter and Graham, temptation proved too strong and she rammed the little horse into the back of Peter's legs with all her force. I had never before seen him so startled. As a small token of my appreciation of the whole occasion, I sent the royal housekeeper a copy of *All About the Giant Alexander* for the royal nursery, and had a most enchanting reply.

The conference gave my representatives a wonderful opportunity to voice their grievances to the senior London management. These were based largely on the fact that they felt they were regarded as second-class citizens, who were expected to perform but to have no say. This entirely echoed what I had been saying week after week at the executive meetings, and received a generally sympathetic response until it came to the final unscheduled speech from an unexpected quarter. This was the traditional London voice saying you get on with the job elsewhere and leave us alone. The resulting turbulence undid most of the good of the previous two days.

Some months later, despite a noticeable tightening of cash resources, Ernst Behrens and I persuaded Graham Llewellyn that it would be very much in the firm's interest to start a new Sotheby office, in Vienna. Here the auction scene was dominated by the state-owned auction house, the Dorotheum. There was general surprise that we had the effrontery to barge into that world of monopoly. Curiously enough, however, I seem to remember that whatever the Dorotheum's thinking was behind closed doors, they did not officially begrudge our appearance on the scene and made quite friendly noises. As soon as rumours began to spread that we intended to open an office in Vienna, I started receiving letters from anxious fathers suggesting that their daughters would be an ideal representative. To me, the way power is wielded in Austria was a revelation. Before we ventured there, I had no idea of the importance of titles or the might of the old aristocracy. The girl we eventually appointed seemed to have a particularly strong blend of qualifications. Nearly twenty years later she is still there. The Vienna office has been a great success.

We launched it with considerable *éclat* with a party in the sumptuous ballroom of the Polo Club in Vienna, just behind the building where the famous white horses are quartered. As the British Ambassador was leaving he congratulated me on the turn-out. He commented that he had never seen such an immense gathering of influential people in one place since his posting to Vienna. I asked Agnes Husslein (whom we had appointed to the post) afterwards how she had put together her list of guests. The answer was that it was substantially the same people who had been asked to her recent wedding.

Another most important outpost which heavily underpinned London sales was Paris. Marc Blondeau, who had recently taken over responsibility for it, seemed to me the ideal representative. He knew all there was to be known about the Impressionists; he knew the people who owned them; he pursued them energetically, but with great tact as soon as it was rumoured that they might want to sell; and he was highly effective in dealing with the French bureaucracy, who procrastinated infuriatingly about issuing export licences. Together with Michel Strauss, London's long-standing expert on Impressionist painting, they were probably the most potent combination ever to have worked on that side of the auction business. When one looks back at the records of the time, such as Sotheby's annual, *Art at Auction*, it is amazing what passed through their hands compared to the tiny trickle of overpriced items today.

*

Even with eighteen years of hindsight, there is no doubt in my mind that my first frantic year as Head of Overseas Operations was enormous fun, and that success made it most enjoyable. In my particular situation, I could look upon what was happening around me with more detachment than those whose entire career was linked with Sotheby's. More important, I could also say (more or less) what I thought. At times not a popular move with the top management!

I had long given up any hope of confining my activities to only three days a week: it would have suited me much better if the week had had nine days; certainly there was more than enough work to fill them. The amount of travel alone absorbed much of it. It was, however, pointed out to me that some people felt I didn't travel enough. I checked. I found that in the first fifteen months I had left Heathrow sixty-six times. The most rewarding development was that the harmony between my overseas offices and the individual London expert departments had improved as the increasing quality and flow of property sent for sale to them in Bond Street began to be appreciated.

The glittering successes of the late seventies had given the firm a feeling of complacency. The general view was that the world could only get better; there would be more and more sales and an ever growing turnover. New staff were taken on in droves, mainly in New

York, to deal with what was thought to be continuing expansion. The possibility that there might be a down-turn never seems to have been considered. So that when it came, not many were prepared for it, and as the deteriorating world economy began to indicate that this was not a temporary blip, panic and fear developed. This in turn led to deep unrest among the staff. The time which elapsed between euphoria and decline was remarkably short. A new tetchiness made itself felt.

Europe had been the only part of the Sotheby group that had yielded a greatly increased profit, £4.7 million out of a total of £7 million for the entire group, including the UK and US, during the year since my appointment. I now had to make clear to the accountants that the budgets for the next year would diminish. This was unwelcome news. It was more or less at this point too that Lord Westmorland circulated a memorandum saying that he would change a second command structure in London which he had only recently introduced. This would confine executive action to a tiny, seemingly secretive cabal. The overseas representatives were particularly outraged. Their increased say in the running of the firm would be virtually annulled. The entire firm gradually became unmanageable and the financial situation more and more precarious. Graham Llewellyn, newly appointed as chief executive, sent me an ominous hand-written note in which he said: 'The whole group is in the most difficult financial situation. Every penny of expenditure needs to be looked at several times and, whenever possible, severely reduced. The scope for entrepreneurial activity at the moment is nil if it involves investment. You cannot invest what you do not have. I can live with the dangers, which will in any case be made easier to live with once the measures we are obliged to take become public knowledge'.

Later, David Westmorland, in desperation, handed over control as chairman to Gordon Brunton, a non-executive director, who was chief executive of the Thomson newspaper and publishing group. I knew him well from my previous, inglorious involvement with Nelson's, the publishers, part of the Thomson Group. He asked me to explain the role of Europe and, in common with others, to prepare a paper outlining my ideas for an improved structure for the future of Sotheby's as a whole. I suggested once more what London had earlier turned down, that the European offices should be merged into a single entity, as a third force of a three-legged structure: the other two being London and New York, each with its own board and managing director reporting to one chief executive. I also suggested that, in due course, the Far East might make a fourth unit, but I was ahead of my time. My letter accompanying the report to Gordon said, 'I wish you luck in your endeavours. It is very sad to see an organisation, to which I devoted ten years of my life, bent on destroying itself from within, at the same time as it faces so many pressures from without'. He responded by saying: 'When the [new] recommendations are made, you will see something of your own hand in them'.

One consequence was that the firm's two directors in charge of oriental porcelain on either side of the Atlantic became chief executives: Julian Thompson in London and Jim Lally in New York. But it was hardly fair to load these two with the job of righting such overwhelming problems. It seemed to me only a matter of time before someone from outside would make a bid for the company. I certainly didn't want to live through a corporate turmoil of such dimensions. It was time for me to go. I went.

Probably no one appreciated the irony more than I that, only two or three years earlier, in the Sotheby history, I had referred to Sotheby's expansion since the War as one of Britain's great success stories. It was more than sad that in such a short time the venerable auction house had moved from one extreme to another: it had now become not so much a house divided as a rambling edifice, totally splintered.

Thus far my dealings with Sotheby's had really been in four parts: the writing of the history, the share offering, the re-organisation of the book department and running and re-shaping the firm's overseas operations.

But if I thought that that was the end of my involvement with

Sotheby's, I was wrong. There was to be another remarkable episode. At the end of 1982, two Americans, Marshall Cogan and Stephen Swid, who ran and largely owned under GFI/Knoll International, a part of General Felt Industries of New York, bought 14.4 per cent of the issued Sotheby share capital, obviously with the intention of making a bid for the whole firm. They later pushed their shareholding up to 29 per cent. The Sotheby management, and Graham Llewellyn in particular, were appalled. What they didn't know was that Cogan and Swid – advised by the merchant bank Morgan Grenfell – proposed to instal Lord Harlech as chairman. As luck would have it, I had got to know and like David Harlech during my spell as publishing adviser to HTV of which David was also chairman. We met several times so that I could brief him about Sotheby's and its personalities. But such was the opposition to Cogan and Swid that their bid was referred to the Monopolies and Mergers Commission, and they retreated back to New York, by Concorde, to await developments.

It is said that it was Peter Wilson who found a 'White Knight', hailed in the press as the tenth richest man in America, a property developer called Alfred A Taubmann, as an alternative buyer. He made a much higher bid than GFI/Knoll: 700 pence per share versus Cogan and Swid's 520. This valued Sotheby's, a company about to make a sizeable loss, at £83 million. The shareholders, who had had rather a rough ride, obviously liked this, but nothing much happened for nine months while the Monopolies Commission undertook its investigation.

However, as far as I was concerned, it meant yet more work on Sotheby's. I was asked to give evidence and to submit a report to the Mergers & Monopolies Commission. This was to analyse my view of what had happened within the firm in recent years. It was made clear to me that I was to pull no punches. I found, to my astonishment, that each member of the investigating committee had been given a copy of my Sotheby history to read, and the secretariat who had approached me even managed to borrow the British Library copy of *The English as Collectors* for good measure!

I commented that even the recent blood-letting of staff (altogether some 700 people were made redundant on both sides of the Atlantic, and a good many regional offices were closed) and the increasingly disruptive effect of the recession with the consequent reduction in sales turnover, seemed to have done little to mitigate the internal dissension until the moment when Cogan and Swid had made their unwelcome entry on the scene. My feeling was that Sotheby's was not capable of healing itself from within. I emphasized too, that whatever assurances the firm might have been given to the contrary, any purchaser would have to bring about major changes to protect his investment. I stressed how important Sotheby's European and Far Eastern offices were to its operation. For the first time I realised, by analysing the figures, that the volume of property from Europe sold in London, in my short period of office, had increased from 28 per cent to 52 per cent. I concluded by saying that the answer to Mr Taubmann should be yes.

The Commission's report appeared in September 1983. They had taken the precaution of getting me to read the final proofs (though *not* the vital part containing their ultimate decision), so that any obvious errors of fact about the auction world could be corrected. I sat reading them, while the courier waited. In due course Mr Taubmann took over. It turned out to be a brilliant investment from his point of view, but today Sotheby's has become a different animal and no one then could have had any idea of the problems that would beset both Sotheby's and Christie's as the new millennium was ushered in, which put their very survival at risk; and forced Mr Taubman to face a trial for price fixing in a New York court and even, eventually, a prison sentence.

CHAPTER THIRTEEN

Cloud-Cuckoo-Land

While my career in publishing and my labours for Sotheby's proceeded, there was always another scenario in the background.

Pretzfeld, which I mentioned earlier, is a piece of pure cloud-
cuckoo-land. It was taken from my parents by the Nazis in 1937 and
dropped again into their laps in 1948 – a huge baroque castle, at that
time housing some 250 refugees, in a part of Bavaria known as
Franconia. The nearest market town is Ebermannstadt; the nearest
university Erlangen; the nearest cathedral Bamberg, and the nearest
airport is at Nürnberg, some forty-five kilometres to the south. The
countryside around is beautiful, a landscape of hills and valleys, with
small compact villages set among forests and fields: the whole rather
reminiscent of drawings by Dürer. The area rejoices in the name of
Die Fränkische Schweiz (Franconian Switzerland).

Little by little the 250 refugees, who mostly came from East Prussia
and had been fleeing from the Russians, were absorbed into the local population, integrated into what was for them a strange society
whose dialect they could only understand with difficulty. Eventually
we were left with one tenant, Siemens, a splinter of the vast electrical
enterprise, and nearly forty individual contracts for single rooms,
which Siemens took over as the refugees disappeared.

My first return to Pretzfeld after the war, with my father, was
amazing in retrospect but seemingly humdrum at the time. Zettner,
our pre-war estate manager – the German word for the job is *Verwalter*
– was still there. At the time of the *Kristallnacht* on 13 November
1938, thirty Nazis, in their brown uniforms, from nearby villages (not
Pretzfeld itself, though a local man let them in) stormed into the
castle – then still fully furnished with antique furniture – and smashed

up anything they could see – the furniture, the mirrors, the paintings, the porcelain, fourteen perfectly preserved faience stoves from the early eighteenth century, the library, many of the windows and anything else they could find. They went about it in an absolutely methodical way, with sledgehammers and pickaxes, working their way round the multitude of rooms on each of three floors. A small band of looters followed in their wake. Then, exhausted by their labours, the 'brown shirts' descended into the wine cellar and drank themselves into a stupor.

It was all observed and noted down in diaries by people who had been fond of my parents and grandparents, to bring up at the time of reckoning, which they felt would surely come one day. Several brave souls persuaded the Nazis to desist from burning the place down, unlike other houses owned by Jewish people, saying it had its uses and a fire would certainly endanger other nearby houses. Some degree of sense prevailed. Perhaps the thought of all that wine in the cellar was the real deterrent.

The Verwalter Zettner was one man against a horde and was not much in evidence during the rampage. But when the band of wreckers had disappeared, he began collecting the broken furniture, the

Hans Zettner. He spent four years collecting all the broken bits and pieces left behind after thirty men spent three days smashing up the contents of Schloss Pretzfeld during the 'Kristallnacht' in November 1938. It took us 30 years to put them all together again.

odd chair legs, the scattered books with their bindings torn off, the
family portraits with holes where the faces had been, and all the other
savaged bits and pieces, and deposited them in the largest room in
the castle, a sort of state room, erroneously called the *Rittersaal* [the
knights' chamber]. It was said to have taken him four years, on and
off, to assemble the detritus. Then he locked up the Rittersaal and
defended it against all comers, of whom there were many.

It was still there, that great mountain of mish-mash and misery,
when my father and I returned to Germany on that first visit after
the war in 1949. At the sight of it my father went downstairs into
the garden and was violently sick. I was too young to be affected,
and started to sort through it. It was almost thirty years before we
finished the necessary task of restoring all that could be saved.

The Bürgermeister of Pretzfeld in the immediate post-war years
was a stalwart Franconian character called Karl Kraus. 'Democracy',
he said to me, 'democracy, Master Frank, is a tender plant. We don't
yet know what to do with it.' He was one of those who had kept a
detailed record of Nazi misdemeanours. He had also made it his
business to find out who had stolen which of my grandfather's many
paintings, left behind by my parents in what was once Curt
Herrmann's studio, when they emigrated from Germany.

My father and I had driven from England in our brand-new Austin
14 with its English number plates. We now toured round the
neighbouring villages in it with a long list of names and addresses to
recover what had been ours. It is perhaps worth recording that petrol
for getting round in our car at that time could only be obtained on
the black market. This appeared to be supplied entirely by the
American army of occupation. We learned this from the simple fact
that when, at one stage during our visit, they were out on manoeuvres,
petrol simply could not be had.

The procedure of recovery, as I remember it, would typically go
as follows. I would knock on the door of a house in a village street; a
sturdy peasant type would open it. 'Good afternoon', I would say (in
German, of course). 'My name is Frank Herrmann, from the Schloss

in Pretzfeld. I have a list here which says you are very kindly keeping three paintings by my grandfather.' 'I don't know what you are talking about', would be the usual gruff reply. 'It says here on my list that you have three landscape paintings hanging in your best parlour to the left of the front door.' Amazement would follow at the accuracy of my information. God knows how old Kraus got hold of it. A slightly shifty look would appear on the man's face. 'Oh, those old

Schloss Pretzfeld: an aerial view of the whole complex in the 1960s.

things: yes, you can have them back. We don't want them.' In this way we collected what finally amounted to two or three hundred paintings and watercolours, most of my grandfather's extant oeuvre. I do not know how I had the nerve to go on doing this, day after day. I would certainly hesitate to be so brazen today. The story of our presence must have got about. But the retrieval worked time and again.

Those were the days when most of the rural traffic was with cows tethered to waggons. All ploughing too was done with cows. There was only one tractor in the village, and there were virtually no cars. We could not, of course, stay in the castle because of all the refugees. Zettner found us a room on the other side of the nearby village church, above the shop of a local butcher called Pankratz Kraus. The furnishings were of the simplest. Every morning we were woken up at 5 a.m. by loud, frantic squealing as old Pankratz Kraus slaughtered pigs. The whole place teemed with blood, intestines, excreta and sawdust. The smells were overwhelming. It was primitivity akin to the Brueghelesque: an almost unimaginable contrast to the sedate life we lived in Hampstead Garden Suburb. We were looked after by the plump daughter of the butcher. She was about to marry a dentist. Years later I met the same lady again, now a white-haired widow and approaching her seventies. She looked like a saintly *grande dame*, a Joan of Arc-like figure, but beautifully attired, exuding peace and dignity. She was a senior church elder. Her transmogrification was an interesting example of how Germany's post-war affluence had changed its citizens.

Now, more than fifty years after that first return to Germany, I can look out of the upper windows of the castle – from what is today the Curt Herrmann Museum – across the peaceful and beautiful valley in which it is situated, and a sense of the historic is always evident.

In 1966 I took over from my father the job of looking after the house and the estate. Since then I have made it my business to get to know the detailed story of the four generations who preceded my own: from my great-great-grandfather, the grain merchant and banker, Josef Kohn, onwards. He was the first Jew allowed to live in the centre of Nürnberg. He bought the castle in Pretzfeld from the Bavarian State in 1852, three years after the Seinsheims, the family who had owned it for many generations (along with forty-seven, yes, forty-seven other estates) was broken and bankrupted in the year of revolutions in 1848. Schloss Pretzfeld had once been, so the story went, the summer residence of the Bishops of Bamberg.

When he died Josef Kohn left his bank to his two sons and the Pretzfeld estate to his two daughters. The most dominant – and, indeed, dynamic – was my great-grandmother, Lina Herz, who survived to a great age and died when I was seven, in 1934. She married a cantankerous lawyer. He died after relatively few years of marriage, and while he left her reasonably well off, she quickly learned financial wizardry and became plain rich. Her only daughter, Sophie, became a pupil of the painter Curt Herrmann, who ran an art school in Berlin. Although he was twenty years older than she, they fell in love and married in 1896. Two years later they had their only child, my father. He survived three years in the army in the First World War, but was severely wounded – in an accident – on the last day of it. After some indecision, he became an architect, and in 1925 married Gabriele Jaffé, oldest of three sisters, offspring of a similarly interesting family, who had achieved renown in Germany as particularly able private bankers. The more I learned about the background of all this – my parents rarely referred to it – the more interesting it became.

But looking after Pretzfeld from 750 miles away was not easy. My father had done it by dint of an enormous correspondence and occasional hectic visits. He, poor man, was bedevilled in the very early 1950s by the resurgence to power locally of a particularly vicious former Nazi mayor who had avoided imprisonment after the war by feigning imbecility. It took a monumental battle to get this man displaced, but after some years, with the help of many other local people, my father succeeded. It left a bitter taste and a difficulty which my brother Luke and I felt had to be overcome.

As we would walk down a village street my mother would point towards someone and say, 'We can't talk to him. He was one of "them"'. Or, 'No, we can't go back to such-and-such a village. That's where another particularly virulent former Nazi lives'. It seemed to Luke and me that we could not keep on going to Germany if this was to be a permanent factor. We gave our parents a gentle ultimatum. If we were to take an interest in things, we should be able to speak to anyone, whatever their background. One would have to forgive even if one could not forget. To their everlasting credit, my parents, for whom this was a huge hurdle to overcome, agreed, and life became a lot easier thereafter.

The *Schirmerin*, close friend of my mother's and benevolent dynamo who controlled a whole dynasty that looked after our interests.

During his most active years, my father achieved miracles of restoration and reinstatement in Pretzfeld. At first there were major financial problems. Eventually, it was the generosity of the German Government that enabled him to make real progress. They provided compensation for those who had been forced to flee and who had lost their possessions and property. He also received a great deal of assistance from the local Inspector of Historic Monuments, Fridolin Stumpf, who helped him to establish a museum for the permanent display of Curt Herrmann's paintings in the same state room that had once housed the mountain of detritus, and to restore the castle chapel to its former glory, including a charming small early eighteenth-century organ.

Best of all, in 1961, the then director of the principal art museum in Kassel suggested a major retrospective exhibition of Curt Herrmann's work to be held there. Kassel undertook a complete programme of cleaning, restoring, framing and cataloguing those of his paintings which had survived and we had recovered. In the event, it was a huge task and it was ten years before the exhibition took place. It proved to be something of a watershed and re-established Curt Herrmann's name as a painter of distinction, after the long years of denigration under the Nazis, for my grandfather's work as one of Germany's two leading neo-Impressionist painters had been labelled as 'degenerate art'.

The other prop to our rising – if very modest – fortunes in Germany that allowed the process of restoration was the continuing Siemens' tenancy of the Schloss. By the mid-1960s my father began to tire of the work this involved, and when I took over the management of affairs from him, it instantly brought me into close contact with the formidable Dr Eberhardt Spenke. In the company of two fellow scientists from Siemens, he had arrived in Pretzfeld early in 1946, having escaped from Berlin. All their worldly possessions and their research equipment were in their rucksacks, and they proceeded to take over three empty offices in the Schloss just vacated by the American Army Signal Corps.

From this unlikely beginning grew a mighty enterprise which continued for fifty-four years, though there are now clear indications that it may come to an end. Spenke was a research physicist with a brilliant exploratory mind *and* a great gift for organisation. He envisioned what turned out to be the semi-conductor. After years of experimenting with selenium as the major element, he turned to silicon and made a breakthrough. It eventually resulted in a Nobel Prize for his genial adviser, Professor Walter Schottky, who had moved to Pretzfeld earlier, and an immense income in royalties for the team of fifteen scientists with whom Spenke had gradually surrounded himself on Siemens' behalf. Many of them lived in the stable block behind the Schloss. The upper floors of the castle became research laboratories and workshops. Visiting scientists from all over the world who came to acquire the patents could not believe their eyes when they saw the unlikely scientific environment in which these had been created.

But brilliant though Spenke may have been, he was a tough nut with whom to negotiate and a man who never spent a penny more than he had to. As the refugees living in the Schloss were resettled elsewhere, he took over their quarters, room by room, so that I found myself with all those forty separate contracts, a constant quest for more space from Spenke's colleagues and very little to show for it in the way of rent. Cautiously, I demanded a single, new contract at a rent that made the whole thing worthwhile. Siemens sent along a couple of professional negotiators and we fought out the new contract, clause by clause. My father was horrified by my seemingly intransigent attitude, but many years of arguments with printers, binders and paper-makers had been a good training ground for this. It was only some years later that I realised that this was the sort of skirmish for which one could bring in lawyers. With some reluctance we consented to the erection of a temporary building in the park behind the Schloss. In return, we got agreement for no less than five years' notice if Siemens decided to quit, *and* a decent rent.

For many months they hesitated about signing the new contract. Then I heard that they had started to put up the temporary building. I sent a cable saying, 'Sign the contract within 48 hours or it is cancelled'. They signed, and we have been on good terms with them ever since. They have been marvellous tenants, even though on three separate occasions since 1966 they firmly decided to move out, and then changed their minds at the last moment and stayed. The research work gradually diminished, and the manufacturing side for high-powered thyristors increased. This ultimately led to the erection of three more hi-tec buildings where there had only been the one.

Spenke retired in 1970 but continued to live in the house he had built for himself in Pretzfeld village. By then we had become extremely attached to him. For many years my visits to him were blessed with long intellectual arguments over the state of the world. They were probing exchanges, stripped of vapid conversational niceties, in search of realities. It was the sort of relationship I can remember with only two other people. One was another scientist, Sir Eric Eastwood, a near neighbour in Essex, who was head of research at the General Electric Company. The third was my great-uncle, Jean Fürstenberg, my mother's step-uncle, a brilliant if rather retiring banker, but a great bibliophile and book collector. He had a mind rather like a refrigerator where sentiment was frozen out. Yet later I discovered that there was an entirely different side to him. He had apartments in Paris and Geneva and a house near Frankfurt: but best of all he owned a wonderful chateau in Normandy where I often visited him. He was married to a Russian lady of great presence, a sharp mind, but little beauty. Some years after they had both died I went to a dinner party outside Zurich and found myself sitting next to a charming, pert lady a good deal older than I. We conversed happily and she took me back to my hotel in her car. Suddenly she stopped, looked at me quizzically, and asked, 'Don't you know who I am?'. Fortunately, I remembered her name, but that was not the answer she sought. We had talked about my great-uncle, whom she appeared to know. 'Don't you know', she asked again, and then, 'Are you not aware that I was his mistress for 36 years?'. Collapse of stout party. I saw her occasionally after that first meeting. It turned out that my uncle had written to her almost daily during their long liaison. She made two other comments about their relationship which I am unlikely to forget. The first was, 'I am rather good in bed, you know', and the second was, 'Poor Jean, he only had one bank. I own two'.

*

Of course, there were frequent highly-charged moments in Pretzfeld when things seemed to go very wrong. In mid-term of the chancellorship of Helmut Schmidt, for example, bureaucracy in Germany began to take on an upward surge and hardly a month seemed to pass in which Pretzfeld did not have a visitation by an official from some authority who asked us to undertake work of one kind or another, which had never been thought necessary before. Much of this was expensive and totally alien to a seventeenth-century building. As we had spent vast sums year after year restoring both the inside and the outside of the whole Schloss to a high standard, entirely off our own bat and without any of the grants that other people seemed to be able to obtain, I wrote a seven-page letter of protest, in English, to the local *Landrat*, the senior elected official in the area. I described in detail the ravages of the Kristallnacht and the horrendous things done to the building both during and after the war, and the work we had done to put it right in the intervening years. I threatened to eject Siemens, by now a major employer in an area in which it was difficult to find work; to close the whole place down; to put a padlock on the gates, and to let the building fall down. This, indeed, was what a great many other owners of similar properties were doing at the time. It was many weeks before I received a reply. No doubt a translation of my letter had been passing through the hands of innumerable official committees. When it came, the response was helpful. We were bothered much less by interfering busy-bodies and the local authority became positively supportive. It was a minor triumph.

In total contrast, more frequent at the time when my parents were alive, total strangers would arrive in Pretzfeld with interesting antiques, such as faience, pewter, small pieces of furniture, and offer them as presents or for patently ridiculous sums, in view of the losses that my family had suffered. Usually, the reason offered was that, as the owners' homes were being modernised, such objects looked out of place, but that they would be right for the Schloss. One could not help feeling that these were acts of personal contrition for what had happened in the past.

During the years that I worked for Sotheby's, I found myself in Germany much more frequently. I often travelled from Sotheby's German head office in Munich to spend a weekend in Pretzfeld. Occasionally the inimitable Ernst Behrens, head of Sotheby's German offices, would come too. He formed a great affection for my grandfather's work as a painter, and (as I have written in chapter 12), it was because of Ernst's enthusiasm that we held a small exhibition of CH's work in Sotheby's galleries in Munich in 1983. The interest this evoked was far greater than I expected and that exhibition really began a dramatic renaissance of my grandfather's reputation. Through

My grandfather, the painter Curt Herrmann.

the exhibition I met Kurt and Gabi Zimmermann who ran an attractive, family-owned art gallery in Stuttgart. They were keen to organise a further exhibition where CH's paintings could be bought by collectors. There had been many requests for this at the Munich exhibition, but we had not wanted to part with any of our paintings.

The Stuttgart exhibition in 1985 was widely discussed in the press and was a virtual sell-out. One particularly fine winter townscape of Berlin – my grandfather had a special penchant for snow scenes – was bought by the Berlin Museum. It was paid for by a lottery for art objects, run by the Berlin city council. The two leading lights of the museum, Rolf Bothe, its director, and Thomas Föhl, his principal assistant, became engrossed in CH's work and came to Pretzfeld to see his other paintings and to study what archival material we had. The public in Berlin also took a great fancy to the painting they had bought.

Eventually, Bothe asked whether he could hold another major retrospective exhibition of CH's work in his Museum. It was now eighteen years since the one in Kassel. We agreed on one condition: that the Museum staff should make a study of the contents of a large and mysterious cabin trunk we had in Pretzfeld. Its four separate drawers were entirely full of unsorted correspondence to CH covering a long period. We found the handwriting of that era very difficult to read. At first Bothe and Föhl looked dubious, but once serious work started on the sorting and transliteration of the correspondence, their excitement knew no bounds. The nearly three thousand letters threw a new, revealing light on the history of German art between 1885 and 1925; and not only German art, because Curt Herrmann had corresponded avidly with many of his painter contemporaries in France, Holland and Belgium.

Most of the work of elucidation and subsequent commentary fell to Thomas Föhl. He proved to be a brilliant art historical detective who found and followed up links, and arrived at cogent interpretations that no one had been aware of before. When the result of all this preparatory work, and the huge number of CH paintings, watercolours and pastels was finally assembled in 1989 and shown to the public, it aroused enormous interest and again wide-ranging press discussion. What really emerged most clearly was not only that my grandfather was a talented painter, but that he had been a very inspired and down-to-earth leader of groups of his often cantankerous contemporaries and had organised innumerable exhibitions on their behalf with great diplomacy and skill. He had done similarly sterling work for his French and Belgian colleagues. Among the most important were Paul Signac, Pierre Bonnard, Louis Valtat, Henry Edmond Cross, Theo van Rysselberghe and, above all, Henri van de Velde. Later, Bonnard came from Paris to Pretzfeld to paint a whole series of portraits of my grandmother, Curt's wife Sophie, and she, in turn, had become so friendly with Paul Signac that he asked her to translate his seminal book, *From Eugène Delacroix to Neo-Impressionism*, into German. The catalogue for the 1989 retrospective was a vast volume which dealt with the varied aspects of CH's activities and also contained a comprehensive selection of the many letters to him that had emerged from the cabin trunk.

You might well wonder how this remarkable piece of luggage came to survive the Nazi period unscathed. My father, as it happened, was a dedicated huntsman. His rifle boasted a telescopic sight years ahead of its time, and his binoculars were of the best. These were items he could not take out of Germany. Nor – he felt – could he take the entire CH correspondence. So the binoculars and rifle telescope were concealed among the letters; the trunk was firmly locked and put into the hands of my father's then dynamic attorney, a Geheimrat Kastl who lived near Munich, for safe keeping. A confirmed anti-Nazi, Kastl nevertheless rose to be a successful industrialist and became chairman of M.A.N., the motor manufacturers. He was the nominal keeper of my father's affairs in Germany after 1937.

After the war he returned the trunk to Pretzfeld, but its locks were broken. When my father opened it he discovered to his horror that the telescope and binoculars had been removed, though the letters were intact. So disappointed was he by this turn of events that he never again bothered about the trunk or its remaining contents.

Thomas Föhl, in the meantime, became a close friend and spent a good deal of time organising the letters into a comprehensive archive. By the time he had completed this work, he had absorbed so much more knowledge about CH than anyone else was ever likely to that we persuaded him to write his biography, for which there had long been a great need. This was finally published in 1996. One of the most interesting discoveries that emerged from it, which had already become clear from a study of CH's correspondence, was his sympathy for the work of a much younger generation of artists: such

Curt Herrmann

Ein Künstlerleben 1854–1929

Thomas Föhl's
biography of the painter.

as the *Blaue Reiter* school, and Expressionists such as Kirchner, Schmitt-Rotluff, Jawlenski and Otto Mueller whose work could not have been more different from his own. During the First World War he had sent them food parcels while they were on active service and had looked after their dependants. In the case of Kirchner, who suffered severe ill health and psychological problems, CH even paid his studio rent for many years. He frequently visited their exhibitions and generally encouraged them. Altogether he was a remarkable man and my brother and I rejoiced that we had been able to bring him back into the artistic main stream of his time.

*

Looking back on it, the double horizon of straight-forward life in England and the cloud-cuckoo-land in Germany was a decided plus. It allowed one to see things from different points of view. Fluency in another tongue also enriched one's thought processes. It was a rare privilege to be able to swop from one to the other, but my anchor remained firmly in Essex.

CHAPTER FOURTEEN

More of the Same

As if Pretzfeld was not enough, a second piece of cloud-cuckoo-land dropped into our laps in 1989. *Gut Wulkow* (literally the Wulkow Estate). It consisted of nearly 300 acres about 55 km east of Berlin. This was after Gorbachev had turned the key and opened the floodgates of liberation from communist dominance in Eastern Europe. The Berlin Wall was breached and Eastern Germany, the much hated and rather mysterious DDR, became reunited with Western Germany, after much pushing and coaxing by Helmut Kohl.

Actually, Wulkow did not exactly drop into our laps. We had to pluck the fruit from the tree piece by piece. When my father had died in 1983, my brother and I cleared his office. There was a file labelled 'Wulkow'. We hesitated. The chance then of ever getting it back in our lifetimes seemed infinitely slim. But I am a great hoarder, particularly where papers are concerned. We kept the file. It contained ancient maps of the property; inventories; correspondence with the British Foreign Office Claims Department that dealt with forfeited property overseas. Our case number was 701.

Wulkow had been bought by two younger brothers of my grandfather, Curt Herrmann, in about 1870. They thought that as a country estate, it was just large enough to support them in comfort. It wasn't. They nearly went bankrupt. My great-grandmother, Lina Herz, the family's financial genius, newly entered into the family, saved them. She bought the whole thing, lock, stock and barrel, and allowed the two brothers to go on living there. But she made plans for its future. Together with a financial partner, a dentist, she hired an architect to draw up plans for a complete garden suburb from which people could travel to Berlin from a nearby railway station: a very early example of commuting. There were to be 150 executive houses, shops, restaurants, a church and a community centre. It was very advanced stuff. But in fact it never happened. Instead, most of the land was turned into fields of asparagus.

Celebrated tea party in Wulkow in 1896. On the extreme left, Curt Herrmann and his fiancée Sophie Herz (seated), my grandmother, just after their engagement. The tiny seated lady wearing a decorative bonnet is Louise Herrmann, the widowed mother of the four brothers around the table, and her daughter, Hella, (pouring tea). Lina Herz, mother of Sophie and, without doubt, the eventual matriarch of the tribe, with the rather masculine head, is third from the right.

My father inherited the property in 1934 and began a course of wholesale restoration. My earliest memory of Wulkow was of a short holiday visit, during which my father suddenly developed appendicitis, and my mother – who could not really drive – took the family Model T Ford and drove my father, my brother and me to Berlin, in the dark, in the pouring rain. We got there but it was a memorable journey.

Now, in 1990, my brother and I travelled to Berlin and met up
with Thomas Föhl. He had sent us reports of conditions in Wulkow
ever since he had been able to travel there freely from West Berlin.

The house consisted of a long, low, single storey building with a
pitched roof (which we called the Longhouse), probably dating from
the middle of the eighteenth century, to which had been added in
about 1840 a tall, three storey tower block of ungainly proportions,
in the Italianate style, so popular in Berlin during that period. Thomas
had told us that all the windows and most of the window frames in
the tower were missing. He had had these boarded up. Much of the
Longhouse was in a deplorable condition and some of the walls were
crumbling, but a squatter still lived at one end.

What met our eyes when we got there was a horrifying sight, even
worse than the recent photographs we had seen. All the old stables,
barns and outhouses, which had formerly enclosed a rectangular
courtyard, had disappeared. No one had bothered to look after them.
They had simply decayed, collapsed and been removed, as we later
found out. Only the house itself had survived because, while it was
still habitable, five families had lived within it, but no one had ever
undertaken any repairs, repainting or work on it of any kind. But
even the five families had been moved out ten years earlier when the
building was no longer considered safe. But there was one other small
survival; a half-timbered, 18th century earth closet. It was the only
toilet there was – and even that leaned over at a drunken angle.

We drove round the forest. There it became clear that the communist forestry authority had felled all the mature trees over an eighty
acre stretch, but, amazingly, had replanted the entire area with spruce
and pine. The trees had reached a height of four or five feet, so they
would have been five or six years old. The shape of the whole forest,
including the much older parts, was remarkable: virtually a giant
circle surrounded by a strip half a kilometre wide of meadowland
which encircled the treed area like a giant race course. Beyond the
meadowland a new area of forest began. We learned later that this
arrangement had been a form of medieval land pattern and that the

course of the river that ran along it had been diverted many years before. We were delighted to see the odd deer in the distance, but more worried by the many stretches of roughly turned up soil, evidence of the sort of mess that sizeable herds of wild boar leave behind after digging for nourishment.

*

We had already decided that our first approach to authority to reclaim the property should be at the lowest level: the parish council. Wulkow was only a tiny hamlet. Its authority functioned in the neighbouring, much larger village of Hangelsberg. The council officers and staff were housed on two floors in a minute wooden building. The Bürgermeister and his clerk were squashed into a small upstairs office. There was barely enough room for Luke, Thomas Föhl and me to sit down. I explained who we were and what the purpose of our mission was. The faces of the two officers were a study in dumbfounded astonishment. I produced what papers we had. Ancient maps and *Grundbuch* (Land Registry) records; copies of the death certificates of my ancestors, the proof that we were their descendents. The Bürgermeister and his clerk had only recently been elected to these posts. They had ousted a long-standing communist clique. The two men were both former academics: one a lecturer in physics, the other in chemistry. The physicist had a sound knowledge of the local history and grasped immediately who we were. Once the surprise of our unexpected appearance had abated there was a warm welcome and as much cooperation as they could muster. We worked out a plan of whom else we would have to visit.

And so began a round of calls on offices where the dawn of change had not yet broken. There was occasional truculence, even resentment. But we spoke German. We were patient. We often had to be diplomatic. Officials were not used to facing the degree of resolve we mustered; we would not accept no for an answer. When occasionally things got very up-tight, we mentioned the fact that we had a case number for a British Foreign Office claim. This would make a deep impression and reduce the intransigence from obstructive burearocrats.

There had been a total change of plot numbering for the individual fields and areas of forest since the documents we brought with us had been compiled. Our first priority, therefore, was to establish what the new numbers were. Eventually we found ours in the office of a lady who was the keeper of the Grundbuch ledgers, the so-called *Liegenschaftsamt*. Everybody spoke of her with the utmost deference and, indeed, when we were ushered into her office she proved to be cold, uncommunicative and totally unwilling to divulge any information unless we could prove to her that our claim was valid. Fortunately we had one document, an old mortgage, which contained a number she recognised. She began to leaf through her records. She sat at a long table, piled high with files. On each file was a sizeable polished pebble to weigh it down. Now my brother always carries such a stone in his pocket with which he can fiddle if tension arises. In an effort to break through the permafrost, he showed her his very beautiful and rare Brazilian agate, and said, 'I see you collect these polished stones, as I do', simply as a gambit of conversation. She took it from him without a word and put it in her pocket. It was the key that unlocked the iron gates. Information gushed from her. It was a beginning. I have to say that it was the only occasion on which any question of a bribe arose. In one instance later on, when the clerk of another organisation had been incredibly helpful to us, far beyond his call of duty, we offered him a small sum at the suggestion of the official accompanying us. The little man in question blushed deeply but said, 'It's very kind of you, but as I have never accepted anything in forty years of work here, it would not be right to start now'.

It took three years to see it all through. Although much of the property, particularly the buildings, had become *Volkseigentum* (State property) and had been used as such, the respect for my Jewish great-grandmother, Lina Herz, was still formidable, and the ultimate ownership of most of our plots was still registered in her name. There had not, in any case, been time between her death and my father's emigration to England to change it all into his. No one during the Nazi régime or the communist administration had had the courage to eliminate her name, despite appropriating her property. This was really the most surprising factor in our prolonged struggle for recovery. It also helped us enormously because, once we could claim direct descent from her, there were no purely legal grounds why we should not get everything back.

Many more visits to Berlin and Wulkow followed, but it was during our second time there that we really struck gold. We desperately needed someone to begin work on the neglected forest *and* to look after what was left of the property. The Hangelsberg Bürgermeister and his clerk, who rejoiced in the names of Schicketanz and Lange, said that they had the very man for us. He had worked for the local forestry commission, but had never risen very high in the hierarchy because he was very independent-minded and totally opposed to communism. But a brilliant organiser and absolutely reliable. He had been indispensable to the forestry management because he looked after a team of 150 women who gathered resin from the forest on a vast scale, and resin was an essential commodity for industry in a country such as the DDR, which had no hard currency with which to import its derivatives from elsewhere in the world. We met the man concerned, Gerhard Pehnke. We took to him at once and asked him to work for us. My brother and I are totally convinced that Wulkow would not now be ours again if it had not been for Gerhard Pehnke's obdurate struggles with all the authorities that stood in our way. He would simply refuse to leave any office until he got what he wanted. He also quickly began to bring our forest back to life.

*

It became obvious that the house would have to be made habitable if Wulkow was going to be somewhere to which one wanted to return. In our early visits we had to stay in a nearby hotel on the edge of one of the many very beautiful lakes in the area. It had once been a holiday haunt for the highest communist functionaries. We started to search for architects and builders. The first three East German builders we consulted said that they would simply put a bulldozer through the building and start again. Builders in the former DDR

were short of subtlety and restoration was not something they had
ever been taught to practise.

The first three architects were over-ambitious and produced
drawings for a motel rather than for a simple country house. It was
Pehnke who found the right builder and the right architect for us.
Both were local. Both grasped the idea of what we wanted at once.
Over a period of several years it was a joy to work with them.

In our initial uncertainty because of the conflicting views we received over how to reconstruct the building, we brought over our
own builder, Peter Loe, from England, to advise on how to proceed.
No one liked the tower block. Its proportions were inelegant, though
it was a landmark for many miles around. But it turned out that,
despite the ravages that ten years' exposure to the weather had
wrought on it, it was, in fact, sounder than the Longhouse. Decision One: it had to be kept, even though it needed new beams, new
floors, new windows and doors throughout. The roof of the tower
block was another problem. None of the architects had been able to
provide what we wanted. In the end we were inspired by a visit to
Potsdam where we saw what we considered the ideal solution. It
was our English architect, Geoffrey Vale, who produced the perfect
design for us after he had seen our photographs.

He devised a flat pyramid in zinc and that is what we constructed,
though we had to import a craftsman from Czechoslovakia to do the
work: no one in the DDR had ever had to work in zinc. Eventually
Patricia and I attended the topping-out ceremony. She has no head
for heights, but bravely climbed up long ladders to get up to the
narrow ledges around the roof. The wonderful internal staircases
ordered from a firm in Denmark had not yet been installed. It was
the first occasion on which we were able to see how impressive the
views were from the top of the building.

I was amazed to see what looked like a 'group' of musicians on the
roof. They were wearing bell-bottomed trousers in black corduroy,
with waistcoats and jackets to match, loose white blouses and flat,
black, wide-rimmed hats that would have been suitable for the can-
ons in Trollope's *Barchester Towers*. The 'group', in fact, turned out to

be our carpenters. Their so-called 'Manchester suits' (because that is where the corduroy had come from in years past) are their every-day working garb in East Germany. They were just rather more clean than usual! The senior among them took a sheet of paper from his pocket and read out a long poem, specially composed for the ceremony. I had to make a speech in return as the builders' client, thanking all the workmen on the job, before we drank glasses of schnapps and climbed back down to the ground floor to partake in a beanfeast, prepared by Mrs Pehnke, with unlimited quantities of beer. With typical forethought our builder had organised a large open lorry with benches, so that they could all be driven home by the one teetotal workman without incurring any problems over drink-driving.

The very first obstacle we had to tackle before any rebuilding could start was to clear the property of the incredible amount of rubbish that had accumulated on it. Not long before 1989 it had been the intention of a local circus owner to acquire it. He had already installed a lot of his property. What was left of the rooms was filled with the sort of equipment a circus owner needs. Fortunately, the deal had never gone through, but by some curious legal quirk he retained the pre-sale rights. There had been a lot of legal chicanery in the dying days of the DDR when hundreds of contracts were hastily drawn up, giving tenants rights to the properties they inhabited but did not own. We lost another house on the estate in just this way.

After the architect had done his preparatory work and we had received permission to start on the restoration, the actual construction work was planned very carefully, phase by phase, during my regular visits to Wulkow. When I was back in England, Herr Hartwig, the builder, would send a fax (at this time still a complete novelty in East Germany) every Friday to outline the work done during the previous week and we would then discuss any problems and decide what was to be done in the following week. Occasionally it would be necessary for him to send photographs so that I could see the problems in detail. This system worked remarkably well, even down to controlling the costs.

I felt it was very important that my children should play a part in what was being done, so eventually one of them chose the fitted kitchen; another the tiling for the bathrooms; a third the furniture for the drawing room. In this way the house was reconstructed and became an airy, welcoming delight.

Even the proportions of the tower block seemed to have improved when it had been replastered and painted in a pleasant colour. We were the first people to utilise the gas from a pipeline under the surface of the road that ran in front of our garden. It was ideal for central heating and cooking. This road had an interesting history. For most of a kilometre it belonged to us. What had once been a farm track round our property was now the main road. The authorities wanted to buy it from us but I thought it was rather fun to keep it. We could always put a barrier across it and levy a toll from passing traffic if we were desperate for cash!

We tackled the second tranche of the building operation two years later. It consisted of the restoration of most of the Longhouse. Many of the 18th century timbers looked a bit dodgy so, thanks to an ingenious scheme devised by our local architect, we constructed a complete internal, welded-steel skeleton to support the roof. In fact, most of the roof timbers had to be strenghtened too and our bell-bottomed friends did a marvellous job. They worked with a sureness of touch that was truly remarkable.

We planned to revive the garden in what had become an open wilderness all round the house. Gerhard Pehnke removed generations of accumulated detritus. He imported topsoil; he sowed grass; he planted hedges – mostly, at our request, of lime; we put in a fence and a gate. He dug flower beds and planted evergreen shrubs and young trees. Today one would never guess what a riotous disaster area it had once been. The keystone to it all were three magnificent lime trees in front of the house, which had already been substantial in photographs we had of the early 1860s. Their scent was delicious and they gave one shade in the very hot summer. The house had, of course, to be furnished from scratch: all that had remained were two rickety old garden chairs. This is where we were fortunate. As the years progressed after

Wulkow: a total ruin, as we found it in 1990

and, sparkling, after reconstruction six years later.

The tower block: before and after reconstruction.

the fusion of East and West, enterprising companies set up supermarkets in nearby Fürstenwalde, and above all IKEA, the Swedish company that supplied well designed furniture (in flat packs that needed to be assembled), had opened one of their warehouses nearby and we placed an order with them of a size that at first they seemed to have difficulty in comprehending. What we bought was not only reasonable in price; it was also elegant. But beyond the merely functional, we imported surplus antique furniture that was stored in Pretzfeld. We found it virtually impossible to hire a carrier from the West to the East. In the end we borrowed an ambulance and driver from a voluntary service, which we packed to the gunwales.

Herr Pehnke sent us regular reports of what was going on. But one day he reported a sudden crisis: the local authority had complained that the wild boar roaming on our property were doing too much damage within the neighbourhood and that we must reduce the number. The number turned out to be in excess of fifty! As it happened, we had been negotiating at a gentle pace with a German friend of one of my authors in the educational field in England about

The Longhouse: unbelievably wretched in 1990 – and a pleasure to live in by 1997.

taking over the Wulkow shoot. He was a glass manufacture in Hannover, but the temptation of taking on a virgin shoot was so great that he didn't mind the distance. Wild boar are notoriously difficult to shoot. They roam only at night and conceal themselves in the forest during the day. But our new friend soon took the matter in hand and shot some, usually by moonlight, and often in the snow,

Wulkow in winter.

and though the herd still seems vast to me, and the damage it does is appalling, it is now apparently more acceptable.

For many years my mother had had an attractive tea service, made by a number of factories after an original design from Strasbourg. It was called Luneville. She was always adding to it so that by the time she died it was enormous. We could never understand her obsession with it until one day she explained that 'If we ever get back Wulkow, that's the service I want to have there'. She had been dead for many years by the time we finished the restoration and furnishing of the house, but we took it over from England, bit by bit, and now the old Luneville service has pride of place there and is in constant use.

CHAPTER FIFTEEN

Loose Cannon

Independence was all very well, but independence embodied the stark fact that there was no cheque in the bank at the end of each month. But though I didn't know it, the years after leaving MM&S in 1976 were to be a glorious amalgam of the things I liked doing best: writing and historical research, helping to run a group of book shops, publishing books for the art market on the one hand and for the popular market on the other, travel on the Continent with Patricia and visiting children at university. Occasionally there were opportunities to use know-how of a financial kind applied to publishing, which proved singularly rewarding. Yet all this was against a background of harsh economic uncertainty and soaring inflation that seemed unending.

First I needed an office. Years earlier my father had shared a pokey office with another architect, Professor Adolph Rading, up a dark, crabby staircase in an old house in Chancery Lane. I felt they deserved better. At that stage, in the mid-fifties, Patricia and I still lived in Bloomsbury Street which was only a stone's throw from the simple Georgian magnificence of Bedford Square. Finding an office in London at that stage was exceedingly difficult, but we noticed that the National Farmers' Union, who occupied *three* houses in Bedford Square, were putting up a spacious new headquarters building at Hyde Park Corner. We alerted my father that there would be space in Bedford Square, and because we were the first to apply, we obtained a twenty-one year lease on 6a Bedford Square, which backed on to the British Museum, and had once been the residence of Lord Eldon. A blue plaque outside the front door told us so. It was also a few doors down from the sumptuous No.1 Bedford Square, where

Geoffrey Hobson[1] – one of the three senior Sotheby directors who had bought the business in 1909 – had lived until the slump in 1931 forced him to move.

The cost of our lease was £3,160 – a laughable sum by today's standards. My father suddenly worked in magnificently spacious rooms on the first floor of 6a Bedford Square. His clients were deeply

The Georgian elegance of Bedford Square. 6a is the left-hand half of the white building. First it housed my father's office; then mine; finally, in 1983, BBA's.

impressed. The rest of the building was let out and the resultant income came to be regarded as my father's equivalent of a pension. After my departure from MM&S, I took over the second huge room

1 See *Sotheby's: Portrait of an Auction House*, plates 31, 32 and 33.

on the first floor which my father had kept for expansion which had never materialised.

An opportunity for bookish involvement soon presented itself. At Hudson's there had been several occasions when other firms of booksellers had made enquiries about joining the bookselling part of the group. One had been from an old-established North Country firm called Sweeten's. By a curious form of synchronicity we each now made contact with the other. The company was owned by three brothers, Christopher, David and Guy Sweeten. Guy was more interested in cars than books and wanted to set up a Saab garage. The question now put to me was would I like to join in his place as third partner?

I travelled up to Preston. There were four shops altogether – smaller ones in Blackpool, Bolton and Wigan: the largest branch by far was on Preston's main shopping street. Christopher, who had trained as an accountant, looked after finances and administration. David was responsible for the buying and shop management. But what particularly intrigued me was that Sweeten's had been one of the first booksellers to introduce computers, largely for stock control, and had made such a success of creating the necessary software, that other booksellers wanted to buy the Sweeten system.

The firm's origins went back to the 1870s when Frank Percy Sweeten had founded it in Blackpool after an earlier career as a publisher's representative selling books in India. His son, Harold, took over the business and some years earlier had been President of the Booksellers Association. He had achieved fame in the trade because he drove around in a white Rolls Royce which was certainly not expected of booksellers. On his retirement he had handed over the business to his sons. Only a little while later the Preston shop had been badly damaged by a fire. This had enabled them to modernise the shop completely. It also inspired Christoper to introduce computers for the all-important matter of stock control. To achieve this he had worked closely with David Wynn, then deputy head of the computer department in Preston's own Technical College.

I liked the thought of being involved once more with a family firm. After I bought into it, I was amazed at the number of other booksellers who constantly arrived to see the computer system Sweeten's had installed. These visits took up a lot of our time. I suggested that we charge such visitors £100 a day. The unexpected result was that we had more such inspections than ever before, and these brought requests that we should organise systems similar to our own for other bookshops. Therein lay the seeds of a business in its own right, which Christopher built up brilliantly. It meant not only adapting the software specifically for each customer, but also supplying him with the hardware. It is important to remember that in 1976/7 we were selling mini-computers which had only been in existence on any scale for five or six years. The world in general still thought of computers as major main frame installations in air-conditioned rooms with special operators. Our 'minis' were comparable to the full-size animals of ten years earlier but at only a fraction of the size and the cost. One of the first Sweeten installations went into Willshaw's, the Manchester bookshop run by my old friend, Hilary Patterson; another into Parry's of Liverpool. Both were members of the University Bookshop Group owned by Blackwell's of Oxford.

My connections with publishers meant that before long we were able to design and instal systems for them which could undertake such tasks as invoicing and producing statements, sales statistics, royalty statements, general accounting functions and even mail order systems. But we were breaking new ground and there were many setbacks and complications. At one stage we became extremely concerned because David Wynn's boss at Preston Technical College's computer department was leaving and we thought Dave would want the job. But instead – to our infinite surprise and relief – he asked whether he could join Sweeten's full time because he so much enjoyed the work he was doing for us.

While I remained in blissful ignorance of the technicalities, I could see, after some years, that we were barking up the wrong tree. We spent most of our time endeavouring to find new customers in order to sell them our hardware and software, while undertaking the maintenance and up-grading of existing installations for purely nominal – if any – charges. The result was that genuine profitability always eluded us. It was only when we began to charge properly for this sort of indeterminate but very time-consuming consultancy work that the computer side of Sweeten's began to flourish. Also, by then, many of the small firms who had entered the computer installation market had gone out of business, while our own enterprise had grown enormously and our services were much in demand.

Each month I made my way up to Preston and stayed with either Christopher or David's family. We got to know each other extremely well. What I had learned at Hudson's came in very useful from time to time, though Christopher and David were such thorough-going professionals that it was not often that I proposed something which they had not thought of already, except perhaps the blindingly obvious. When, for instance, I first saw the Preston premises, there was a whole floor above the main shop which was not used except for storage. I suggested that it should be turned into a selling area. The result was a very considerable increase in our turnover.

I also enjoyed visiting the lesser shops, of which we opened more in due course. We kept precise records day by day of the takings in each branch. What I found remarkable was the extraordinary consistency of the sums concerned year by year when one considered that the books stocked varied enormously. We often experimented with eliciting various forms of statistical information. It was surprising, for example, that for every six male customers entering our main shop, there were only four women, and that we had almost exactly ten thousand customers in the Preston shop in an average week.

My association with Sweeten's lasted twelve years. Financially the years of recession rendered bookselling almost profitless. We had exactly the same sort of problems with bank managers as we had had at MM&S, though eventually the totally unnecessary extremes from one particular such character drove us to change banks, which I had always rather dreaded. However, it turned out to be a change for the better to an extent we could hardly have imagined. We had found someone who was supportive rather than obstructive. Yet there were times when we sailed so close to our expanding overdraft limit that I had to help out with temporary loans.

What helped us most on the computer side was our gradual entry into the publishing world. The scope of each installation was more extensive than it had been in bookselling. There was less haggling over price and even the payments came through more speedily. Although a good many of the publishers we worked for were those with whom I was involved in other ways, I was able to say to them with complete confidence that Sweeten's would do a better job than most, and indeed in almost every case we went on up-grading such equipment for years.

*

While my work on the Sotheby history at Bond Street continued, I would often need to consult Peter Wilson, Sotheby's chairman, over what had occurred at particular sales he had taken, or about sparsely chronicled pre-war events. It usually involved a prolonged hassle with secretaries to get an appointment. He existed almost permanently in a state of high tension. I was therefore all the more surprised when one day he rang me up in Jim Kiddell's office to ask whether 'I could spare the time to come and see him'. He outlined a proposition that sounded intriguing. His son, Philip, had for some ten years worked within the firm to oversee the production of various books which Sotheby's had published, in particular the annual review of their sales, *Art at Auction*. In the previous year Philip had set up his own independent company and Sotheby's had concluded a contract with him under the terms of which he would be responsible for all books published under their imprint. As long as a small consultative committee approved of any project he put before them, he could widen the range of the publications as he wanted. The quality of authorship and production standards, however, were of paramount importance. While the books concerned would come out under the Sotheby Publications imprint, in general Philip would provide the necessary funds.

In return he was given the sole right as an outsider to use Sotheby's enormous mailing lists. There had been long delays over some publications in the past and it was clear that a good many things had not gone according to plan. Peter Wilson and his son, it seemed, both felt that my publishing expertise would be of useful assistance in the fledgling enterprise.

Philip and I met. We talked things over at length. We liked each other and I agreed initially in 1977 to plan working one day a week at his offices, which overlooked Covent Garden, formerly the site of the earliest Turkish baths in London and latterly the headquarters of the National Potato Federation! I had only been there a number of weeks when our financial administrator, Ernie Collman, an old Sotheby stalwart, suddenly died. He had owned a magnificent old Rover, and the car had broken down. He pushed it some way along the road. The strain had been too much for him and he died on the roadside of a heart attack. Our need for a replacement was obviously instant.

Dear Tom Nicholas, lately of MM&S, had recently retired. He had moved to the seaside in Kent, was totally bored with taking his dog out for its daily walk and was delighted at the thought of helping us at Covent Garden. He not only sorted things out, but initiated a completely new and up-to-date accounting system which gave us much more management information than we had previously had; and he thoroughly enjoyed himself laying down the law to us. We even got Christopher Sweeten to put in a computer system while we were at it, and although Tom and Christopher looked at each other rather suspiciously at first, they worked well together. And once Philip Wilson himself had also mastered the system he was never happier than when he was working at the computer. The whole exercise did wonders for the stabilisation of our financial controls, without which no publishing concern can exist successfully.

The project that dominated our life was *Art at Auction*. It was Sotheby's principal marketing tool. Vast quantities were sent out each Christmas to the firm's clients – and to bookshops generally – and there could be no question at all of any delay over timely delivery. At that time the book contained no fewer than 448 pages, mostly in colour, and the quantities printed were enormous.

The history of this illustrated record of sales was interesting. It was John Carter, Sotheby's representative in New York from the mid-fifties onwards, who had insisted that he needed a document to show prospective clients what the firm's achievements had been. The firm's policy previously had always been to concern itself more with the present and the future. As a result of John Carter's insistence, a thin, limp pamphlet of twenty-eight pages in brown paper covers, with a frontispiece in colour of a major Van Gogh (Les Usines à Clichy) which had recently been sold for £31,000, came out in 1956/57. Sotheby's had borrowed the colour blocks from the Museum of Modern Art in New York to save costs. The following year a similar pamphlet of thirty-six pages appeared, now in 'Sotheby Green' covers. This time there were two colour plates. By the third year, 1958/59, Sotheby's had two watershed sales under its belt: the Jakob Goldschmidt sale of seven Impressionist pictures sold for £781,000, and the sale of the Duke of Westminster's *Adoration of the Magi* by Rubens for £275,000, and the business had become thoroughly PR conscious. The annual, still called *Sotheby's* but now in a cover showing a drawing of the front of Bond Street by Harry Buser, came out the following year and ran to 144 pages, but with no colour. The year following, for the 217th season (1960/61), it came out in the same format but had increased to 192 pages and contained a charming introduction by Cyril Connolly entitled *Sotheby's as an Education*. Christie's had caught on and produced a similar publication. By 1961/62, the fifth year, *Sotheby's* had a hard cover, cloth binding and a jacket, lots of colour plates and had expanded to 224 pages. Again there was an introduction, this time by Frank Davis, the doyen of auction room correspondents. For the following four years the format grew again and the title changed from *Sotheby's* to *The Ivory Hammer*. The first *Ivory Hammer* contained a short story by Ian Fleming, and each year thereafter there was an introduction by a well-known figure in the auction world. There were also numerous articles by the firm's experts on specific sales. The volumes were no longer purely an in-house production but were published by Longman's. The volume for 1966/67 had been the first to state quite clearly that it was edited by Philip Wilson, but was published by Macdonald's. Over seven hundred items sold in the preceding year were illustrated, but the greatest change of all was that the volume now carried the title *Art at Auction*, and thus it remained until 1984. Macdonald's gave up after four years. Then it was Thames & Hudson's turn for a couple of years. The imprint finally became that of Sotheby Publications in 1972. The simple truth was that the work involved in putting the book together was greater than any outside publisher could manage in the limited time available. The selection of the items to be included and the infighting among departments for the maximum space within each volume required an editor with the skills of a super-diplomat and an altogether unusual degree of tenacity.

*

I soon found that, small though we were as an enterprise, the number of books we were offered for publication, not least through the Sotheby connection, needed to be sifted very carefully. Our close links with a business as commercial as an auction house did not seem to daunt academic authors in the least. Many of the projects we considered at our weekly editorial meeting represented years, if not decades of scholarly work. The processes of editing, design and production needed to be tackled with patience and *gravitas*. Our small team and its advisers worked fastidiously to bestow on each volume the clarity of presentation and elegance it deserved. All the more reason, therefore, to ensure that our marketing and distribution were of the best. When I joined Philip Wilson it fell to me initially to make the necessary new arrangements for representation and selling, both in the UK and overseas.

The cost of producing such lavish volumes was immense, and it was therefore necessary for us either to secure subventions from learned bodies or munificent patrons, or to sell sufficient quantities to overseas publishers – mostly, of course, in the US – to ensure profitability. Philip worked wonders to produce acceptable contracts on the one hand and accurate costings on the other. Our policy at that time was to print quantities of each title that would last for a good many years and would, in general, not require reprinting. We expected and got slow but steady sales and, of course, with the help of Sotheby's far-reaching mailing list, our export sales were relatively high.

For all these reasons our visits to the Frankfurt and other international book fairs became of supreme importance to put forward our plans and obtain firm commitments from what were like-minded publishers or university presses elsewhere. Our meetings with fellow publishers therefore became just as hectic as those of Martin Dunitz had been at Ward Lock years earlier. Philip and I had appointments that started early in the morning and went on till late in the evening each day. It fell to me to keep a record of all that went on, for it was only too easy after a frantic day of negotiation to forget what had been agreed. And all such deliberations had to be confirmed by letter when we got home and translated into agreed printing numbers, special proofs, revised time schedules and, most importantly, financial transactions.

Frankfurt on its own was not enough. We travelled frequently to American book trade conventions and similar events in Europe. The journeys that stick most clearly in my mind were those involving the search for museums to add to a series of museum guides we had recently started. On another occasion I undertook a uniquely exciting trip with our senior editor, Anne Jackson, to spend some days in Lugano, Switzerland, to visit the celebrated collection of Baron Thyssen-Bornemisza. The Baron had decided that he wanted printed catalogues of the collections that had been started by his father and added to enormously by himself. There had, of course, been several publishers who were keen to undertake the publication. We had worked hard to prepare a submission but we did not know enough to judge how many volumes for the different categories of material, ranging from Old Master paintings to Expressionist pictures, from antique silver to ancient carpets, would be required. Simon de Pury, the curator of the collections, showed us around. (He was later to join Sotheby's and eventually became Head of European Operations, the job I had had. He then made himself independent as a dealer and more recently joined his business with Phillips.) But frequently the Baron would himself accompany us round the collections. At one stage, after we had decided on virtually everything that should be included in the volume on the antique silver, I noticed a pair of magnificent silver tureens in a room we had not previously visited. It seemed to me at a glance that they were the ones that had recently been through a much-discussed auction of silver by Christie's in Geneva, and had become the talk of the town because they had fetched the then highest recorded price for a silver item. But the identity of the buyer had remained a mystery. I asked Baron Thyssen whether they were the pair I was thinking of. He confirmed that they were and then added laconically, 'Yes, I suppose that they should go in'. There were to be nine volumes in all. The Baron too joined Sotheby's holding board years later.

In New York at another time Philip and I heard that Mr and Mrs Jack Linsky, who had a remarkable collection of French art and furniture, wanted a multi-volume catalogue of their collection. Mr Linsky had made many millions out of inventing the office stapler. With the help of their principal adviser/dealer we spent much time studying the contents of their large New York apartment to see how many volumes would be needed. I was particularly impressed by the paintings that hung on both sides of a dingy corridor that led to the kitchen quarters, which no one took very seriously. When Peter Wilson heard what we were doing he got very excited. To *sell* the collection would be a great coup for Sotheby's. He asked me to give him an idea of the worth of the collection which, as it happened, chimed almost exactly with the extensive valuation later undertaken. But the Linskys seemed unwilling to reach a decision about what to do, and eventually left almost everything in their collection to the Metropolitan Museum, where it occupied several rooms in the Department of French Decorative Arts.

Fairly frequently we decided to proceed with volumes where the risks of publications were entirely ours and the outcome was successful wildly beyond our expectations. Thus John Harris's book, *The Artist and the Country House*, which broke new ground in detailing the history of British country house and garden view painting over four centuries, sold spectacularly as a Christmas book in the year of its publication. The reputation of Sir Alfred Munnings, famous as a painter of horses, was not particularly resonant in 1978, a hundred years after his birth. But we went ahead with publishing an extensive illustrated book on his oeuvre nevertheless. Soon thereafter interest in his paintings increased significantly and our stock soon melted away. Another success was a series of slighter books on themes where the collecting interest was strong. Elizabeth Bennion's *Antique Medical Instruments* was the first of this genre which we published. It was followed by Gerard Turner's similar book on *Nineteenth Century Scientific Instruments*. But most successful by far was the first book on the subject of *Corkscrews for Collectors*, by Bernard Watney and Homer Babbidge. The two of them had practically invented corkscrews as a collectable, and their book reprinted again and again. It was also translated into a number of languages. After Bernard Watney's death in 1999 Christie's sold his corkscrew collection and the prices reached astronomical heights.

Throughout my publishing career I had been involved in books on the history of English delftware. It will be remembered that F H Garner's seminal book on the subject was the first I had dealt with at Faber's in 1947. Now I became deeply embroiled in getting Frank Britton's catalogue of *English Delftware in the Bristol Collection* into publishable form. Frank, a former Rolls Royce engineer with an enquiring mind, had spent nearly ten years researching the project. I mention it particularly because we designed the book in what seemed to me the ideal format, where each piece catalogued was illustrated right next to its description. Considering the specialist subject matter, it sold out relatively quickly and changed hands at a considerable premium from the moment it went out of print. Louis Lipsky was a Polish architect who also became fascinated by English delftware. His particular enthusiasm was for pieces which contained inscriptions and, above all, dates within the decorations on each piece. His collection was so extensive that at first we considered bringing out the catalogue, fascicle by fascicle, as a part-work over several years. But then he died unexpectedly; the collection was to be sold by Sotheby's. Michael Archer, an old friend and senior curator in the Ceramics Department of the Victoria and Albert Museum, and chief priest in the study of delftware, spent several years turning Lipsky's huge listing into publishable form under the title of *Dated English Delftware*. These two books on delftware were helped along by subventions: this enabled us to include far more colour plates than would otherwise have been the case.

CHAPTER SIXTEEN

The Simon Saga

In contrast, in 1978 Philip Wilson and I published in paperback a summary of the cream of the contents of the London National Gallery, entirely in colour, with some 230 plates, for only £4.95. The book was an instant hit and reprinted again and again. Basically it was the brain child and work of a friend of Philip's, an American expatriate, John Clarke, who lived in Florence and ran a photo agency for works of art, called Scala. The book was also printed in Italy. It soon occurred to us that it should be the cornerstone of a series of similar books on other well-known museums.

When Patricia and I went to Vienna, we explored the Kunsthistorisches Museum there, and I at once realised that both the paintings and the enormous collection of decorative arts would make wonderful additions to our museum series. I asked to make an appointment to see the director and was granted an interview at 9 a.m. on the following morning. The museum itself had virtually no guides to its own contents, merely a collection of postcards. I left a copy of *The National Gallery* for the director, Friederike Klauner, to study. She turned out to be a fairly fierce lady (not far off retirement) with bright red hair, and an amazing title. (Titles are an important archaic phenomenon on the Austrian social scene.) She started off the conversation by saying that she was pleased that we could converse in German, but she could think of no reason why she should meet me as she had refused all previous offers from publishers – and there were many – to produce just the sort of guide we had in mind. But then she went on to say that she considered our *National Gallery* a sound piece of work at a very reasonable price and in the circumstances she was prepared to withdraw her usual objections.

I hope I didn't show it too clearly, but I was jubilant. I explained my thought of having two volumes, which obviously she liked. I asked whether she could suggest possible authors on her staff and she forthwith introduced us to Rudolf Distelberger and Wolfgang Bohaska. Each then showed Patricia and me round his own department so that we could select the sort of paintings on the one hand, and decorative works on the other, that would make essential illustrations for the two volumes. I was particularly smitten by the Italian bronzes and the hardstone and ivory carvings produced in Prague and Vienna during the 16th and early 17th century, which were virtually unknown in Britain. Most had at one time belonged to the Austrian Imperial family, the Habsburgs.

It was one of the rare highlights of a long publishing career when everything clicked from the word go. In the event, it took much effort and longer than we thought to bring the two volumes to final fruition, but their publication led to another most useful association. We persuaded the distinguished Munich publishing firm, C H Beck, to act as co-publisher with us of the German edition of the two books. This meant that they would supply the Kunsthistorisches Museum with stock for their bookshop – obviously the single most important sales outlet. My own principal contribution to the whole series was that every volume should contain a fairly detailed history of each museum. This had rarely been regarded as of general interest, but now proved to be what the public wanted. Most such introductions, in fact, required a great deal of research, and gave the series something of an academic imprimatur. In due course it included volumes on the Victoria & Albert Museum, the Louvre, the Neue and the Alte Pinakothek in Munich, Madrid's Prado, the National Maritime Museum in Greenwich, the National Galleries of Scotland, the National Gallery of Ireland, the Rijksmuseum in Amsterdam and a host of others.

A year or two earlier, before the breakthrough in Vienna, Philip and I went off to the West Coast of the United States of America to attend the Annual American Booksellers' Association Fair. It was

being held that year in Anaheim, near Los Angeles, better known as
the seat of the first Disneyland. These annual fairs gave us a most
important opportunity to show our books to the American book
trade. Philip and I decided that our presence in that part of the world
would also allow us to call on the major museums in the area, and
we made appointments to see the Huntington Museum in San Ma-
rino, the then relatively-newly-established Getty Museum in Malibu
and the Norton Simon Museum in Pasadena. Huntington said yes
to our proposals, as long as we divided the volume into three parts:
the Library, the paintings and the botanical gardens. When it was
published the book turned out to be one of the most delightful in
the series. Getty dithered and asked for innumerable variant proposals, and eventually – after many years – did their own thing. Norton
Simon? Well, Norton Simon became a saga all of his own.

We met the great man himself, which was apparently unusual. Was
he great? History will judge. He showed us round his collection, accompanied by his then director, Thelma Holo. After studying major
collections for twenty years I was stunned. It was astonishing that
one man, even a rich man, should have assembled such a diverse collection of prime works of art by major masters from the fifteenth to
the twentieth century, in the space of a quarter of a century. It represented a body of paintings, watercolours and sculptures that surpassed
the great majority of the best regional museums in the States. I was
intrigued how he had achieved this and I was soon to find out.

Mr Simon asked us to put our proposals in writing, with the full-
est details of costings. Eventually, to our surprise, he said he wanted
us to go ahead. We sent him a contract to sign, but after several polite reminders he failed to do so. He, in turn, asked us to propose an
author. We tried, but there seemed to be a universal reluctance on
the part of suitable art historians to get involved. We should have
taken notice. Instead I agreed to see him on a further, unconnected
visit to the States, to persuade him to sign the contract so that we
could at least start planning the book.

By the time I met him, his turbulent and successful business career was largely behind him. He was seventy-three. But the millions and the deep grooves on an ageing face remained. It seemed astonishing that such a career was largely based on the successful marketing of tomatoes. But as far as I was concerned, his mind was now wholly devoted to the cause of art, or at any rate that part of it that came within his purview. I spent a fascinating weekend in Pasadena with Mr Simon, during which he explained what parts of his contract he didn't like. I suggested that we should sit down and re-draft the parts he didn't like. 'What, without a lawyer?', he queried. 'Why not?', I said. 'We draft our own contracts all the time, and there is nothing very complicated in what you want.' We got on well, sitting, as I remember, in an untidy study on rather uncomfortable cane chairs (on which, at one stage, I tore my trousers). I don't believe Mr Simon had ever worked on such a matter himself. Normally he stated what he wanted and one of his many legal advisers did the rest. I remember he didn't like our clause over shipping, how the finished books were to be sent from Italy to California. He drafted a highly complex, long-winded clause which seemed to repeat the same basic thought over and over again, which I found unacceptable. He agreed that I could re-phrase the essentials. I did it in fifteen words. He mulled over the result for a long time. He admitted he could see nothing wrong with it, but he didn't like it. I said politely, 'You don't like it because it seems too simple to you.' He gave one of his rare, very rare, smiles and accepted my wording.

After a couple of hours we had revised the whole thing to his liking and I asked him to sign it. 'Sign it?' He looked at me questioningly. I said 'Yes, if you want us to go ahead'. He looked astonished, but signed. I didn't say anything. It was only later that I learned that Mr Simon never signed contracts if he could avoid it. He hated entering into any firm, irrevocable commitment.

We then discussed the matter of authorship. I explained that so far we had drawn a blank. Could he suggest anyone? With his far-reaching contacts it seemed a likely possibility. But he said no, he was not prepared to put anyone forward. Then, in a rash moment, I said that I had written *The English as Collectors* and many articles on collecting. Would he like me to tackle the job? To this day I don't understand why he said yes, but he did so enthusiastically. I explained that this was not part of the publishing contract and I would want a modest fee. Would $2,000 be acceptable?' I asked. The publishing contract would pay for my expenses of the necessary visits to Pasadena. He seemed to think that such a fee was reasonable. I said that it would need a separate undertaking, in writing. A simple letter, signed by each of us, would do. There was no need to put it into writing, he said. I could – and should – rely on his word for it.

He and I then wandered round the gallery and he gave me a running commentary on the great majority of works on display: not just the art historical details, but where the painting had come from, the ups and downs of negotiating the purchase, the price he had paid, and what his different advisers had said. He had a firm policy always to consult several advisers, and if their opinions on authorship, condition and dating conflicted, so much the better. He could then select the facts that satisfied him. It was quite clear that he enjoyed the uncertainties of the chase as much as the actual acquisition.

One of the leading auctioneers who dealt with Simon for many years commented to me in a letter, 'He is possibly one of the most difficult clients we have, as no matter what dealings he is involved in, he has to come out on top. His philosophy of collecting defies any rational description in so far as he is just as happy to sell paintings as to buy them, if the price is right. He has a horror of committing himself to any course of action and likes to juggle five or six options at the same time until the very last minute'.

It was this hesitancy that caused a furore at Christie's when he had agreed beforehand on a strange system of bidding, depending on whether he was standing up or sitting down, and then confused the auctioneer, the very experienced chairman of Christie's, Peter Chance, by not sticking to his own pre-arranged ploys. It was at the sale of Rembrandt's charming portrait of his son, Titus. Initially the painting was knocked down to the Marlborough Gallery, at £740,000.

Simon got up and caused a fuss. The auctioneer put the picture up for sale again – the dealers present, in general, felt that he should not have done so – and Simon bought it for £20,000 more. It was one of his acquisitions the possession of which gave him most pleasure. It eventually appeared on the cover of our guide to the museum.

The painting on the back of the same book, *The Resurrection*, by the Flemish fifteenth-century artist, Dirk Bouts, is said to have had a not dissimilar story attached to its acquisition. It was coming up for sale at Sotheby's in London. Simon sent his then director, and his wife – the former actress Jennifer Jones – to the sale with precise instructions on how high they could bid. Unbeknownst to them, he then continued the bidding on the telephone from California, and the painting was eventually knocked down to him.

Auctioneers have a strict policy not to part with goods sold until they are paid for. When Simon asked that the painting should be sent to the States immediately after the sale, but before he paid for it, this was pointed out to him. He responded by saying, 'You know me well enough. Of course I shall pay for it'. The painting was despatched, but no payment reached Sotheby's. Simon answered frantic calls for the money by saying 'How do I know that you sent me the original? For all I know, it may be a copy. I need time to establish the authenticity of the painting'. It was many months before the matter was settled. Probably, it was thought, only because Simon wanted to print a reproduction of the picture on his annual Christmas card and even he didn't want the recipients to know that it had not been paid for. It became another of his favourites.

On my final afternoon on that trip to Pasadena, Simon offered, and I eagerly agreed, to tell me the story of how he had bought the rump of the famous Duveen Gallery in 1964.

When Joseph Duveen died in 1939 he left the business to his nephew, Armand Lowengard, and to his long-time principal assistant, Edward Fowles. As the war bit, the London and Paris houses of the gallery were closed and Fowles moved the business to the States, where, of course, it had been, in palatial offices, many years earlier. It took Fowles some time to re-establish the gallery. His principal sales over the years were to the Kress Foundation. When eventually he wanted to retire, he heard that Norton Simon might be interested in buying what was left of the business, and Simon did so for what was rumoured to amount to $15 million. There were about 150 works of art, many with questionable attributions and a lot in very poor condition. A considerable proportion of this residue had been bought by Duveen with the assistance of Bernard Berenson, who had, of course, been Duveen's adviser on Italian paintings for many years.

The importance of the multitude of paintings that passed through Duveen's hands is barely credible today. Most went to well-known Maecenae such as J P Morgan, Frick, Widener, Altman, Kress, Jules Bache, Huntington, Mellon, Mackay and Rockefeller, and today a vast majority of the paintings adorn the walls of the great museums in America. One of Duveen's major European clients was Calouste Gulbenkian, who made his money in oil and was said to be one of the richest men in the world. Gulbenkian, a great collector, was a difficult, often mean-minded, man and one of the few who more than once got the better of Duveen in their transactions. In many respects, his unconventional ways of doing business resembled Simon's own and I later often wondered whether Simon had noticed this similarity.

But Mr Simon became a different personality as he talked about the Duveen acquisition. His otherwise permanent sense of detachment deserted him and he positively sparkled with enthusiasm. He took me into the museum basement and pulled out many of the paintings from where they were stored. There was no doubt that what excited him most about the acquisition was the correspondence that related to the many masterpieces the house of Duveen had sold, and the arguments there had been about attribution. He constantly stressed how much he would have liked to have been part of that earlier generation which still had so much choice of really great pictures.

*

In order to complete the writing of the Simon catalogue, I made three trips to Pasadena. I divided my days there into eight hours of researching in the museum, eight hours of drafting the text and eight hours sleep in the Pasadena Hilton. It was extremely hard work. The first essential was to choose the 240 paintings that were to appear in the book, and then to construct the text around them. I knew even then that Mr Simon was a great one for selling pictures, or swapping them. He and I made a verbal agreement that he would not part with any painting that we had selected for the book until after it was published.

By the end of my first visit I had drafted the text and I gave it to him for consideration. Once more, to my astonishment, he said he liked it, and that with minor alterations it would do. Little did I know what was in store. Mr Simon liked it on the day I gave it to him, but he had utterly changed his mind a week later. I tried to avoid the endlessly repeated phraseology used by his PR department. The many articles on the Norton Simon collection based on this always seemed to express precisely the same sentiments and facts.

What was actually used in the book was my seventh draft, many months later. I had written at one stage to Thelma Holo, 'The script did indeed arrive back in London last Wednesday, but my heart sank when I read it: you have turned a soufflé into a suet pudding. Your revised version in no way does justice to the brilliant sparkle or originality of the Norton Simon collection or its creator. The text has become flat and boring, and limps along with the triteness of a press release'. It was, in fact, the heavy scrawl of the 'creator' that was recognisable all over every sheet of the text. Although his ultimate objective in life was obviously to be remembered as the creator of an amazing collection, he apparently wanted it described in the most conventional manner possible.

The whole production of the book was one long fight. First it was about my text; then about the quality of the colour proofs; then the layout and the juxtaposition of the paintings. Even the size of the printed book came into play. Always someone was having a change

The NORTON SIMON MUSEUM

'The whole production of the book was a long fight'.

of heart. It may have been under the signature of a host of museum assistants, but it was not hard to guess who had instructed them to write. The carefully balanced layout became grossly overloaded with additional subjects. Repeated journeys by my colleagues to Pasadena – an expensive trip from Europe – became necessary. Every time matters were agreed in the museum they were changed the moment the exhausted colleagues got back to Italy or the UK.

Philip and I were becoming more and more concerned as expenses mounted, and we had to write over and over again stressing that these could not be part of the originally agreed schedule of prices. Eventually, when relations between us and the museum had reached a nadir, we were shattered to hear that the Norton Simon Museum had handed the whole matter over to the London law firm of Goodman Derrick, run by the famous and formidable Lord Goodman, and that all future communication was to be through them. The contract that Simon had signed, which, of course, gave us the publishing rights in the Pasadena Museum collection, was the first target of attack. Clearly Norton Simon bitterly regretted that he had put his signature to it. Philip and I had a dismal summer. Our very survival was in doubt.

But, but we were lucky. The lawyers we used – who were, of course, at that time also Sotheby's – were Herbert Smith, long-established, dynamic and not infrequently innovative. Our problems were in the hands of a charming and intrepid lady called Mrs Perutz. She really enjoyed battling with Goodman Derrick. As their arguments grew fiercer and fiercer, she fought back with vigour and subtlety.

In the end we won. The accusations were withdrawn. The book was printed in vast quantities. We were even paid, though not, of course, on time. The critics liked the volume. The public bought it in large numbers. We breathed many sighs of relief.

Then came the final irony. Norton Simon wrote to us personally whether we would undertake a new and revised edition for him. But we had learned our lesson about dealing with tycoons. They made up the rules as they went along. Once was enough.

I wrote to Mr Simon to ask for my miserable author's fee. At first there was no response at all. After repeated requests I was told that there had never been any separate arrangement for the writing of the text. In the end, I asked an extremely distinguished New York attorney to draft a letter on my behalf. He did, and I sent it off. Back came the reply from a new director of the museum that if I dared to bring the matter up again, Norton Simon would regard it as so insulting that he would put the matter in the hands of his lawyer. Put not your trust in princes!

CHAPTER SEVENTEEN

China for the West

This was the title of one of the most successful books which Philip
Wilson and I published. It was a detailed catalogue by David Howard
and John Ayres of the famous Mottahedeh Collection of Chinese
porcelain, mostly of export ware. The Mottahedeh's were friends of
mine in New York. Mildred Mottahedeh, a veritable tornado of a
woman, and her Persian husband Rafi, had built up a thriving business that created facsimiles of well-known examples of earlier
porcelain wares, largely for sale in museums. They were most anxious to establish a printed record of their collection and asked me to
find a publisher. Such a book fitted admirably into the Sotheby/Philip
Wilson publishing programme. The Mottahedehs were more than
willing to provide a subsidy and, indeed, to take a significant proportion of the whole edition for sale through their own business.
We published a huge and sumptuous two-volume book at a price a
shade below £100 in 1978. Today, twenty-five years later, it is much
sought after and changes hands at £800. After the death of both the
Mottahedehs, their collection was sold by Sotheby's in two large
tranches, several years apart, and is no more.

Mildred involved me in another great adventure around the time
when the book came out. She tremendously admired the products
of the Spode porcelain works of the very late 18th and early 19th
centuries and much regretted that so few of the magnificently decorated patterns had ever been re-issued. She was most anxious to do
so herself. I did not know then, of course, that I too would become
absorbingly interested in Spode products only a few years later, when
Patricia and I began to assemble an extensive collection of Regency
porcelain in the form of dinner, dessert, tea and coffee services. This

followed on our earlier interest in English delftware, which we had begun collecting from the moment we were married.

The recent history of the Spode works had been one of decline and the ownership was complex. For some years it had belonged to Carborundum, Terry Maher's old stamping ground. Then Carborundum had itself been taken over. Part ownership had subsequently passed to the Royal Worcester company, who had made efforts to revive Spode. It was at this stage that I was asked to act. I did so through my old friends at County Bank. Negotiations lingered on for a long time and eventually took on quite a different character. Nelson Rockefeller, one-time Governor of New York and a former U S Vice President, as well as a great personal friend of the Mottahedehs, planned to inaugurate a series of reproductions of his own magnificent art collection. It was a project launched with much éclat, but not without contention. Mildred was one of the moving spirits behind it. Spode were asked to undertake some of the facsimile work. The Rockefeller millions were to come into play through a joint venture company. Then Rockefeller suddenly collapsed in his office and died of a heart attack and the whole thing fizzled out. Mildred, however, never gave up. She never did. She continued to ask me to act on her behalf on other matters for several years and eventually we found a smaller pottery in Stoke which worked for her firm.

It was David Howard, one of the authors of *China for the West*, who had, many years earlier, introduced me to the Mottahedehs. He too was an old friend, and was the author of an earlier book which had become a classic, *Chinese Armorial Porcelain*, a listing of all the known services made in China, principally during the eighteenth century, for rich or noble European families. It was published by Faber & Faber in 1974. Patricia had been David's house editor in a freelance capacity and for three years he had come down from Yorkshire for frequent weekends to turn his enormous script into publishable form and to match it with some 2,000 illustrations.

In 1980 *China for the West* was to take on an altogether different meaning for us. Philip Wilson had got to know a Yugoslav publishing house, *Jugoslovenska Revija*, which, in the days of Tito concentrated on encouraging tourism to Yugoslavia. They published books on the Yugoslav countryside and culture in English and other languages. The firm was headed by Bato Tomasevic, an imaginative publisher who was married to an Englishwoman: they had met as students at Exeter University. Bato had been gradually building up a group of about twenty publishers from different countries, who met each year at Motovan in Istria on the Baltic coast in order to discuss common projects and to enjoy themselves. He now proposed to organise a visit by the members of this group to China to see for themselves the country not much more than a year after the reign of the notorious 'Gang of Four' had ended, and China was slowly rebuilding everything that the Gang had set out to destroy in their ten years of supremacy during the period generally known as the Cultural Revolution. One has to remember that there had been a long-time warm relationship between China and Tito's Yugoslavia, based on a less restrictive form of communism known as 'self-management', and the two countries' mutually intense hatred of the Soviet Union[1]. The common bond was to undertake the publication of a new, largely visual book on the country that was in the process of being put together under the aegis of *Jugoslovenska Revija*. The text was to be in as many languages as might eventually be required. The core of the book consisted of 250 illustrations, in colour. They represented the cream of some 24,000 transparencies of Chinese rivers and mountains, its crowded cities and agricultural landscapes, its temples and antiquities, taken during the preceding year by twelve young Chinese photographers, who had systematically toured the nineteen provinces of China. It was to be China as the Chinese saw it.

Philip and I decided that it was an unusual opportunity to visit a

---

1 I never cease to be grateful that there was so little love lost between China and Russia at this stage of the world's history. Together they would have given the Cold War an infinitely more dangerous edge.

country we were unlikely to see on our own. We felt we might also find interesting publishing material, so we signed up for the tour. We flew to Belgrade to meet the rest of the party, publishers from eleven countries. Two days later we set off on the sixteen-hour flight to Beijing, stopping only at Dubai.

Naturally we were flying on a Yugoslav Airlines charter flight. Although we were virtually the only passengers, the accommodation was spartan and a major problem hit us as we took off. The passenger door would not close! Three burly flight attendants exercising all their strength eventually got it shut. Bato, who had been involved in the notorious Munich air disaster in 1958, turned the colour of newspaper, but the pilot decided to fly on and to have the matter attended to in Dubai. At Dubai they couldn't fix it and our door was closed again by even more flight attendants. However, we got to Beijing, until recently still called Peking, without further incidents.

None of us, to be honest, knew what to expect. There was talk of a rigid bureaucracy in a police state, of poor planning and primitive hotels, and total segregation from the Chinese people. After all, virtually no foreigners had been allowed into Red China for almost two generations. But one thing we had been told was that the weather would be at its best in May.

In fact, a relaxed and friendly atmosphere, brilliant organisation and a great eagerness for knowledge of the West became apparent from the moment we arrived in the huge public hall at the brand new airport in Beijing. There to welcome us were twenty-five men and a single woman, who were all dressed in dark blue, buttoned-up tunics, uniform blue trousers to match and peaked caps. They had arrived to meet us after their working day was over: the heads of twenty-six Beijing publishing houses. There were speeches of welcome, polite clapping (Chinese clapping is more decorous than ours), friendly hand shakes and smiles between every member of our party and every one of theirs, occasional shouts of recognition with the several Yugoslav members of our party, close hugs and even kisses (a habit apparently learned in Yugoslavia), a limited exchange of visiting cards, but absolutely no conversation. The linguistic barrier was absolute. Fortunately we soon learned to overcome this through the six interpreters attached to us. (Three spoke English, one Serbo-Croat, one German and one Japanese.) Also accompanying us throughout the tour were three or four members of the staff of the Chinese National Publishing Administration who had spent nearly a year organising the trip, and whom we came to know extremely well.

We were at once provided with a beautifully printed itinerary. We

上海市出版界欢迎南斯拉夫
"评论之友" 访华团

WELCOME
TO
"FRIENDS OF REVIJA"
DELEGATION TO CHINA

SHANGHAI PUBLISHERS

April 30, 1980

eventually visited five cities, including principally Shanghai and Beijing. We travelled 3,600 miles. The hotels, by and large (many built by the Russians), were excellent, the food was superb, though strange at times, even for habitués of European Chinese restaurants.

The buses and trains were extremely comfortable. A special railway carriage, provided for us on our trips by train, dated from long before the Second World War and had its own kitchen. The frequent banquets to meet different groups of Chinese were wholly enjoyable. Tea-drinking ceremonies soon displaced our hankering for coffee (I had brought some with me, but gave it away). But of course we were offered a standard of luxury that the majority of Chinese rarely enjoyed. We visited temples and factories, museums and palaces, schools and communes, historic sites and famous gardens, innumerable 'Friendship Stores' and occasional antique shops.

As soon as we had settled into our hotel after arrival in Beijing we all opted for a two-hour walk round the city. What struck us from the moment we got onto the street was the density of the teeming crowds wherever we turned. The impression of sheer multitude was strengthened because the vast majority, both the men and the women, were invariably clad in the dark blue trousers and buttoned up tunics. The women were not allowed to wear jewellery or make-up. It was truly an Aldous Huxley-like vision. Progress along the pavements was snail-like. People stared at us in disbelief. Most of them had rarely, if ever, seen a group of Europeans. Three or four of our party had red hair; several, particularly the Scandinavians among us, were blond. We heard one phrase repeatedly used when mothers pointed us out to their children. We asked our Chinese interpreters what it meant. 'Look at the barbarians; look at the barbarians' was the answer. In fact, a novel experience which took some getting used to, was the immense interest and curiosity we aroused in public places wherever we went. There was no hesitation in coming quite close to us. The Chinese wanted to see us at close quarters. Our polaroid cameras, in particular, were regarded as pure magic and drew crowds wherever we were seen to use them.

We were indeed a thoroughly international group: several from the US, including Ed Booher, a former president of McGraw-Hill, and Alfred Vandermark, the then current president; several from Germany, Switzerland, Italy, Japan, Norway and Holland. A group

of Bato's colleagues from Yugoslavia, a three-man team from Yugoslav Television, Philip Wilson, myself and one other publisher from
Britain.

We were constantly regaled with statistics. Those about publishing stayed in the mind. There were 160 Chinese publishing houses in
1980, 84 of them in Beijing, 30 in Shanghai and the rest scattered
through other provinces. Above them was the National Publishing
Administration. This in turn controlled various regional publishing
bureaux who allocated finance, paper and production facilities to
the individual publishing houses. There was a great shortage both of
paper and printing facilities. In all, there were fewer than a hundred
plants capable of printing books, yet they had produced four thousand million books in the previous year (1979), with an average run
of 230,000! Educational, technical and practical books were given
preference, for obvious reasons. In each house the senior editor was
king; it was he who decided what would and what would not be
published.

Decisions on printing numbers and all aspects of marketing were
in the hands of the National Bookshop Organisation, which had five
thousand retail outlets. Not surprisingly, few of the publishers we
met felt that the number printed of their own volumes was sufficient. One of the great problems for us was that China at that time
did not adhere to the international copyright conventions, though
the British Publishers Association had sent two deputations to China
to persuade them to do so. The P A's hard work, we were told, was
on the verge of bringing about a change of heart. We crossed with
one such party in Shanghai. It was headed by none other than Peter
du Sautoy, my one-time boss at Fabers thirty years earlier.

The days not devoted to sightseeing gave us an opportunity to see
what books the Chinese were offering us for publication and to negotiate with them. As far as Philip and I were concerned not much
was suitable for our list. However, there was a book on ancient Chinese bronzes which we thought would intrigue the museum world
and collectors who could afford such valuable artefacts. When we

started discussing the financial side of buying copies of the book (it was to have an English text), we began to realise something quite extraordinary: Chinese publishers had no comprehension of the profit motive. 'Why', they asked, 'could you not sell it for the price you paid us? Why should you want to add something extra?' It was not easy to explain capitalist finance through an interpreter, but we gradually succeeded. The next stage, we discovered, was to write a letter of intent, reserving the rights in the book to ourselves, explaining how many copies we required, the price we would be prepared to pay, how we wanted copies shipped to the UK and when. This would lead to another face to face negotiation, when the terms suggested would usually be altered. There was as much of a learning curve in all this for us as for them. We were especially intrigued by an immense new Chinese-English, English-Chinese dictionary, which was being prepared by a vast Shanghai publishing house. Some 150 people were at work on the project and had been for some time. This required a whole sequence of letters of intent, but though the Chinese negotiators seemed delighted by our interest, nothing, as far as we were concerned, ever came of it. It all seemed perfectly feasible while we were on Chinese soil, but the thought of writing to England and corresponding regularly over the detail to another continent seemed a total barrier.

The evenings were devoted to a concatenation of banquets where we made informal, social contacts through our highly active interpreters. The most dynamic of the English-speaking ones had been a leader of the Red Guard, one of the Gang of Four's elite troops. As no more than a boy, with an automatic rifle in his hand, he had been personally involved in arresting the former ministers who had ruled China. He could never get over the fact how easy it had been. Now, following a change of heart, it was riveting to hear him speak of his experiences. One of our number was a Professor of Political History at Berlin University who had made a special study of this era, and his well-informed questioning elicited the most astonishing responses. The young man in question had built up a huge collection of the printed ephemera of those times and, to his great joy, our German professor was able to take home a large part of it.

For the rest, the Chinese publishers were clever, gentle individuals, thirsting to hear about publishing in the western world. Only a year or so earlier many of them had still been imprisoned or lived as labourers to do the most menial work in remote parts of the countryside. Some seemed still to be recovering from the harshness meted out to them.

One of the topics of conversation that seemed dominant was the size of the Chinese population and the enormous rate at which it was growing. The point had been well and truly driven home to us on one of our long train journeys. As the landscape unfolded before us it seemed like a giant market garden. It was mostly women in huge hats who were working the land and who waved cheerfully as we passed them at our normal slow pace. At one stage we observed a new road being built, with masses of men in coolie hats, with heavy panniers of soil over their shoulders. It led to an interesting exchange with our guides. 'A couple of bulldozers', we said, 'could do the work more effectively in half the time than all those men.' 'But', came the answer, 'where would we find employment for those men otherwise? The Chinese population is approaching a billion people, nearly a quarter of today's world population.' There was little one could say. Later on we were shown several housing communes to see how the population actually lived. Often we went right into people's homes, which they seemed delighted to show us. The living space usually consisted of a single room, beds rolled up during the day, a cooker and some chairs, all on an earthen floor. Sanitation was as primitive as it could be. Often the rivers we saw were simply open sewers. The sheer crudeness of life was best demonstrated to us when we went up the Yangtze on a four-storey pleasure steamer. The principal function of this outing was a grand meeting to explain how publishing worked in China. But we spent many hours on the top deck looking at the river traffic. Several times human corpses floated by. No one took the slightest notice.

As it happened, we shared the deck with a group of three English-men from a division of Jardine Matheson, who were ship-brokers. They explained that, unlike the rest of the world, the Chinese were prepared to buy vessels more than ten years old. The day before they had had their long annual negotiations with the relevant Chinese purchasing authority. In previous years these had always begun with a fierce and lengthy diatribe about the iniquities of powers from the West, which had to be listened to in silence. On the previous day the very same man who had been the most vituperative in the past, apolo-gised for his former ill behaviour and explained that his superiors had always insisted on this opening gambit.

*

Obviously our little party was taken very seriously by the Chinese authorities. Co-publishing in general, and the dissemination of the new book on China in particular, seemed of great importance to them. So on our final day we were taken to spend more than an hour with one of the Vice-Presidents, Wang Ren Zhong. It was he who had swum the widely publicised eight kilometres down the Yangtze with Chairman Mao twenty-one years earlier. But that had not saved him from eight years of imprisonment, much of it in solitary confine-ment, and three years' banishment subsequently to labour in the fields. So he certainly knew about the Cultural Revolution at first hand.

The Vice-President told us, 'Western nations have left us far be-hind. Now we must modernise. We must concentrate particularly on education. We will do it in our Chinese way. Our approach to widening the knowledge of China elsewhere must be to mention both the good parts and the bad parts; the two side-by-side. Our publicity must be based on facts'. We were allowed to ask all the questions we liked. The problem of the dramatic population growth came up. We were thus the first foreigners to be told of the new government policy that had only just been formulated that, as of the following year, couples in China were only to be allowed to have one child. If they had more they would lose state benefits and income. It did not take us long to realise the significance of this information.

I had been asked by *The Times* to write for them an account of our journey. When I mentioned the population control idea to them they would not believe it and it was omitted from my article. Their regular China correspondent was then asked to establish whether it was true. It took him three weeks. Then it made headlines. On the other hand, my own local Essex paper ran a double-page spread feature about our journey. I mentioned Wang Ren Zhong's statement to us. It was picked up very speedily by the national media.

Sadly, during the last week of our journey many members of our group were seized either by a most virulent form of influenza or intestinal problems. I was victim of the Asian flu. I reckon my life was saved by a kindly American lady in our party who gave me some tetracycline tablets. The other English publisher in our party, John Spears of the Harvester Press, contracted some fell disease that laid him low for many months after our return home.

In contrast, during our travels we had been constantly tempted by goods in the many Friendship Stores we had visited. I came home with several lengths of wonderful brocade silks, bought from the textile mills that made them, jade jewellery for ridiculously low prices and a superb little seventeenth-century bronze of a fish. At that time antiques could only be sold if they were no more than one hundred years old, as certified by a special museum seal. I spotted my fish in a monastery shop. I looked at the elderly monk quizzically and pointed at the museum seal. He smiled and rocked from side to side. I assumed it was his way of saying, 'You know what these museum people are like. They don't know a good thing when they see one'. He was obviously pleased that I had recognised it for what it was, packed it up most carefully and patted me on the shoulder as we parted.

We were genuinely sad when it came to saying goodbye at the airport. Even more local publishers turned up to bid us farewell than when we arrived. Only now we knew who they were. It was particularly affecting parting from one or two of the Publishing

Adminstration staff. We had formed a genuine attachment to them, despite the language difficulties. It was unlikely we would ever meet again and they had become real friends. We had all taken part in a tiny but memorable breach of the bamboo curtain.

The spirit of increasing liberalism prevailed and grew until the fearful decisions for new repression at the time of Tiananmen Square. One got the feeling that the old men then in charge remembered with great clarity and alarm what had happened to their aged predecessors at the time when the Cultural Revolution had taken them unawares.

And the books? The one on China that had been the catalyst for our journey did not seem quite right for the Philip Wilson list, but it was ideal for another publishing house for whom I was working at the time, Frederick Muller, of whom more later.

I had been very sad that a second major trophy had totally eluded me as I was informed that there was a whole queue of English language publishers anxious to buy the rights. This was a large illustrated volume on the amazing Terracotta Army of some six thousand life-size warriors of the Imperial Guard that had been excavated from a tomb near Xian, 'the City of Eternal Peace'. But in the end that too came my way and was published by Muller's. Both books were a great success, to some extent because they were the first two to emerge from what we all hoped was a new China. As the text of the first book said, 'China is so vast, so varied and so old that it cannot be easily understood'.

CHAPTER EIGHTEEN

The Tale of Beatrix Potter: an Interlude

In the early 1980s B T Batsford were regarded as one of the most successful and stable middle-ranking publishers. The chairman, Alex Cox, was a one-time South African barrister and we used to lunch from time to time, so that after my experiences at MM & S he could pick my brains about possible ways of expanding. He foresaw quite clearly that the future favoured only the bigger publishers. He had already completed a successful property deal which gave his company ample capital for growth. He had also acquired Seaby's, a firm in the numismatic field, who not only traded in coins but also published a journal and books on the subject; although it had to be pointed out to him that their most valuable asset was an enormous mailing list.

Then, one day, quite unbeknownst to me, Batsford launched a *partial* takeover bid for the old-established publishers of that most famous of children's book authors, Beatrix Potter. Frederick Warne was the very same firm that Pat Matthews had approached with similar aims and talked to me about, before FNFC actually acquired Ward Lock, whose family shareholders were more amenable to such a step than Warne's. A very high proportion of the Warne shareholders were direct descendents of the founder of the firm, Frederick Warne. They were not impressed by the price Batsford offered and after a great deal of hassle, Batsford only acquired $1\frac{3}{4}$ per cent of the total equity. However, Warne's defence had turned a searchlight on their own finances and this had made it very clear to the shareholders why they had received so little in the way of dividends in recent years; for all was not well in Warne's publishing offices in Bedford Square where they were housed, literally a hundred yards from my own office.

It so happened that one of my wife's fellow District Councillors was married to a great-granddaughter of Frederick Warne. Henry Frost was a well-respected Essex farmer, renowned for his direct manner of speech. When Henry rose in the council chamber to comment on a matter under discussion, he was listened to with the utmost attention because the other councillors knew that his speech would be short and pithy, but so well considered and replete with common sense that it would brook little argument. Patricia and Henry had at one stage both stood for election as Chairman of the District Council, and when Patricia won the contest, Henry had behaved with the utmost dignity and courtesy. So we knew Henry and his wife Joan pretty well, and they often asked on social occasions how the world of publishing was faring.

Soon after the Batsford thrust, they became anxious about Warne's future. Henry asked me if I would be prepared to go to see the firm's recently appointed chairman, David Bisacre, and find out more about Warne's future plans. I duly wrote to Mr Bisacre asking for a chance to talk to him, explaining that this was as a result of a request from one of the principal shareholders. To my surprise, Mr Bisacre asked that such a meeting should take place a good many weeks ahead. This gave me a chance to make a very careful assessment of Warne's publishing activities.

When eventually I arrived at 40 Bedford Square (my own offices were at No 6a), I was ushered not into the chairman's office as I expected, but into the large and impressive board room. Seated round the table were all the Warne directors, the firm's auditors and accountants, their lawyer and a representative of County Bank: twelve or fifteen people in all. I could see that this was going to be fun. I was introduced to everyone present and asked to explain precisely whom I represented and about my own background in publishing and bookselling. I then asked whether the chairman wanted to give me a run-down of the business, or whether he would prefer me to ask a series of questions. He opted for the questions, as I had hoped. I had prepared them in two parts: firstly, those relating to the generalities of Warne's publishing activities and the recent history of their profitability – or lack of it – and, secondly, those relating specifically to statements which he, as chairman, had put out in the firm's last few annual accounts and his letters to shareholders, following the approach from Batsford.

Warne's were quite exceptionally fortunate in that, not only did they have the right to publish and sell Beatrix Potter's books and to make a turn on that, but Miss Potter had also given them her copyright, so that the firm benefited from an additional huge volume of royalties (not only on her books, of course, but also on the massive sale of licensed character merchandise). Everyone was fully aware that this copyright had only ten more years to run. The law permitted such right to prevail for fifty years after an author's death (though since that time the copyright period has been extended to seventy years under European law). Warne's now proposed to prolong the ten year period of copyright exclusivity by selling the television and video rights in animated films of all the twenty-three titles by Beatrix Potter.

Collectively these titles yielded a total profit of half a million pounds a year, and represented Warne's principal publishing activity. In addition, they published the popular 'Observer' series of about a hundred small but densely illustrated information books; books on transport; adult reference books, including the now very dated Nuttall dictionaries; books of an educational nature and wall charts; and a well-known but antiquated series of guide books. Thus there were seven categories of titles.

It emerged that the firm was losing considerable sums of money on the last six categories when set against the income from Beatrix Potter. I hammered the board very hard on this, and, understandably, they did not like it. My impression was that the publishing was perfectly competent, but barely relevant to the changes in public taste;

and there was certainly little hope of any genuine upturn in the results – despite improved housekeeping – which would do the
shareholders any good in the long term. It was a clear case of the
same *malaise* that I had encountered when I took over at Ward Lock.

Warne's had already sold a loss-making bookbinding business, but
still maintained a publishing branch in New York, staffed by some
fifteen people who looked after US sales, but also spent a lot of time
protecting the Beatrix Potter copyright from local infringements.
Overall it was losing a packet in the process.

I had learned in the last few years that the nature of publishing
had changed so much that draconian steps were needed if there was
going to be anything left for the shareholders in a few years time.
Either a firm had to be very big to survive or it had to have a niche
market with not too much competition. Warne's did not fit into
either category.

I therefore propounded a radical shift of course which, to my surprise, met with approval not only from the Warne directors – I suppose
it was a relief that somebody had the courage to propose such a total
volte face which they must all secretly have hoped for – but my proposals drew cheers and loud thumps of approval from the auditor
who kept repeating, 'That's what I've been telling them for ages'. The
plan was to sell off the stock and copyright of all books and series
except those by Beatrix Potter. This I felt would not be difficult even
in the then uncertain financial climate, particularly if Warne's could
act without being subject to undue pressure. In fact, I was able to
suggest a number of possible purchasers. This would enable the firm
to reduce its staff from over sixty to about fifteen; it would also allow
them to give up and sell their remaining lease in Bedford Square and
to let out their substantial warehouse in Dorking, Surrey.

The holding company would be left with the stewardship of the
warehouse, the control and exploitation of Beatrix Potter, both in
the UK and the US, and a considerable pile of cash to invest in new
ventures of appropriate validity and profitability. I even went so far
as to suggest that the actual publishing of the Beatrix Potter books

should be leased to another publisher, one that had displayed a proven sales and marketing dynamic in the last few years. I felt there would be great competition to undertake this.

My belief was that the publishing trade would applaud these moves by an old-established and well-loved firm emboldened to take into account the stark realities of the then very prolonged recession in the world of books. I stressed that it was important to treat the staff who would be made redundant with the maximum humanity. Some of them could move to other firms with the series on which they had been working. Finally, I stressed that it would not be easy for an internal executive management to bring about such a major shift of business activities, even though they themselves regarded it as necessary.

Happily, once the meeting had approved of these proposals, they allowed me to continue to dominate the meeting with further questions and suggestions. I urged them to bring forward their Annual General Meeting by several months and suggested that the chairman should accompany the Annual Accounts with an honest and informative statement for the benefit of the shareholders – and there were several hundred of them – who might not be able to attend such a meeting to hear him speak. (He did so, even at times using my wording.)

It was only near the end of the long session that my continued cross-questioning elicited what seemed a major factor in the board's plans for future strategy, which they seemed particularly reluctant to reveal. I could only assume that this mystery move might involve the appointment of a well-known and successful publisher to the board.

I left the last word to Warne's auditor and chairman, who both said repeatedly that what I had proposed – radical though it seemed – was the only satisfactory long-term solution for the future viability of the company and for the benefit of the shareholders.

I then reported to the family shareholders with a long memorandum of what had occurred and suggested that for the time being they should hold onto their shares. I was now representing not only

Henry and Joan Frost but also various sisters, brothers, uncles and aunts, and two members of an earlier generation. Among them was 'dotty Uncle Norman', who lived in Brighton and was regarded as so eccentric that he had been made a ward of court, but his official mentor put his charge's sizeable shareholding into my care. Uncle Norman's principal interest in life was toy trains, but he telephoned me at one stage to express enthusiasm for my activities.

As a parting shot, both the auditor and the representative from County Bank had asked me what I considered to be the correct valuation of the shares. I could only reply that I felt it should be much higher than the figure put forward in the Batsford offer.

David Bisacre and I continued to correspond in a desultory way, and the date for the AGM was eventually advanced by three months. But the announcement of it was accompanied by a bombshell. The board stated that, following the approval of a motion to be put to the meeting, they proposed to appoint an individual, who was virtually unknown within the close-knit confines of the publishing world, to take over the running of the firm. There was an immediate outcry that the terms being offered to the man concerned were excessively generous to the point of madness, and the family shareholders whom I represented – and a host of others who had heard of my involvement – demanded that I should vigorously oppose the motion at the AGM. This was not a role I had ever played before, or envisaged as part of my investigatory brief, but the family persuaded me that it was essential. Batsford had asked their solicitor to look into the background and he had reported that the 'contender', as he now became known, had not been too successful in his previous posts. However, I felt it would only be fair if I could meet him and make my own judgement. We did indeed meet for lunch, under what must have been ticklish circumstances for him. We got on well enough, but I was, after all, acting as adviser to the shareholders and I could not see him pulling off the task he would face in the light of the plan for the future now generally agreed. In any case, he seemed to have other ideas.

In the event I got up at the AGM, asked the difficult questions I had already put to the board at our first meeting and opposed the resolution for the appointment of the 'contender' on behalf of what had by now grown to be a small majority of all the shareholders, whose proxies I held in my hand. The motion was not carried.

So far so good. There then occurred another unplanned development. Interestingly enough, Henry Frost had written to me at one stage: 'Personally, I never believed that important things on this earth happen as a result of conscious planning; rather, as in this case, an unimportant episode . . . sets off a chain of circumstances and emerging possibilities . . .'. One of Warne's other shareholders was friendly with the chairman of a printing company called Sir Joseph Causton, and that firm now put in a bid to buy Frederick Warne, but at a price which County Bank and I considered far too low. But the very act of a further bid seemed to give us licence to seek other bidders; in fact, to launch a sort of auction for the company. This had been at the back of my mind for some time and during a holiday on Mediterranean beaches I had idled away the time by working out, with sums scratched into the sand, what the right share price should be. Many years earlier, Chapman & Hall had published a book on Discounted Cashflow and I now applied the principles of this to work out what income and profit from the sale of the Beatrix Potter books alone would yield over the next ten years, while they were still in copyright. The results astonished me. They were much higher than anyone had dared to contemplate. I put my calculations to County Bank on my return to London. They did the same sums and came up with the same answer. I hardly dared mention this to the shareholders in case I raised their expectations to what might be an unattainable level.

More bids now came in and, as news of this spread, the excitement and expectation among my shareholders grew. Henry Frost was marvellous. He often acted as funnel for the communications from other members of the family and gave me wonderful backing. He also had a wry sense of humour which, under the circumstances developing, was particularly welcome.

The highest bid by far came from the large publishing and

newspaper conglomorate, S Pearson & Son, and they were acting on behalf of their subsidiary, Penguin Books. Their negotiations were carried out by Lazard Brothers, a merchant bank also within their own group. I still felt that the price per share they offered was not high enough and I was asked to meet their representatives on the umpteenth floor of some high-rise office block in the City. Henry and Joan Frost had already talked to them to impress on them that our group of shareholders was unlikely to accept their offer. It was now up to me and County Bank to explain the reasons, and to persuade them to increase it. We did, but it took a long time. Eventually the figure reached exactly the one I had calculated. Offer documents began to fly; various shareholders' meetings took place and the final price was accepted by all concerned with literally no dissent. A number of my delighted shareholders became millionaires overnight. Even Batsford were more than pleased. They got nearly five times the price they themselves had offered only twelve months earlier. Henry Frost reported to me the chairman's statement verbatim at a final, Extraordinary General Meeting held at the Hotel Russell to sign and seal the deal, which I had not attended. 'This is – er – , I suppose, the final meeting of the shareholders of Frederick Warne as a separate company. Er – I suppose – er – that this is a sad occasion. We have made – er – arrangements for the Beatrix Potter material – er – to be treated sympathetically. Er – thank you all for coming. There should be – er – a cup of coffee for you soon.'

Initially there was no doubt that the book trade felt I had pulled a fast one over Penguin. But Penguins did the sensible thing. They made new printing plates of Miss Potter's original illustrations which still existed, and issued her books, looking much fresher but still under the Warne imprint. Warne's elderly printing plates had been so worn out that the more delicate and subtle colour tones were barely discernible on the printed page. It was a huge investment for them, but it gave the books a new lease of life, and nothing could have pleased me more than when Pearsons said in a subsequent annual report what a useful and profitable purchase Warne's had been for Penguins.

CHAPTER NINETEEN

Muller's:
a Bit of a Foozle

As if Sweeten's and Philip Wilson and Sotheby's were not enough to occupy my time, there was also Frederick Muller. After having worked so closely with David Reed and Jonathan Cohen of County Bank during the merger of MM&S and Pentos, we kept in touch. Such short but intense encounters forge close links. It was not long after I had parted from Pentos that David reported that one of his clients was most anxious to buy a publishing firm. Could I help? The client was Harlech Television, whose programmes covered Wales and the adjacent areas. They were said to be a prosperous thriving company. I met Lord Harlech and his colleagues who explained what they were looking for and why. They felt that there might be useful opportunities for collaboration between one medium and the other, what the pundits like to think of as synergy.

I set about looking but it was one of those rare periods of economic calm when there seemed to be no publishers on the market. But eventually I heard that the Australian newspaper group, Australian Consolidated Press, controlled by the Packer family, wanted to dispose of Frederick Muller which they had bought many years earlier. In the first few years of the Australian ownership of the company, Muller's hit the headlines when they published Grace Metalious's out-and-out best seller, *Peyton Place*. Sir Frank Packer came over to the UK once a year for the flat racing season, but as far as Mullers' staff was concerned, it was usually to sack one or other of the senior management of the firm in order to keep it on its toes.

Muller's had been founded in the mid-1930s by Frederick Muller, the sales director of Methuen's, the very same man who had introduced Ernest Shepard to Kenneth Grahame as a possible illustrator for *Wind in the Willows*. Muller had left Methuen's in a huff because he could not get on with the then newly-appointed managing director, E V Rieu (who much later in life achieved fame as a translator of Homer's *Odyssey*). Muller had resigned from his own firm in 1956 soon after its sale to the Australians, in fact to start up another very short-lived set-up called Frederick Press; short-lived, because he died in 1961.

At the time I became interested, Mullers' managing director was Vic Andrews. Formerly sales director, he had taken over after an earlier MD had fallen victim to one of Packer's annual clear-outs. Vic had managed admirably considering that there had been no new cash injections for years. At a time of considerable inflation he had had to move the company from its highly central offices in Fleet Street to a much cheaper site, out on the industrial environment of London's North Circular Road. Despite this, he had a reputation for being an unusually perspicacious staff talent spotter, though he had great difficulty in hanging on to them out in the sticks. The publishing survived by a scatter-gun approach to finding new books to publish. Few titles earned sufficient to make a real contribution towards overheads, let alone useful profits. Hefty advances for good authors were therefore something the by now impoverished firm could ill afford. Muller's principal sheet anchor was Patience Strong, who wrote inspirational verse that was extremely popular with her own devoted public. After careful study of all aspects of the company I was not over enthusiastic about recommending it to HTV. What was needed above all was a really creative editorially talented team that – backed by sufficient resources – could evolve a long term publishing programme for specific markets. If HTV really wanted to get into the book world and not just make a sizeable investment with little return, they would need a second, editorially orientated firm with a proven record of success *as well* as Muller's. I reported this to HTV and they said 'All right, find one'. I succeeded fairly quickly. The second firm of my choice was a small 'packager' who had produced excellent material for various major London publishing houses. The packager's problem at that stage was that they were financially weakened because a US publisher had recently failed to pay them for a major delivery of a specialist encyclopaedia. I strongly advised HTV to consider these two firms together, and not one or other in isolation. But HTV's financial director, a doughty Welshman, nearly choked at the thought of taking over debt, and the purchase of my packager was rejected. The deal with Australian Consolidated to buy Muller's, however, went ahead. I was asked to stay on as editorial adviser and to become a director of Muller's. I could see a bleak period ahead, but my usual optimism prevailed.

The HTV board agreed that the policy of issuing single, totally unrelated titles which had a short shelf life and did little to support each other, should be replaced. I expounded to them on Methuen's various splendid series of books that constantly reprinted and to which it was relative child's play to add new titles. I explained that it would take time to establish anything similar and would need considerable investment, but HTV agreed that we should think in such terms. The hope was also that the odd star title might be culled from their televised material.

If I am to be honest, by the end of the first year of HTV's ownership of Muller's, what had been principally generated were a series of long memoranda from me on what needed to be done at Muller's, and the sort of series they should publish for a semi-educational market I knew to exist; but there was scant evidence of such material coming through. Our vivacious chief editor suddenly had to quit because she was going to have a baby. We also lacked a production manager and a sales manager. It was the Nelson scenario all over again. But this time, although I was a director of the company, I was an outside, part-time adviser and had little executive control. I found a good new production manager; Vic found an excellent sales manager. But I could not agree with my colleagues that the replacement chief editor they had found was the right man for the job. In the event he turned out to be completely overwhelmed by what was expected of him. The piles of work in his office grew higher and higher – unsigned contracts, unedited manuscripts, un-corrected proofs, jacket roughs which needed approval, overseas rights unsold, unanswered letters. The whole editorial process seemed to grind to a halt until Vic Andrews was driven to interfere by sitting in the editorial office to start reducing the piles of work: the last resort in publishing terms which one does almost anything to avoid because inevitably it causes resentment and often confusion. The delays set back the launch of our new Muller programme by many months and cost us dear in disappointed booksellers, disgruntled sales representatives and – above all – in a greatly reduced cashflow. It turned into a disaster from which it proved seemingly impossible to extricate Muller's. HTV's financial director asked for more and more figures, but it was not figures we needed: it was new books.

At the height of this critical period, as I was setting off to London one day from my home in Essex I must have been looking particularly glum. Our dear old gardener asked whether I was feeling all right. I explained. 'A bit of a foozle, is it?', he asked. Muller's was indeed a bit of a foozle.

Inevitably my editorial involvement became much greater than had been envisaged. After all these years I had wonderful editorial contacts, and until Vic's approaching retirement two years later, when we hoped to replace him with a new managing director who was also an experienced editor, finding a high proportion of the new books was up to me.

After much investigation and research, I wanted Muller's to branch out into a number of new areas. One was science at the level of late school/early university and wide general library interest. Our American and export contacts clamoured for this too and HTV seemed very interested. My principal adviser for this was Sir Eric Eastwood, whom I have already mentioned (see page 261). At this stage he had fairly recently retired after a final career as research director for the

vast General Electric Company (now again called Marconi), and enjoyed extra-mural chores such as advising a publisher. His principal
benefit to us was his extraordinary knowledge of able individuals in
the scientific world. One only had to mention a subject and he could
at once pinpoint one, two or even three possible authors. We held a
meeting – another think-tank – in Cambridge, together with two
outside editors I had already found, and Tony Garratt, a former chairman of BAT, the HTV director who was now responsible for Muller's
progress (or lack of it!), and Eric. Our own recently appointed senior editor, supposedly the linchpin of such a meeting, typically failed
to turn up. Primarily, we laid down the ground rules for a series of
biographical encyclopaedias on chemists (including bio-chemists),
biologists, engineers, mathematicians, physicists and, possibly, astronomers. The editor who had already begun work on the volume
on chemists was there, David Abbott, author of several highly ac-
claimed and successful scientific school textbooks, and a polymath
with a positively demonic energy and an unquenchable thirst for
work. He produced his texts at a pace which we had the greatest
difficulty keeping up with. As a former schoolmaster he was also
remarkably astute in deciding at what educational level our books
should be aimed. But the editorial work involved in finalising the
series for production was, in the end, much more complex then we
had envisaged at this early stage, and it was several years before the
series saw the light of day.

Another major contributor to these encyclopaedias at that
Cambridge meeting was Gareth Ashurst, an outstandingly
knowledgeable Durham senior science master who later produced
an excellent study of *The Founders of Modern Mathematics* for Muller's.
Other individual titles which we considered that day were a book on
'Exploring Electronics'; a work on scientific measurement aimed at
a young audience, which the author eventually called *Yardsticks for
the Universe*; a proposed book on the pharmaceutical industry which,
sadly, never materialised, and a book which Eric Eastwood himself
was going to tackle on the future of research in industry. He died

quite unexpectedly soon after producing a brilliant synopsis. Brilliant because it foreshadowed exactly the general lines on which research work developed in practice over the next two decades.

He also enthused about another book he wanted to write himself on 'The Early Communicators'. He obviously had Marconi in mind. He commented dryly that he was particularly familiar with the subject (having worked at Marconi's for thirty years!). He also offered to provide a synopsis for a book on major figures in the world of nuclear physics. He had obviously correctly sensed the spirit of our meeting. He thought that 'The Particle Pundits' would make a good title. I had rarely seen Eric so animated and expressing himself with such fervour. It was wonderful to behold. Clearly he relished the idea of becoming a catalyst in areas of science which he felt were insufficiently appreciated among the teaching world. But it was not to be.

In any case, it was all very extraordinary that I, the great non-scientist, was bringing all this about.

So much for science. Muller's already had a useful list of books on films. This was intriguing. In my days at Nelson not that many years earlier, we could not raise an iota of interest in the subject in book form, either by the public or the book trade, when we had had an opportunity of acquiring really informative material on the subject of movies from America. But Muller's had succeeded where we at Nelson had failed, and we now proposed a series of books on music, side-by-side with those on films. But finding authors in this field proved difficult, and when we did they were invariably slow to produce their manuscripts.

HTV was keen that we should pursue titles on business subjects. The hope was that they would lend themselves to adaptation for television. With the help of a number of friends at Spicer & Pegler, a sizeable firm of accountants and management consultants with a small publishing arm of their own, we found possible authors for a series of books on such topics as British banking, the commodity market, the Inland Revenue and *Understanding your Pension*. One partner of

Spicer & Pegler came up with particularly good sample chapters on
'The Annual Audit', and a friend at Price Waterhouse, as it then was,
on 'Headhunters'.

There were books whose gestation went through without a hitch
that greatly redounded to Muller's credit. I had long admired the
reports by the *Manchester Guardian* correspondent in Germany,
Terence Prittie. We met, and I suggested he might enjoy tackling a
book on Germany's post-war Chancellors, Konrad Adenauer, Erhard,
Kiesinger, Helmut Schmidt and Willy Brandt. We called the book
The Velvet Chancellors, and it was a phrase which was quickly absorbed
into the vocabulary of international politics. My one-time loyal craft
author from Ward Lock, Valerie Janitch, came up with an idea for a
book on objects which people could make at home and then sell, in
order to make a bit of money on the side. She called it *Crafts on the
Counter*. It was taken up by a good many women's magazines and
earned quite a bit of money on the side for Valerie. Finally, completely out of the blue, a farmer's wife in Aberdeenshire, Vickie
Crabtree, sent us a synopsis for children on the basics of British agri-
culture, called *Farming Today*. Living as I did in rural Essex, I was
surrounded by farmers, and they all regarded it as a magnificent effort. However, we had great difficulty in getting it reviewed in the
press, but once we had succeeded the book sailed away. Another
former Ward Lock friend in the gardening world, Ian Walls, wrote
two books on modern greenhouse methods for us and introduced
us to a colleague, Lila Dick, whose *Modern Nursery Stock Production*
became essential reading matter in the garden centre world.

So it was not all gloom, but after a while my principal task was to
help to find a replacement for Vic Andrews as managing director.

At Philip Wilson's office I had met Anthony White, an art historian
turned publisher. He had spent five or six years with the Paddington
Press, a small, dynamic publishing firm which, unusually, had equally
large bases in London and New York, and published simultaneously
for the UK and the US market. But things had gone horribly wrong
in New York in 1979 when Paddington's US distributor was faced

for the first time with 'returns' (that is, books sent back unsold to the publisher without payment) at an unprecedented level of 40 per cent. It demonstrated all too clearly that, despite constant such temptation, one should not have a company split between two sides of the Atlantic unless there is a very clear division of profit centres. The unfortunate Anthony White was now having to wind down the UK end of Paddington Press and would then be looking for a new job. One advantage for us was that he would bring a number of yet unpublished projects with him. HTV liked the thought of employing him and he arrived at Muller's as managing director designate with the principal task of improving the sales and marketing, and to accelerate the removal of the log jam on the editorial side.

HTV also at this period acquired the publishing business of Anthony Blond (called Blond & Briggs, whose most famous publication had been E F Schumacher's widely influential *Small is Beautiful*), and these events enabled me to retire gracefully to concern myself more fully with Sotheby's. In all, I had spent six years with Muller's. My stint there had made it clear to me that the day of the small general publisher was really over, which is why I was forced somewhat later to recommend such draconian action when it came to deciding what the future of Frederick Warne should be.

The most touching element of my parting from Muller's was, once again, the stream of letters from the many authors with whom I had worked and their gratitude for active counselling on their various projects. As always, it was the relationships with authors that mattered most: but what would be their future in the long term? One always hoped that their very intensive work would be rewarded with success.

Sadly this was not the case in Muller's own ultimate fate. HTV eventually lost interest, particularly after Lord Harlech's tragic death in a car crash. There had never been the synergy they had hoped for: although Anthony White had managed a few cooperative ventures. I always found that television management were too much under stress with their normal work to consider turning screen material into books. Those who subsequently have made a success of it have found the need for special liaison staff. Eventually, Anthony White and Anthony Blond jointly took over the Muller business for a token payment but went into liquidation only a few years later.

The ultimate judgement about the revival of firms such as Muller's had to be that it no longer worked. The rust had penetrated too deeply. Lubrication merely prolonged the agony. Dozens of small publishers simply faded away. As far as my view of publishing was concerned it was the end of an era.

I was asked to undertake crisis-management in a number of other firms, but I didn't take this up.

CHAPTER TWENTY

The Last Lap:
Bloomsbury Book Auctions

In 1983 Sotheby's and Christie's were having a hard time. Indeed, everyone in Britain was having a hard time. Sotheby's decided to lay off a lot of staff. They planned to make redundant a number of people with whom I had worked closely in the book department. In addition, Sotheby's decided that they would no longer accept the less expensive book (or artefact) for sale. It would be better, they thought, to confine themselves to selling items worth £500 or more. This form of exclusion started me thinking. Perhaps there should be a new auction house that dealt with the less choosy end of the market; rather like the late and much lamented Hodgson's of Chancery Lane (which Sotheby's had absorbed some years earlier and which I, of all people, had been directed to close). If someone was to set up a new auction house, why shouldn't it be me? I was fifty-six; young enough to have a crack at a new venture. I decided it was *going* to be me. After all, having studied the business so closely for seven years while writing the Sotheby history, and later while supervising a great flow of material for sale by auction to London from elsewhere, I had a pretty good idea of what was wanted and, even better, how to organise and run it. What was needed were bookish experts and premises.

One of my tenants who occupied the capacious basement in our splendid Georgian house at 6a Bedford Square had just gone bust. He had organised trade exhibitions for British industry in Iron Curtain countries, but his customers had recently failed to pay him. My brilliant brother, Luke, suggested that this was the ideal administration centre for my auction house. If we needed posher surroundings to see prospective clients, we could always use my own or my late father's sumptuous offices on the first floor. As far as the actual sales were concerned, we would hold them in the ballroom of one of the many nearby Bloomsbury hotels, just as Samuel Baker, the founding father of Sotheby's, had done 250 years earlier. The cost of this, as we discovered upon enquiry, was surprisingly reasonable. The hotels hoped to entice our buyers to eat – and drink – on their premises. So that was the question of premises settled. The offices would not even cost me anything.

Then David Stagg, who had been the dynamo of Hodgson's in Chancery Lane, and had latterly run the Fast Sales I had invented for Sotheby's new premises off Bond Street in Bloomfield Place, reported that he and his friend, Peter Collingridge, were about to be made redundant. Come and work for me, I said to them. So he and Peter came, replete with redundancy payments and second-hand cars. We needed a porter and a really good administrator. Stagg persuaded Stephen Cain to join us as porter, and Julia Ladds – blonde bombshell, who was the most outstandingly competent administrator by far in Sotheby's book department – also came to work with us.

We had begun to settle into our basement when one day Stagg asked whether he might tell Lord John Kerr, head of Sotheby's book department for the last eighteen years, what we were up to. Of course, said I. Only a few hours later Lord John phoned. Could we have lunch? We did, and he asked whether he could join us. Nothing could have delighted me more. Here was the ideal and distinguished chairman for our new business.

We planned the whole operation extremely carefully. One of the things that had bothered me most at Sotheby's were the constant lapses in administration which drove clients to distraction. I was determined that our system was going to be as dependable as we could make it. After we had devised the whole of our methodology (for which Julia Ladds should receive the most credit) we submitted the entire procedural plan to Spicer & Pegler, a firm of accountants and management consultants, and asked them to test it to destruction. They found a few things wrong, but after eighteen years we are still using the same system, though for some five years now it has all been computerised.

We then announced our arrival on the auction scene to the press. Geraldine Norman, at that time *The Times* saleroom correspondent, did us proud. Lord John, David Stagg and I were photographed together in Bedford Square outside our office, and a huge photograph of us appeared in *The Times* the next morning, the caption announcing that three ex-directors of Sotheby's had started a new firm. Within half an hour of our arrival at the office that morning, London's two leading antiquarian book dealers, Maggs and Quaritch, had rung us up to wish us well and to say that they would back us. When the press came to see us a little later they asked where the books were, looking with surprise at the empty shelves in our rooms. We explained that we had no books as yet, but we had a lot of faith. In fact, we certainly intended to go out on regular drives in order to find property to sell, but the astonishing thing was that for nearly ten years we never had to do so: the books just came pouring in.

I thought it would be a courtesy to tell Sotheby's what we were doing. I had a meeting with Julian Thompson, who had only recently been appointed as Sotheby's London chief executive, but he had too many other problems on his plate to take much interest. As Lord John wrote somewhere: 'Sotheby's, who had long been used to employees defecting to the trade, had not, if ever, been used to ex-employees establishing a new auction business. They pondered their reaction long, but in the end publicly decided on benign indifference'.

*

An auctioneer's catalogues are all important: they are the firm's ambassadors, salesmen and recording angels all in one. The information conveyed had become steadily more sophisticated as knowledge improved. Lord John laid down a cataloguing style which all could follow. It was particularly important to describe books with all faults, so that people who could not come to view the sales would not be disappointed if they bought books sight unseen. At first it worried me that we included so much negative comment. But in the long run it was this very factor that enhanced our reputation worldwide. We also took a lot of trouble over the design of the catalogues so that they were as readable and elegant as we could make them without an

A typical fan of our (bright orange) catalogues that pushed their way through the antiquarian book trade every two weeks. Later they occasionally grew in format.

extravagant use of space. With my previous typographical experience, design generally became my bailiwick; also our publicity. My aim was that people should instantly recognise our advertisements from our colophon and house style. There was soon too much for me to deal with and we took on my former colleague from ABP, Andrew Burrell, to undertake the design work for us.

We had all been busy for months collecting names and addresses of possible clients. We now mailed several thousand of them with a leaflet offering them a 'founders' subscription' to the twenty sales a year we proposed to hold. Imagine our astonishment when we had a 29 percent response, *with cash*. It was enough to set us up comfortably without any help from the bank. In fact, for eighteen years we never had a bank overdraft.

Another factor I regarded as most important was to treat all our customers – whether they were buying or selling a £1,000 book or a £10 one – with courtesy and respect. A friendly atmosphere was essential in a new business in a community as competitive as the auction world. We wanted the saleroom experience at BBA to be fun. But we also wanted to avoid the colossal overheads that the big auction houses had to bear. At BBA things were going to be simple. Lord John coined our splendid motto, 'No Frills'. He had bought the ancient auctioneer's rostrum from Sotheby's for £250 some time after Hodgson's saleroom had been closed. The rostrum was now given a new lease of life for Bloomsbury Book Auctions.

The first few sales were not wildly distinguished, but proved that our systems worked, and property began to come in at an accelerating pace. Few lots at first exceeded £100. A four-figure result was a land mark. But the sale results really took off in our sale No.10, devoted to 'Printed Books, Autograph Letters and Historical and Musical Manuscripts' in November 1983. The well-known bookseller, Bernard Breslauer, had come over from New York to bid for our lot 13, the first Aldine edition of Plutarch, the Greek text, in a fine contemporary Venetian binding of 1519. Our copy had a good provenance going back 150 years. We had estimated its value at £800-£1,200. Mr Breslauer had to pay £12,500 for it.

We also had on offer a number of interesting musical manuscripts, 'the property of the estate of a lady recently deceased'. It included a Johann Sebastian Bach fragment from his cantata *Eine Feste Burg ist unser Gott*. It sold for £8,000. The next lot was Chopin's signed, autograph manuscript of his *Cantabile in B Flat Major*. This had been reproduced in a facsimile edition in 1925, and then thought lost. Our copy was sold with an invoice from Maggs Bros of 1923. Our estimate was £8,000-£12,000. It went for our first real record at £35,000, to a London dealer. A little later in the sale we had an interesting letter from George Washington of 1795. This was bought by a New York dealer for £2,400. We were pleased with the price, but it would be infinitely higher today. Also included in the sale was a first edition with a dust jacket of Ian Fleming's *Casino Royale* of 1953. This title became a sort of barometer for the health of the antiquarian book trade. In 1983 we sold our copy for £500. Everyone was astonished. Thereafter copies sold for steadily increasing prices, reaching £5,500 in the late-1990s, and then descending again; but increasing to £11,000 at another auction house in 2001.

Conversely, Tolkien's *Lord of the Rings*, a first edition in three volumes, with dust jackets, moved upwards in a straight line. It fetched £650 in our 1983 sale: by 2001 the price for the same book had reached £12,000. We sold two copies in one season.

In the first eighteen years of our auction house activities we were able to chart a fascinating pattern of how fashions, in general, affected prices. The most outstanding examples of increasing interest were in the four titles by A A Milne, which I had turned into paperbacks at Methuen. When we started I was reluctant to pay £45 for a first edition with a jacket of *Now We Are Six*. By 2001 we sold a copy at nearly £4,000.

By the spring of 1984 it had become clear to us that our premises in 6a Bedford Square were too small to cope with the flow of books we were now receiving. We also hankered after a saleroom of our own in order to avoid the fortnightly major upheaval of moving sales to hotels. We started a search for new premises and very quickly found the ideal place in a quiet side street off Rosebery Avenue in Islington, a stone's throw from Sadlers Wells theatre. This was a one-time toy warehouse, on four floors, with passenger and goods lifts. The ground floor seemed almost as if designed for an excellent auction room. At first there were doubts if clients would move so far out of

BBA - the three musketeers: the author with his partners, Lord John Kerr and David Stagg, outside their new premises in Hardwick Street in 1984.

the central part of London they were normally used to. We also needed planning permission to convert the premises to our use. In the end, we had to take a gamble and move before such permission came through because local civil servants were on strike for many weeks. It was a nail-biting period, but all was well in the end and our first sale took place at 3 & 4 Hardwick Street on 16 November 1984. At first some buyers grumbled at having to go to an unaccustomed area, but they soon came to like a district where the traffic was less intense and parking was a possibility.

Our determined policy of courtesy to our clients had a remark-able result in the summer of 1984 when it landed us with a truly wonderful library, which we sold in two entire sales in September and November. The collection was so obviously valuable that we brought out the catalogues for it in a much larger format than was our norm. The books in question had been assembled with infinite care by a dealer in Old Master drawings and prints, named Wynne Jeudwine. He was a man of wide interests. His hobbies had included skiing, mountaineering, painting, and for many years he had been the editor of *Apollo* before Denys Sutton (whose library we were to sell many years later) took over. Jeudwine, who was much loved in the trade, had done so well that he spent the last ten years of his life studying in the British Museum reading room in order to put together a collection of books to illustrate the theme of 'Art and Style in Printed Books', on which he wanted to publish an analytical study. He was a man after my own heart who cared primarily about typography, fine printing, illustration and binding, and he wanted to find the best available copies of the most outstanding examples of books in all languages that demonstrated these characteristics at their best. He had already written the first part of his study on the fifteenth and sixteenth centuries, and hoped to publish a second volume on the seventeenth and eighteenth. But he became ill with cancer. Because he felt so strongly that he did not want to be a burden on his friends, he committed suicide, but not before he had instructed his executors to sell his library through 'those nice people who have recently started an auction firm in Bedford Square'. He had apparently been to see us on several occasions but we never knew who he was.

We took great care to catalogue Jeudwine's books in a manner that would do justice to their quality. Lord John surpassed himself with the scholarship he bestowed in particular on the early books, and the press was quick to recognise that this was a sale out of the ordinary. *The Times Literary Supplement* wrote, 'Last week being the occasion of the tenth International Antiquarian Book Fair, the London auction houses all had sales, the most distinguished of which was that held on September 18 by Bloomsbury Book Auctions of fifteenth-and sixteenth-century books from the collection of the late W B Jeudwine . . . The sale aroused great interest and prices consequently were high. An American collector paid £15,000 for the most expensive lot, a copy of *Aesop's Fables*, two parts, in one volume, folio, Basel, printed by Jacob Wolff of Pforzheim, 1501'. It was a notable example of early German woodcut illustration.

Buyers had come from far and wide. Béres of Paris bought prominently and paid enormous prices for two rare 16th-century bindings. So again did Breslauer. There were only 130 lots in the sale, compared to our norm of 300 to 400, but only a minority sold for £100s rather than £1,000s. The total was well over £250,000. For us it was a watershed. A second Jeudwine sale did no less well.

In the following year, 1985, we had two even more outstanding and profitable sales. Lord John had established himself as the leading auctioneer of Hebraica and Judaica at Sotheby's over the years, and the Yablon collection was our first such sale. Ralph Yablon was the father of our non-executive director, Tony Yablon, and in his lifetime he had not only rescued all the Scrolls of Law (Torah) the Nazis had seized in Czechoslovakia, but he had also, in 1969, acquired the library and ancient manuscripts of a distinguished Hebrew scholar to add to his collection. It contained early items that rarely appeared on the market and the announcement of our sale caused quite a stir.

The catalogue had been prepared with the help of Lord John's friend, Chimen Abramsky, a distinguished professor of Hebrew and Jewish Studies at University College, London, and long-time adviser to Ralph Yablon.

Such sales are principally attended by rabbis, who all seemed delighted to welcome Lord John in a new environment. We asked one particular such rabbinical scholar-dealer, who seemed anxious to buy some of the most expensive items, how he was going to pay for them. The answer was, 'In cash'. He did indeed spend a very great deal of money. After the sale, he came into my office and asked if he could close the door for a moment. He then took off his belt and lowered his trousers. To my astonishment he had a cord tied round his waist from which dangled, at intervals of a few inches, fat wads of banknotes. He then unhooked several of these, put them on my desk

and dressed again. Our financial controller spent a long time checking them all out. However, not all payments were so straightforward,
and sadly we suffered a considerable loss from another purchaser – a
New York private collector – who only paid in dollars after an inter-
val of many months, when the pound sterling had greatly decreased
in value.

The second major 1985 sale took place over two days, in October
and November. This consisted of a collection of nearly five-hundred
early printed books which had been sent to us from Germany. There
were actually over 250 true incunabula (books from before 1500) from
almost every known printing centre in Europe. As far as we were
concerned, it was the first and last occasion when we had this material in such quantities.

In the meantime, we had received a number of very different properties which we proposed to combine into a single sale at the end of
November. John Braine, renowned author of *Room at the Top*, whom
I had got to know vaguely when we published his books at Eyre &
Spotteswoode, came to ask if we would be prepared to sell his diaries. He had used them as background material to many of his novels.
It was most unusual to sell literary diaries while their author was still
alive. Lord John and I debated it, and thought, why not? I went to
see Braine in his flat in Hampstead. It was very spick-and-span. Someone obviously looked after him well. But he was not a happy man
and, I thought, was probably rather ill. But we had a pleasant chat
about publishing in former times and I agreed to have a shot at selling the diaries, though I warned him that a public sale might not
come off.

He had only recently recovered them. They had been with his
former wife, from whom he was divorced, and his son and a friend
had agreed to bring the trunk in which they were stored over to
Hampstead in their ancient Citroën 'deux cheveux'. As luck would
have it, their car caught fire on the way, and it was only with difficulty that they dragged the trunk out of the car before the vehicle
was consumed by flames. There were 130 volumes and nearly 20,000

pages in a large assortment of different-sized exercise and notebooks. In 1964 – twenty years earlier – Braine had written 'No matter what I say, I cannot do without some form of diary. I need to be able to think things out, and I can only think on paper'. I felt our catalogue needed a good interpretative and historical introduction to Braine's work and I got John Bright-Holmes, my former colleague at Eyre & Spotteswoode and for many years Braine's editor, to write it. He made a brilliant job of it.

Braine was in fairly desperate need of money, and we put an estimate of £25-£30,000 on the collection. The sale of the diaries caused a great deal of press interest, particularly among television companies. But in the event, the bidding only went up to £15,000. When the sale was over, Braine gave an interview with a mass of floodlights on him, sitting on one of our orange chairs, with a gnarled stick in his hand. He was very calm and dignified, and exclaimed prophetically, 'The diaries will only be of real interest and sell when I am dead'. The fact that they had not sold was probably more of a news item than if they *had* sold. The BBC mentioned it on on every news bulletin that evening, and thus more people heard the name 'Bloomsbury Book Auctions' than we could have reached by advertising for many years.

Braine died soon after, and we then sold the diaries, for precisely the sum he wanted, to the Brotherton Library in Leeds, who collected the writings of North Country authors both in book and manuscript form.

The same sale also included a series of very fine and intimate letters about his difficulties as a writer from the First World War poet, Edward Thomas, to a friend in Essex called Jesse Berridge, to whom the poet looked for comfort and moral support for many years. They continued to correspond up until his death in action in 1917. Unfortunately, the letters had been published in a small edition some years earlier and no one at our sale seemed to want them; though again they were sold to an avid buyer later, but not by us. Also in that memorably unhappy sale was a collection of German *fin de siècle* drawings that had appeared in various German satirical magazines, such as *Simplicissimus* and the *Meggendorfer Blätter*, which attained a wide readership. But they did not accord with British taste, and relatively few of them sold.

But most memorably awful of all was the fate that befell what we considered a marvellous collection of late 18th century French scientific manuscripts, the work of the Marquis of Condorcet (1743-1794), Joseph de Lambre (1749-1822) and Dominique Arago (1786-1853). Arago had been director of the Paris Observatory, but was also much involved in political reform, such as the abolition of slavery in the French Colonies. Most important of all, it was his work on which the true length of the metre was established. On the basis of this very fact, Lord John sent a copy of our catalogue to the Paris *Institut de Longitude*. The property was owned by a Dutch dealer and had been sent to us by our Belgian agent. It had been catalogued after a great deal of research by a young man called Rupert Powell, who wanted to join BBA as a cataloguer. We took him on with great delight on the strength of his work.

Not many days before the sale, we had a phone call from the Bibliothèque Nationale in Paris, warning us that they regarded these papers as French national property, and thus inalienable. They asked that we should withdraw them from the sale. We made urgent enquiries about how they had come onto the market. What had happened was that the relevant papers – and many others – had, since 1906, been stored in a wooden outhouse in the garden of the Paris *Observatoire du Park Montsouris*. When it was decided to demolish this building because it was in such a ruinous condition, a local contractor had been called in to clear the contents, for which he had been paid a small sum and for which he had received a receipt. He had provisionally left them in a skip on the roadside for a while, where they had been spotted and reported to the Bibliothèque Nationale who came to examine them, but took no further action. The contractor had then sold them to the French book trade, and our consignment had passed through three hands before coming to us. Others of the same groups of papers had been sold in France outside Paris, in Holland and Switzerland. But the French authorities were unmoved, even when presented with the three relevant receipts. At their request Interpol called on us to stop the sale. We had little option but to do so. In fact, after many months of correspondence with lawyers, the French Ministry of Education sent us an apology, withdrawing all charges. A year later, however, they came back and said they had been wrong to apologise and wanted the papers returned. More expensive legal wranglings ensued, but after we said firmly that we and the owners would require compensation before returning the material, we never heard another word. Ten years later, by which time the ownership of the papers had changed several times, we finally sold them, by private treaty.

It is interesting to record that in the spring of 2001 a report appeared in the British press that 'tens of thousands of priceless historical documents are being left to rot, fade and distintegrate in the attics of the French National Archives', side by side with photographs of these deplorable conditions. Nothing much had changed.

So altogether the sale of 28 November 1985 was not one we were likely to forget. It showed us how lucky we had been during the two previous years, and how generally fortunate we were thereafter. Fortunate in one particular respect, in that, after Jeudwine, we found two other continuous providers of wonderful material for sale whom we began to regard as our patron saints.

The first was the celebrated dealer in architectural books, Ben Weinreb, who supported us nobly until he himself got into trouble many years later, when it was our turn to help him. By then, he and I had become close friends. The second was a shadowy, very elderly former book cataloguer, simply known as Clarabut, who provided us with magnificent books at frequent intervals. Even after his death, his sock drawer continued to provide inestimable five-figure treasures.

As purchasers, on the other hand, two collectors supported our sales particularly nobly over the years. The first was the papermaker,

George Mandl, who had a truly vast collection of autograph material and signed and association copies of books which he kept in a
wonderful eighteenth-century Swiss paper mill. The other has been
Ken Bernard, an American book collector who was active in the Cali-
fornian construction industry. On the first occasion he asked me to
bid for him it was for some eighteenth-century Irish gardening books.
The prices went way beyond the commission bids he had left with
me. I had to explain very carefully after the sale that I could not go
beyond the sums he had specified. This surprised him. 'In future', he
said, 'I will suggest a base figure, but I want you to bid up to what
you consider reasonable beyond that.' In this way he acquired what
must be a most remarkable collection of pre-1600 books, which were
his particular interest. There cannot be many members of the Cali-
fornian construction industry who had mastered four or five of the
ancient languages. Again we became close friends.

*

One often hears the apocryphal story of auctioneers 'taking bids from
the chandelier'; that is, simply bidding up a lot without any actual
bids from the room. What the public only very seldom hears is that,
frequently, we get very high commission bids for items which subsequently sell for a much lower figure. Thus, we might receive a faxed
bid for a rare book for £4,000. When it comes to the sale, the bidding stops at £1,800. That is the price at which the client is invoiced.
It sometimes makes one gnash ones teeth, but the fact that this is
our invariable practice has several times appeared in the trade press,
and clearly recognition of this form of integrity has done us a lot of
good in the long run.

   By and large, the pattern of sales continued with occasional very
pricey highlights for truly wonderful books. The number of sales settled at about twenty-five a year. For a while we increased the number
of sales of Hebraica and Judaica. We were the only London auction
house still selling such material. But ultimately it proved unreward-
ing. We also began specialist sales of early photographic material.

We found this existed in large quantities. It seemed for a while that it might follow the trend of extreme popularity which it enjoys in America, but it didn't. But what was a success from the word go was the sale of prints, drawings and, in particular, antique maps. Such sales of visual material came about when we were asked by Basil Harley, a fellow member of the Double Crown Club, if we could sell the archival prints of the Curwen Studio. The high-quality printing firm in Plaistow – Curwen Press, which Faber's had used occasionally in the past – had gone out of business some years earlier, but the production of limited editions of individual prints by well-known contemporary artists continued as a separate enterprise. But that too was finding it difficult to make its way. We had never catalogued anything similar, but the sale of about a hundred original prints by Henry Moore, and three hundred more by artists such as Edward Bawden, Barbara Hepworth, David Hockney, Howard Hodgkin, Elizabeth Frink, John Piper, Ben Nicholson, Lynn Chadwick, David Gentleman and many others, was a great success and brought us into contact with that market.

The sale of the diaries of John Braine to the Brotherton Library made it clear to us that such sales of working papers, authors' manuscripts and correspondence – when carefully catalogued – was something we should undertake more often because universities found it most useful as research material and were on the look-out for it. But the cataloguing could be very labour-intensive and it was more than we were able to handle, on top of the unceasing flow of books, without additional help. Then one day we had a request to sell just such material, which consisted of the writing and correspondence of Christopher Hassell, biographer, poet and lyricist. It arrived in the office, beautifully organised and already excellently catalogued. It was very quickly bought by Cambridge University Library. The consignor was Dr Gillian Patterson, at one time Hassell's secretary and his literary executor, and more recently a senior administrator at the Royal College of Art. As I got to know her better, it seemed to me that, with her additional penchant for biographical research, she

would be the ideal person to catalogue other such specialist collections for us in the future, and thus began a partnership between us
that, after a few years, had brought us into close touch with many of
the most important institutional and academic libraries in the UK
and in America; and proved exceedingly profitable from Bloomsbury's
point of view. The only difficulty was that we never knew when such
collections would arrive. We must have sold fifty or sixty in all, but
four in particular stay in the mind.

One day I received a neatly hand-written letter, signed by a name
that rang bells from an earlier period in my life when I had been
strongly interested in the art of the short story. The name was H A
Manhood, some of whose work had figured in various selections of
short stories published before and during the war. He asked whether
I would be interested to sell his personal library and his manuscripts
to some major institution where they would be available for research
in the future, as he realised that the work of his own generation would
be eclipsed in the short term, but hoped that interest in it would
later revive.

Manhood was born in 1904. He began to achieve literary success
in about 1928, but soon after that he tired of urban life and bought a
four-acre plot of land near Hsenfield in Sussex. On it he placed an
old railway carriage which he converted for comfortable living, and
there he beavered away, coming up to London only to see editors
and publishers. He made himself self-sufficient by growing his own
produce. After life on his own there for some years, he married.

He became one of Britain's most prolific and talented short story
writers. His novels too showed a remarkable degree of imagination
and received very considerable acclaim. His publisher was Jonathan
Cape, and with encouragement from that firm's distinguished editor, Edward Garnett, Manhood was soon considered to be one of
the two or three leading novelists of his day. After the war he began
to resent growing editorial interference with what he wrote, and he
was appalled by the puny payments he received for his very considerable output. So in 1953 he stopped writing, bought more land, went

in for brewing cider and never wrote another word.

I went down to Sussex to meet him and his wife. She always referred to him as Manhood. On arrival, I was treated to lunch consisting of a huge portion of home-produced smoked salmon and home-brewed cider. The railway carriage still existed but he had been living in a simple bungalow nearby for some years. There, spread out on a large table for me to study, was his entire output: notebooks of ideas, early drafts, finished hand-written manuscripts, typescripts, *all* his correspondence with editors and publishers, including his invoices and payment receipts, the reviews of everything he had written and all the various editions (his American publisher had been Viking) of his published titles. The final manuscripts of his novels had, in each case, been bound in magnificent vellum bindings by his Cambridge friend, Sandy Cockerell. There were also all the letters he had received from his contemporaries: Henry Williamson, Hugh Walpole, John Galsworthy, H E Bates (a great admirer of Manhood's) and, above all, rather more than a hundred letters from Edward Garnett, not only about Manhood's own work but also full of literary chit-chat about other Cape authors from T E Lawrence to D H Lawrence. There cannot have been many authors who had retained the documentation of a lifetime with such meticulous care.

Despite this, it did not prove easy to sell the material by private treaty. The nearly forty-year gap since Manhood had been active as an author militated against him. But Lord John and I were delighted that his talent was eventually recognised and the virtually unprecedented completeness of his output appreciated when it was bought for the British Library by their modern manuscripts curator, Sally Brown. Sadly, Manhood had died before the transaction was completed, but his widow was able to live in comfort on the proceeds.

Another item that Sally Brown bought from Bloomsbury was just as fascinating in its own way, but its importance stood out a mile. This was a long cycle of letters, from 1935-1952, which T S Eliot had written (on Faber notepaper) to a young man from the West Country who had ambitions about becoming a poet, and had asked Eliot

for a meeting. Eliot obviously took to the young man from the word
go and must have recognised in him some of the frustrations and
difficulties he himself had had to face as a young man. The letters
not only conveyed a remarkable analysis of what Eliot set out to
achieve in his own verse, and the extent to which he worked at hon-
ing each piece before allowing publication, but also what he thought
of his contemporaries and how he felt about being the publisher of
their work. There can be little correspondence in which Eliot had
been so frank. 'I do not feel that I have much in common with contemporary poets', he wrote, 'and modern verse often seems to me to
show a defective ear and a lack of vitality in language'. As time passed,
we came across quite a number of other Eliot letters, most of which
also finished up in the British Library.

*

One of my mother's two sisters, Aniela Jaffé, had left Germany in
the very early 1930s. A women of penetrating intelligence, she became firstly a junior secretary on the staff of Carl Jung, the
psychoanalyst, and later on his principal assistant. She had occasionally come to visit my brother and myself while we were in the
children's home in St Moritz, and had taken me on a memorable
walk up to the St Julier Pass. We stayed in touch – and met from time
to time in Zurich, particularly towards the end of her life. One day,
very early in my publishing career at Fabers, I suggested to her that
she should consider writing a biography of Jung as she had come to
know him so well. No doubt other people had also encouraged her
to do this, and she soon started planning the book. Jung himself
became enthusiastic about the project, but when I heard that he was
taking a hand in helping to write parts himself, I warned her that she
would have copyright difficulties in the future if she did not get him
to give her a written note to say that the rights in the text were entirely hers. Fortunately, she heeded my advice, and Jung gave her
just such a note. When the book appeared, under the title of *Memories, Dreams, Reflections* by C G Jung, and my aunt's role was simply

given as 'Recorded and edited by Aniela Jaffé', it was wholly typical of her self-effacing disposition. But the book, which came out after Jung's death, was an enormous success, reprinted again and again, and was published all over the world in many translations. When, many years later, her rights in the book were indeed challenged, Jung's note protected her. She thoroughly enjoyed the fame it brought her and I remember her excitement at being recognised as a celebrated author in a Zurich shoe shop.

Aniela took a keen interest in Bloomsbury Book Auctions and through links with her I was asked to advise on the sale of all the letters that Jung had written to Sigmund Freud. It was to be a most exciting challenge and I got to know the correspondence between the two men extremely well. It took place between 1906 and 1914, and charted their relationship from the time when Jung was an admiring young professional writing to the master, through a period of strong affection between the two men with long exchanges of experiences and theoretic formulations, to gradually growing disagreement and a final rupture. The complete correspondence had been published in 1974 with approval by both the Jung and the Freud families, though Jung during his life time had had some misgivings about revealing the intensity of the relationship. In the event, it turned out that the letters that I was asked to sell included quite a number that had not previously been published.

It seemed to me that Jung's letters should go to the institution which already had the other half of the correspondence, Freud's letters to Jung. These were in the possession of the Library of Congress in Washington DC. They were indeed keen to possess the other half of the correspondence, but sadly were unable to raise the necessary funds, despite receiving a major donation towards them from Paul Mellon, an enthusiastic Jung supporter. The Jung family had a voice in the disposal and, at their request – after very lengthy struggles to find the money – the letters passed to a Swiss university. Coincidentally, years later I was asked to undertake a valuation of an extensive Freud family correspondence which belonged to an English university and it was fascinating to read in detail letters that Freud had written to others while he was corresponding with Jung.

*

The unquestionable high point of the private treaty sales which Gillian Patterson and I tackled was that of the working papers, correspondence and extensively annotated library of the novelist Graham Greene. He had sold the great majority of his manuscripts during his life time. What we had to sell were the letters which Greene had received during most of his career as an author, and copies of his replies. So from the point of view of the scholars of the future, the archive contained virtually the complete correspondence which he had carried on. It came about as follows. After he had received the letters in France, where he lived, he dictated his replies onto dictaphone cylinders and sent them each week to his sister, Elizabeth, who lived in England and acted as his secretary. On his occasional visits to England, Greene would pre-sign quantities of his notepaper so that his letters could be sent straight out after being typed. The correspondence was then carefully filed by Elizabeth. By the time we became involved, Greene had been dead for some years, and Elizabeth had suffered a stroke. It was her son, Greene's nephew (and, as it happened, a bookseller), who was selling the material at Greene's behest in order to raise money for his sister's support.

For various reasons, Gillian and I had no more than three weeks to identify and catalogue – by groups – some 50,000 individual documents. We had asked librarians and individuals, who had made it clear that they were interested in buying the whole collection, to contact us, and we then sent out some forty or fifty copies of the catalogue, with a suggested guide price. To our surprise, not a single library in Britain expressed more than token interest in the material. Most of the private collectors too found the sheer volume of what there was overwhelming. So eventually a battle developed between three American university libraries, which continued for almost three months, and left me extremely limp at the end of it. After protracted negotiations, the drafting of many versions of a contract (which Bloomsbury never normally issued), and the granting of an export licence for the few parts of the collection that were more than fifty years old, the papers and books went to Boston College in Connecticut. (Over the years they had established a substantial collection of the original manuscripts and working papers of several famous British Catholic authors.) We sold the Greene archive for a seven figure sum in dollars. It was only some months after all the excitement had died down that I discovered that its value had been established by a specialist London bookseller, not long before we became involved, at £30,000.

*

Although we never received such a sum again for any private treaty sale, by dint of such sales we managed to build up healthy financial reserves which gave BBA great strength at times when the general economic outlook seemed gloomy. But the market for antiquarian books never suffered as much as the art world. We were often asked at the height of the recession in the 1990s how much prices had shifted downwards. Our considered view was that a figure of 10-15 per cent seemed to be the answer. As far as I can remember, during nearly eighteen years in business since we had started, there was not a single year when we did not make a profit, however small it might sometimes be.

The most awful financial blow we received was in the eighth or ninth year of our existence, when the government introduced a new business rate – or local tax – throughout the country. Our rateable value – the sum on which the actual rate percentage is levied, had not only recently been adjusted upwards on our premises to £4,200, but the new assessment was to be £74,000. We were completely pole-axed. We appealed. And the result? Our rateable value was even further increased to £76,000. Such valuations were apparently based not on what a building was actually used for, but for what it *might* be used for. So it was explained to us that, although we used 3 & 4 Hardwick

Street principally for the storage of books, we might convert it into a luxury hotel. The result was that for some years we were the only business that survived along our road, Hardwick Street. Sixteen others departed or went out of business. As the person responsible for the firm's 'money and marketing', I was determined to build up a healthy reserve to allow us to overcome any more such misfortunes. The private treaty sales enabled me to do just that, but fortunately we never suffered any similarly debilitating blows.

In 1999 my stalwart help-mate, Gillian, went on holiday to France. As on all such previous occasions, she departed leaving my office peppered with little yellow 'Post-It' stickers reminding me to do this and that, and telling me what she would tackle on her return. But she never returned. She was suddenly taken ill in Avignon, when it was discovered that she was suffering from advanced cancer. It was the first death in the Bloomsbury family.

The 'keepsake' that BBA produced after ten years in business. The cover is, of course, in bright orange, BBA's house colour. The two angels' heads indicate that it is the second edition.

CHAPTER TWENTY-ONE

Behind the Rostrum

Our success at BBA was fundamentally the result of building up a particularly good team; people who were not only competent in their own right, but who worked well together. Initially we had compiled job descriptions for everyone on our staff, but after a while they became superfluous. Everyone knew what he or she had to do and got on with it.

Our company's actual name was Kerr, Herrmann & Stagg, and we traded as Bloomsbury Book Auctions. The third founding director, David Stagg, had trained with Ben Weinreb and then moved to Sotheby's, first to Hodgson's Rooms in Chancery Lane and then to run the 'Fast Sales' in Bloomfield Place. David's infectious laugh constantly echoed through our offices. He had started by looking after all aspects of staging our sales. For many years he was our managing director. Later on we primarily needed his gifts as business-getter and he became responsible for bringing in a large proportion of what was sold in the rooms. This was in part by reacting to letters and phone calls offering us books for sale that had to be looked at, often valued and then collected; and in part by means of trade gossip. David also had an uncanny gift for picking out the most interesting (and valuable) volume from a wall of books without a moment's hesitation.

Dido Arthur was the next to join us. She lived in Essex and had been a student of my brother's in the history of art department at Leicester University. She had then worked for me part-time, sorting out the 42,000 old auction catalogues I had amassed for the writing of the history of Sotheby's. We had practically invented BBA so that we could sell these *and* so that she could fulfil her dearest wish of

working in the antiquarian book trade. Her cataloguing skills soon
stood out and it was not long before she became our senior cataloguer with a particular penchant for skilful lotting, which was much
appreciated by professional book buyers. She developed an interest
in printing history, typography and private press productions, and
organised a whole series of such sales which became very popular.
She has semi-retired from the firm on a temporary basis to have a
string of babies.

Rupert Powell came to us straight from Southampton University
where he had read French and German, which we needed badly for
our cataloguing. His interest in books stemmed from his mother, a
bookseller who specialised in the literature of the First World War.
Rupert soon took in hand our sales on mountaineering and Polar
exploration. The first such sale was made up of the private collection
and the stock of a well-known specialist bookseller, Louis Baume of
Gaston's Alpine Bookshop. I was appalled at the thought of an entire sale on the subject but I could not have been more wrong. It
brought in buyers from all over the world. Similar sales have continued to do so and we have become known as the principal auctioneer
in this field.

In 1996 when Lord John and I felt that we wanted to take it more
easily, Rupert became our managing director and rapidly developed
a gift for taking a host of decisions at great speed. Both he and Dido
became directors quite early on in BBA's existence. Rupert was also
an enthusiastic advocate of direct marketing and developed this to a
fine art, with a system which has, in turn, allowed us to develop a
huge global database of book buyers with special interests.

At different times, Lord John and I allowed Rupert and Dido –
not so very long after they had started working for us – prolonged
leaves of absence from work in the office so that they could travel
and explore the world. This proved to be as beneficial for them as for
us.

While Lord John is our auctioneer supreme, David, Dido and
Rupert are all excellent auctioneers and take their turn in the ros-

trum. As most sales last between two and three hours, such work is quite a strain. It had always bothered me at Sotheby's (and I believe Christie's did the same) that reserves were given in the auctioneer's catalogues in a code, for security reasons. We decided from the start that our reserves would be in plain figures. This has reduced the strain, and certainly the errors.

After Lord John joined us in 1983, he and I quickly decided that he would look after cataloguing and making up our sales, and I would cope with general management, staff and finance. I also, as I mentioned earlier, took on the advertising and publicity for many years. Lord John has a natural gift for the consistency that is required to keep up the production of catalogues on a steady basis so that they appeared four weeks before each sale – the period that was needed to send them out to clients all over the world. This gave them plenty of time to study the books on offer and then to send in their bids. Such consistency is something I would find very difficult to maintain. However, matters have been helped today, firstly by fax facilities which have largely replaced the posting of commission bids, and more recently by dint of the fact that our catalogues appear on the Internet and an increasing number of prospective buyers e-mail their bids to us. Bidding by telephone during the actual sale, which used to be the exception, has also become much more common. It means that we have to have quite a number of staff in the auction room to make the necessary calls to clients.

Lord John and I regularly consulted each other when there were problems, and our long partnership certainly proved to be the happiest of my life. In the eighteen years we have worked together we have not exchanged a single cross word; in fact, we have almost always been in agreement when it came to settling uncertainties. This degree of amity allowed us to take risks together which, in a less friendly atmosphere, or a business that we did not own, would not have been possible. It was simply that if the risky venture came off we benefited; if it failed, we would not do it again. The thought of blame simply never arose.

My partner, Lord John, at his desk. It was he who put together our catalogues for many years. On his left, behind the umbrella, a wheel from a wheelwright's set of tools. Collections of artisans' equipment often came our way.

Although bookish matters always came first, as a firm we devoted a great deal of effort to the financial side of the business. Because of careful estimating and the restraint most of our vendors showed over reserves, the percentage of books that remained unsold after an auction was very low. It rarely rose to as much as 10 per cent, which by auction house standards generally is a healthy phenomenon. This meant that our cash flow was strong and steady. We gave long-term credit only in exceptional circumstances, when we thought someone was having a difficult time, or when someone had spent a particularly large sum with us during a sale. The generality of the book trade accepted this discipline in a very good-natured way.

After my one-time Ward Lock colleague, Christopher Lock, had

The author at work at BBA. We became known for our friendly, cheerful atmosphere, but the business, nevertheless, called for very detailed controls.

started us off on sound and accurate financial record-keeping, we were lucky to find as early as 1984 a former English badminton champion as our financial controller. Pat Havers ruled us with a flexible rod of iron. Her bookkeeping was a model of what such work should be and together she and I made a formidable team of credit controllers. Before her arrival, we had tended to be rather slapdash about this aspect of things until one of our carriers, of all people, told us that the trade regarded us as rather 'lacksadaisical'. Not for long, it didn't. Things got back onto an even keel very quickly. In the many years Pat was with us our vendors were paid out on the dot of the three weeks that were stipulated in our terms of business. As time went on, I was able to leave more and more of the overall financial

control to her so that I was able to devote more of my time to building up the business in other directions.

*

When we started BBA we took the decision that we would group
the books we had to sell under such categories as English or continental literature, art reference, travel and topography, economics,
science and medicine, Private Press and Limited Editions, natural
history and so on, so that buyers with particular interests would not
have to sit right through a sale but could attend only those parts
which mattered to them. This worked out pretty well. Thus, when a
major section of continental literature would finish, the dealers and
collectors would stream out, and those interested in Modern Firsts
would already have arrived for the following section. Right from
our first sale we gave buyers the opportunity to collect and pay for
the books they had bought during the sale. This practice worked
perfectly both before and after we computerised our procedures and
buyers particularly appreciated these features of sales which were by
no means universal throughout the auction world.

After a few years two things happened: firstly, we sometimes got
in so much material that we would devote an entire sale to one subject – such as mountaineering; and secondly, we were asked with
increasing frequency to sell entire libraries or collections more or
less devoted to a single theme. Sometimes it was the name of the
owner of the collection that would attract buyers; sometimes it was
the subject matter; very often a combination of both. We had had
three such sales early in our existence: the ceramic library of Jim
Kiddell of Sotheby's; Howard Nixon's books on bookbinding (Nixon
was the greatest authority on the history of bookbinding in his day),
and the Jeudwine collection – but then there was a long gap before
other such sales came our way.

The sale of Bob Forster's books stays in the mind as an important
such example. Bob was a dealer whom all the trade knew and loved:
a bear of a man with a growling voice. But he was kindness

personified. I had got to know him particularly well because, while I was writing the Sotheby history he seemed to be the only bookseller from whose regular duplicated book lists I could select catalogues of earlier auctions that were historically important. Just as in the case of *The English as Collectors* I had learned to depend on a steady stream of vital books from Ernest Seligmann, Bob's supply of catalogues and relevant old auction material was indispensable. By the 1970s he specialised principally in bibliography, though there were sidelines one knew about vaguely, such as books by D H Lawrence. Bob came to buy at BBA pretty regularly until, in his last few years, he discovered the joys of luxurious travel and frequently went abroad.

There was another link between us. He had been brought up in the Essex town of Maldon (our own nearest market town) and had been a pupil of the local grammar school, now called The Plume School.

The school was named after the Reverend Dr Thomas Plume, a seventeenth-century divine, born in Maldon, with a strong affection for the town of his birth. Plume was an enthusiastic buyer of books and formed an unusually sizeable library of some seven thousand volumes during his lifetime. Although he spent most of his professional career as Rector of Greenwich (to which, surprisingly as a convinced Royalist, he had been appointed by Oliver Cromwell's son Richard), he decided to leave his library to the town of Maldon after his death. He converted a ruined medieval church in the centre of the town to house it. While the library was to be on the first floor of this building, a new grammar school was to be established on the ground floor. The wonder of Plume's library is the diversity of the subjects it includes besides the obvious one of theology, which Plume clearly needed for the compilation of his weekly sermons. He bought and read books that covered every shade of religious, scientific and political opinions. He must have had an amazingly enquiring mind, interested in most aspects of the growing corpus of knowledge of his time. I discovered that after he had decided to expand what had been a working library into a more wide-ranging one that would suit the local intelligentsia, he was probably one of the first regular buyers at book auctions when they started to take place in London in the area around St Paul's in the late 1680s.

Plume died in 1704 and the school and library were opened soon afterwards. The library is still there today, a veritable time capsule, looking much as it did three hundred years earlier. I took an active interest in it as soon as we moved to Essex. By dint of the comparative study of the various inventories compiled throughout its long existence, it was discovered that a considerable number of books had 'disappeared' during the nineteenth century. A group of like-minded Maldon citizens formed an association called 'The Friends of Thomas Plume's Library', whose objectives were to assist the trustees by helping to find funds for the restoration of the existing books and, more

Humphrey Spender, our near neighbour in Essex and famed photographer and painter (left), with his brother, the poet, Sir Stephen Spender, outside the Plume Library. They had just attracted a large audience in order to raise money for the 'Friends of Thomas Plume's Library'.

important, to set about funding further copies of the missing books. Our aim was to make the library as complete as it had been when founded. I became chairman of this body. The project appealed to Bob, because of his association with the town and the grammar school, and he became one of our active supporters. To date we have replaced some 150 of the missing books, six of them being the original copies we had owned, with our shelf marks on them.

What I did not know until some time after Bob's death in 1997 – when his wife had asked BBA to sell their remaining stock and Bob's private collections – was that he had been born Vladimir Voronin, offspring of a prosperous Moscow family in the carpet trade; that he had arrived in England in 1921 after the problems of the Russian revolution, and had been brought up by his maternal grandmother, Lily Forster. He had joined a Russian relative, also living in England, who was a second-hand bookseller, and gradually established his own business. To his intense chagrin, during the Second World War Bob had been dismissed by the RAF in 1942 when it was discovered that he was of Russian origin, and that his mother had remarried a German citizen. Later in life he made up for this disappointment by devoting much of his time to the police. He joined the Metropolitan Special Constabulary and retired in 1979 with the rank of Commandant. He was also a passionate cricketer.

The catalogue we prepared of his stock became something of a collector's piece in its own right. There were more than 750 lots and it took three sales sessions to dispose of it. The most important part by far was Bob's superb collection of works by and about D H Lawrence. Bob's friend – and, indeed, *our* friend – John Collins of Maggs, a one-time Sotheby cataloguer, wrote an introduction to it which revealed what was to most of us the totally unknown background to Bob's life. This attracted wide general interest.

Although we were slightly worried that, because D H Lawrence was no longer quite the literary magnet he had once been, Bob's collection might prove a bit of an overdose of Lawrenciana, we decided to catalogue the books as single lots. In fact, it was the right decision. Although there was a disappointment here and there, most items sold, and sold at very high prices. Only twelve out of the 311 items were bought in, and most of those were pirated editions. One of the thousand copies of the 1928, privately printed Florentine first edition of *Lady Chatterley's Lover*, in the original mulberry covered boards with a slightly tatty jacket (Lawrence collectors are fussy!), sold for £2,600. A collection of sixty autograph letters Lawrence had written to his literary agent, J B Pinker, between 1914 and 1917, which included descriptions of two major works, *The Rainbow* and *Women in Love*, sold for £5,500, and a single letter from him to Katherine Mansfield reached £900.

Bob Forster's bibliography did just as well. There was a very good selection of specialist library catalogues, but it was just before prices for such things took off. Eighteen months later they would have been much higher, but such is life.

Our sale proved a worthy memorial to a remarkable member of the book trade.

*

Earlier single owner/single theme sales had included the extensive working library of the distinguished economist, Sir Arnold Plant (1898-1978). This had taken place in January of 1994 in two sessions. It contained not only individual volumes of great rarity by Alfred Marshall, David Ricardo and Adam Smith, but also many multiple lots that included books rarely seen at auction, which the dealers specialising in economics loved. One volume, A A Cournot's *Recherches sur les Principes Mathématiques de la Théorie des Riches* of 1838, still contained a postcard from a Cambridge bookseller of 1933 offering it to Professor Plant for 2 shillings (10 p), post free. It now fetched £3,800. The total for the sale reached six figures. Before it came our way, the owners had been offered £3,000 for it.

*

Two years later, within the space of a single month, we sold two further enormous named private collections. The subject matters could not have been more diverse. But in the book auction world – just as in publishing – the diversity of the subject matter is part of the fascination.

Mario Max Witt had run the family-owned bookselling business of Rapoport in Rome. He had spent years forming a personal collection of books on seafaring and every facet of maritime endeavour, in a host of languages, ranging from the 16th and 17th centuries to the present day. We had divided them into a series of sections from diving and oceanography, through law and insurance, submarines and torpedoes, to naval tactics and manoeuvres. Witt had died unexpectedly before he could complete a detailed catalogue of the library, and his widow had been unable to find any institution that would keep the collection intact. Again, though so specialist, the sale was a great success. The number of lots unsold was a fraction more than one per cent: a remarkable result.

*

When I had been at Methuen's we had published a book in 1966 entitled *The Art Nouveau Book in Britain*. One of my book handlers, Christopher Holgate, had surpassed himself in its design – an ingenious pastiche – and the volume was awarded several prizes for its distinguished production. It was also one of the first volumes where all the many illustrations were integrated into the text. It was typeset in England and printed by offset lithography in Holland. In essence, it was a study of the vital intervening period in book production between Victorianism and the 'modern': that is, from the 1890s to the very early 1900s. It included Art Nouveau and the Arts and Crafts Movement, the works of William Morris, Charles Ricketts, and illustrators such as Beardsley, Arthur Rackham and Jessie M King. The author was the journalist, John Russell Taylor. No one before had considered the era in this ground-breaking way, and it caused people to look at such books in a much more enlightened and less critically dismissive way.

I had not realised that the basis of the book was a thesis Mr Taylor had written while he was a student at the Courtauld Institute, and that Nikolaus Pevsner had been his director of studies. This I learned from the introduction to our catalogue after Mr Taylor had decided to sell the collection on which the work had been based. He had tracked me down from Methuen's to BBA. By now, the books he had assembled thirty years earlier had become eminently fashionable and our two-session sale of nearly five hundred lots was, like the Witt one, a virtual sell-out.

*

Eaton Square is in the heart of Belgravia and is probably one of London's finest – and most expensive – residential locations. Lord John and I were invited to look at the contents of No. 112, a vast mansion hidden behind trees, with famous political associations, in 1998. Its faded opulence reminded one of Mentmore. It had belonged firstly to Leo Amery, a Tory grandee and stalwart supporter of the tradition of Empire. Amery had been in and out of government for most of the period between the First and Second World War, and had been Secretary of State for India during Winston Churchill's government from 1940 to 1945. The house was famous for two pieces of political plotting that had taken place there: the downfall of Lloyd George's coalition government in 1922, and a Tory rebellion to oust Neville Chamberlain as Prime Minister in 1940. It was Amery who had pointed at Chamberlain in the House of Commons and quoted Oliver Cromwell's famous speech when dissolving the Long Parliament in the year 1653, by exclaiming: 'You have sat here too long for any good you have been doing. Depart, I say, and let us have done with you. In the name of God, go'. Chamberlain went hours later, and Churchill took his place.

After Amery 's death in 1955, his son Julian had lived in the house. He also had had a long political career behind him when he died in 1996, aged seventy-seven. The vast library in the enormous principal drawing room of the house reflected both father's and son's interests. While fascinating, it was neither easy to sell nor to catalogue. This was an instance where we had to undertake a good deal of multiple lotting, though eventually we found quite a number of books that were interesting in their own right. Often these were association copies from celebrated political and literary figures dedicated to the Amerys. Principal among them was a copy of the first edition of Adam Smith's *The Wealth of Nations*, inscribed by Raymond Asquith to Leo Amery in 1910. It fetched £17,000. Amery had been a keen mountaineer and explorer, and his signed copies of photographs by Herbert Ponting also fetched impressive prices.

While we were dealing with the books at 112 Eaton Square, Christie's were dealing with the furniture. Due to an early misunderstanding, they had been under the impression that they were also to sell the books and had already grouped them for cataloguing. I was intrigued to note how differently from BBA they had tackled the job. But the Amery sale was important for Bloomsbury Book Auctions. Because of the political links with the house, it was much discussed in the press and later brought us a good deal of property from sources previously unknown to us.

The Amery library was part of a two-day sale. The second day was given up to the library of H A Feisenberger (universally known as 'Feisy'), a one-time and particularly erudite cataloguer at Sotheby's who had been one of the first people to appreciate the importance of early scientific books. Feisy's sale went extremely well and the result cheered him up, only days before he died in California. Feisy had a distinguished near look-alike in Christie's book department, called Hans Fellner. We were very pleased that, only a little while later, he too entrusted us with the sale of some of the books he had collected.

*

We were never very happy about the extent to which the wider public knew of BBA's existence. The sad answer was that, in general, they didn't. Sotheby's and Christie's, after all, had had a head start over us of nearly 250 years. Though after a few years we began to make our mark in the world of active collectors of books and the antiquarian book trade. Publicity has to be an essential concomitant of the auction scene. But advertising is expensive and while we gave ourselves a useful budget for it each year, it could only very rarely go beyond publicising specific forthcoming sales in the press. These we generally coupled with witty press releases before and after sales which the newspapers sometimes, but not often, picked up when they struck a chord. Later we sent fliers to those names on our database whom we knew to be interested in specific subjects, such as the D H Lawrence Society when it came to Bob Forster's sale. But the general flow of direct mail in the UK was now so immense that we never really knew to what extent such efforts hit the right target. What had surprised me when I began compiling the advertisements for BBA's sales was the occasional direct response generated by trade press advertisements. I remember receiving sixty requests for the catalogues of one of our first children's books sales. This was vastly different from publishers' book advertising which, for all one knew, amounted to little more than posting letters over the edge of a cliff. In any case, the cynics said one did it only to please the authors!

All this amounted to what one might term the old-style publicity. For several years now we have had a website and every sale can be viewed on the Internet. But the jury is still out on how effective the new style media really are. At present they represent a small addition to turnover, but they are certainly not a substitute for the traditional, old-style forms of promulgation.

Occasional articles by ourselves (Lord John and me), or by journalists, portraying BBA, did help and usually brought in enquiries. When the *Book Collector* wrote of us soon after we started, 'Bloomsbury surprise by their variety', that was a comment we could plug and people did take notice. The most charming comment was made by Lord John when he was asked to write in *The Times Literary Supplement* on the general state of the book auction world, and he wrote, 'Now what has happened since the summer? It would require a super-human ordinance of self-denial not to say that Bloomsbury Book Auctions has happened'. People liked that. In 1995 I gave a long talk to the Double Crown Club on 'Serendipity in the Saleroom', which David Chambers published with a number of illustrations in the Journal of the Private Libraries Association. That sort of thing helped too.

The public also liked our occasional more exuberant forms of puffery. After five years we published a large format newsletter in which we explained what we had achieved, who we were (with many photographs) and what we were going to sell in the near future. Large quantities of *The Bloomsbury Bugle*, which is what we called it, disappeared like the driven snow.

After ten years in being we produced a catalogue-sized keepsake of twenty-four pages in our now well-known orange covers, called 'A Celebration'. By this stage we had a lot more to report. We actually had to reprint the keepsake because many people felt it was going to be a valuable item one day, and they ought to keep a copy. In it we reported that, during our ten years of existence, we had sold some 80,000 'lots' of books; we had issued 25,000 invoices, 9,600 property receipts, and we had held 210 sales.

In the early 1980s lectures were still a much more common feature on the social scene. We decided to stage an annual lecture on different aspects of book collecting. They required a good deal of organisation and we felt that if we did not make a nominal charge we would never know how many people were going to attend.

In the first year John Maggs spoke on 'The London Bookselling Tradition'. In the second Ben Weinreb talked about 'The Architect and the Book'. The irrepressible and much lamented Jock Murray spoke in the third year on some of the difficult authors he had had to deal with as a publisher. Jock's was a brilliant performance. He had apparently spent a long time rehearsing it in front of a mirror, and I was sad that we had not had the sense to tape it. Finally, we had Frank Brenchley on his vast collection of the works of T S Eliot which he had assembled and then generously donated to Merton College,

Oxford. After that I became uncertain whether 'our' sort of people still really wanted lectures.

We devised another neat little gimmick for a while which seemed to give a lot of pleasure. I always felt that when someone had worked their way right through a catalogue of, say, 380 lots, they needed a short snap of light relief. We gave them 'tailpieces' – short, pithy quotations from the literature of books about books. Sometimes I would link them with a recent event. Thus, when George Mandl died we included John Milton's celebrated defence of the freedom of the press which had been read at the memorial service for George at St Bride's Church in Fleet Street, and we were also able to pay tribute to him.

I really enjoyed ferreting through my own shelves to find suitable material. Often, I am ashamed to say, I would find them in books I had not even remembered that I had. Several catalogue subscribers joined in with suitable extracts. I seem to remember that we had a useful stream of quotable quotes from California, and there were letters of appreciative comment too. But the computerisation of cataloguing made it very difficult to include the tailpieces, and sadly the feature died.

*

ANOTHER SIDELINE: HUGO'S

When I started BBA it was by no means certain that it was going to have an assured future, and once again there were several parallel occupations that filled my time.

Hugo's was my last fling at practical publishing. The firm had been founded by a talented Frenchman with a flair for languages and teaching in the last quarter of the nineteenth century, and in 1984 it still specialised in providing books, but also tapes, for language self-tuition. It was owned by three octogenarian ladies, and Peter Lock, my former colleague at Ward Lock, was closely related to them. After more than a decade of the demanding world of Pentos, Peter wanted a change. So when Pentos decided to concentrate on bookselling and sold Ward Lock to the one-time family publishing firm of Cassell's – who had themselves undergone several changes of ownership in recent years – he opted out. I suggested to him that he should devote himself to revitalising Hugo's, which had reached a point where its survival was not altogether certain.

Peter went away and thought about it, and eventually came back to say that he would take it on if I joined him as a part-time adviser. When we looked into it, Hugo's sales figures were so appalling that even now I hardly dare commit the figures to paper. I said I would help for a couple of years: I stayed for nearly fourteen. Our principal asset was Hugo's name. It meant something both to the general public and to the book trade. Apart from a series of pocket-sized dictionaries, it was known principally for a long-established series of courses called *French* or *German* or *Spanish in Three Months*. The texts were grammar-based and devised in such a way that they could be used on their own, but it was infinitely easier to learn from them, if used in conjunction with the tapes, which we also supplied.

But the texts had not been revised for many years and the covers looked drab. A major process of re-vitalisation was needed. We launched an energetic programme of refreshing the texts; we gave the series attractive new covers; we improved packaging to include the tape with the book, and we began a vigorous sales campaign both in the UK and further afield. We found an enthusiastic ex-Prentice Hall co-publisher in the States and, above all, we besought W H Smith, then the UK's largest stockist of books, to back the series.

It all worked. After two years our sales were rising at a healthy rate and we were beginning to make a small but useful profit. Our chief editor, Robin Batchelor-Smith, was a genius at devising the tapes and managing the complexities of their production so that they really integrated well with the books; and Peter, with thirty years of selling experience behind him, performed wonders in the book trade. Title by title we expanded the *Three Months* series, a generally complex procedure, so that eventually we had included courses in Greek, Portuguese, Dutch (a surprisingly popular language), Danish, Turkish, Arabic, Swedish, Norwegian, Hebrew, Polish, Chinese and, above all, Japanese. One of my principal tasks was to find the authors.

We also started new series. We up-dated our 'Phrase Books' and combined them with simple tapes of their own, and then called the combination *Travel Packs*. They sold for under £5.00 and were extremely popular. I made sure that our phrase books had the best restaurant menu translations on the market. When Eastern Europe threw off the yoke of communism we had phrase books and tapes ready in Czech, Hungarian and Polish. The Hungarian one stumbled (it is an incredibly difficult language to learn), but the Czech one sailed away as more and more people were anxious to see the beauties of Prague.

I did not have the courage to give our Japanese course the subtitle *In Three Months*. It seemed to me impossible for anyone to learn that difficult language in twelve weeks. We called it *Japanese Made Easy*. It came out at just the time when the West became intrigued by the then miracles of Japanese industry and production and we sold an unbelievable 27,000 copies, many with the expensive tapes, in the first couple of years. Later on, we devised a special language series for businessmen, in French, German and Spanish. We had courses specifically adapted for learning while driving a car: we called them *French at the Wheel*. We published specially graded simpler and also more advanced courses in the most popular languages.

But above all, we kept to our principal niche activity – teaching languages. We were constantly being tempted into related forms of publishing. My most important job as Hugo's editorial adviser, it turned out, was to suppress any such deviations at our editorial meetings, however tempting they might sound. It was this concentrated specialisation that brought us success. And for the best part of a decade the company – or at least its trading turnover – grew and grew, despite an increasing number of competing courses from other publishers, most of which, fortunately, confined themselves to French, German, Spanish and Italian.

We had moved the business from central London to a quiet village in Suffolk, and that had helped to reduce our overheads. Then in the early nineties, we began to have the same problems as other publishers. With less money about, people travelled less, at least for pleasure, so they needed our courses less. Another problem which had worried me for a long time was our dependence on W H Smith. That firm was losing its traditional grip on the market, but fortunately we had seen the signs early and diverted our sales elsewhere as far as possible.

Initially, when we started in 1983/84, a substantial part of Hugo's turnover stemmed from a bi-annual direct mail-order splurge in the *Radio Times*, before the holiday seasons. We took a full-page advertisement – a very costly undertaking for a small publisher – and made special offers. The results could be spectacular. After a few years we felt that an advertising agency might do the job better than we could but the results of their efforts were disappointing. Eventually the public became capricious. There were so many temptations in other directions. We abandoned the mail-order approach. We found other sales methods that were more rewarding.

In the meantime, the three aged aunts had died and their shares had been passed down to a younger generation. As none of them seemed to want to become involved with the business – though they enjoyed the considerable dividends – it was decided to sell Hugo's. Our choice eventually fell on Dorling Kindersley as a safe home. But sadly our identity there soon seemed lost. Dorling Kindersley itself was sold to Penguin's a couple of years later, where perhaps the Hugo identity may yet one day be given a new life of its own.

Of course, there had been the usual ups and downs that any business suffers, but the revival of the firm had fulfilled more than most the criteria I had set myself in 1976, that as far as possible I would concentrate on jobs that were fun. Hugo's had been fun.

*

BACK TO BBA

Socially we were never very active, perhaps because our motto was still 'No Frills', and we were frightened by the constant round of parties that Sotheby's and Christie's held for beautiful people which featured prominently in their monthly *Previews*. When we had first announced our arrival on the auction scene, Lord John and I were astonished by the number of people who rang us up and said 'I expect you are a bit short of start-up capital. I should be very happy to make an investment in BBA'. There must have been fifteen such offers. We said no politely in each case, but we felt we ought to express our gratitude in some way. When we were selling a particularly fine collection of rare Parisian Private Press books, with illustrations by such renowned artists as Picasso, Braque, Pissarro and Derain (generally known as *livres d'artistes*), we staged what we privately called our 'Patrons' Party'. It was fun to see the slightly bewildered faces when they met each other and could not quite conjecture what the *raison d'être* behind the gathering was. We never told them. But one or two of them bought examples of the Private Press books.

After our tenth year in business we instituted a social event each year which gave great pleasure. We organised a dinner in the magnificent library of the Travellers' Club for some twenty individuals who had bought prominently at our sales. It gave us an opportunity to talk to our regular clients much more intimately than was ever possible in the saleroom, and frequently it converted what had been a casual acquaintanceship into a much more friendly relationship. Above all, it created a feeling of trust.

*

In 1996 my daughter Lucilla began to attend our board meetings. She had a lengthy background of financial and banking experience. I was a great believer in regular such meetings. It was essential to consider how we were faring both in a financial and an operational sense away from the hurly-burly of the day-to-day business. I usually wrote the minutes of such meetings and construed them in such a way that they recorded not only what decisions we had taken, but also reflected a history in outline of the firm's activities. It was Lucilla who – after becoming a director of the company – ultimately triggered a major change of policy in our sales that began to take BBA into a stream of profitability that had often eluded us.

After a sticky 1997 and 1998, the profits in the twelve months following burgeoned. It gave us all the boost of increased confidence that, after fifteen years, we needed. As we now had ample resources to do so, we began to plan a radical overhaul of the business (which followed naturally on computerisation a few years earlier) and a renovation of the physical state of the premises. The neo-Dickensian appearance of our offices was all very well, but we feared that it might easily lead to a loss of efficiency as we grew. And grow we did.

People outside began to notice and it was no surprise to us in the strong economic climate that then prevailed when we began to receive overtures about selling the business. Among the informal ones there were none which we considered in the least suitable. The first formal one taught us what our true worth was. The second confirmed it. The third seemed much more interesting – after all, Lord John and I were 146 years old between us and we had to think of the future – but we said no yet again. It came from one of the five young book dealers who, just after we launched BBA, we had privately designated as having the potential to lead the trade in due course. Four of them made it. One of them now was the putative buyer.

In former days I had on many occasions had to urge him to pay his bills which, to be fair, he always did eventually, even if it was with post-dated cheques. Although we had said no to him too, he was ostentatiously persistent. It was probably this characteristic that had brought him so far. In the end, Lord John and I were asked to write down the conditions under which we would be prepared to part with BBA. I thought such an offer was too good to ignore. Lord John thought the same. We wrote down exactly what we wanted, not only for ourselves but also for our staff and for the continuity of the business. Our principal concern was the mass of 'warranties' which lawyers always insist on writing into a sales agreement nowadays, under which any unexpected or unrevealed financial charge arising after the sale, has to be borne by the sellers. We asked that there should be NO WARRANTIES. Unheard of, said the lawyers – both ours and the buyer's. But our request prevailed. The contract we signed contained no warranties. Of course, it made us that much more prepared to continue to help the business. Lord John and I both agreed to stay on at BBA as directors for a further two years.

By the time we sold the business we had held nearly four hundred sales. I had devoted nearly a quarter of my life to it, longer than to any other job. I distilled into it all I had learned during my earlier career: BBA was efficient (people kept telling us so); it was a friendly and a happy place; our clients liked it; it kept fifteen people in reasonable comfort. When we had a particularly rewarding sale or season, we distributed the profits as bonuses to everybody who worked for us. Thus, the Graham Greene sale had resulted in three bonuses in a single year.

It would be quite wrong to pretend that it had all been milk and honey. There were many difficult moments, but by and large BBA was the ideal business in which to finish a long career within the world of books, because it was the books, after all, that mattered more than anything else.

*

But of course there were other things to consider. I mentioned earlier that Patricia and I had been avid collectors of ceramics. Our first love was English Delftware, a form of tin-glazed earthenware, made between 1680 and 1770, principally in Bristol, Liverpool and London (Lambeth) and charmingly decorated in a relatively simple and naive manner. Even before we got married we had set out on expeditions to find it.

On one occasion we had gone to Ipswich in Suffolk where we

knew that a wondrously impressive antique shop, called Green & Hatfield, had recently acquired an extensive group of polychrome dishes and chargers. They had earlier belonged to Drs Willett and Phillis Cunnington, my authors of books on costume at Faber's. I had explained to my parents that we had gone to look for antique furniture. When I showed my mother the four superb pieces of delftware we had bought, she commented drily that one could not sleep on delftware and a bed might have been more useful.

Little by little, after our marriage – even though money was short – we built up a sizeable collection. Such colourful plates and dishes looked splendid on the walls and shelves of our ancient house. Several times articles on our collecting habits appeared in specialist publications.

Sometimes on my travels around the country while visiting printers and binders in my book production days, I found that one could pick up charming early nineteenth-century dinner and tea services for relatively small sums. These gradually replaced the carefully chosen Wedgwood services with which we had started married life, after the hurly-burly of family life had taken its toll of the plates, cups and saucers we were using. We finished up with much more chinaware than we needed.

It gradually dawned on me that there was an important era which people who really collected pottery and porcelain with a purpose ignored: but those who were interested in furniture had long discovered. It fell, so to speak, between two stools. The period concerned coincided roughly with the Regency: King George III's illness manifested itself to a serious extent in 1788, and King George IV died in 1830. The more we looked at the porcelain produced during that time, the more we liked it. It represented a great flowering of inventiveness of design and decoration in the potteries of Staffordshire and Worcester.

There was, of course, a reason. The great Josiah Wedgwood had died in 1795 and many alternative producers emerged to challenge the elegant simplicity of the neo-classical style which had dominated his wares. Then, not only did the government impose a crippling tax on what was imported, but the East India Company stopped bringing vast quantities of Chinese porcelain into London because the dealers there – who bought it on arrival at the docks – would not pay enough for it to make the trade worthwhile. The company therefore sent the bulk of such Chinese porcelain to America instead. This cessation of supply caused a frantic search for an alternative source of services, which inevitably benefited the existing potteries in Worcester and Staffordshire: hence their sudden burgeoning and hugely increased output. One of the major potteries, Spode, for example, produced 4,000 different decorative patterns between 1800 and 1833.

What interested us while seeking whole services of any one particular pattern, was the skilful way in which the potters had adapted quite complex patterns to a great multitude of different shapes. Nowadays, when large services appear on the market, they are usually broken up by dealers and sold as individual pieces. This seemed a shame to me and I decided – in a rash moment – to start collecting and assembling services from the Regency period in as complete a form as possible.

I attended auctions and fairs and began to study what was available. I also bought a mass of specialist books on specific manufacturers, which proved invaluable: books, as usual, were to the fore. Long-term social habits soon became discernible. The well-decorated services had often been kept as 'best' and not much used. In many cases they consisted of so many pieces in the first place that they were split between siblings when there had been a death in the family. On several occasions we bought one half of a service in one auction house, and the other would come up for sale in another in a different part of the country several years later. We were then able to reunite the two. Dessert services were often in almost mint condition, even after two hundred years, because they had been displayed in glass-fronted cabinets and hardly ever taken out for use. It became quite clear that the principal source of damage had been clumsy hands among the kitchen staff when washing up after meals in the inconveniently shaped porcelain and zinc sinks that existed in relatively affluent homes during the nineteenth century.

We gradually discovered how many pieces made up a typical country house dinner service. There would have been enough for twenty-four people: three dinner plates for each person, plus one soup plate and two side plates; a couple of large soup tureens with their own covers, stands and ladles; at least three sauce tureens; four vegetable dishes and between twelve and seventeen meat dishes 'in sizes', that is varying from vast two foot venison dishes (which were expensive because the potters found them difficult to fire), to quite small nine inch platters. The Scots called them all 'ashets'. Our ancestors were too parsimonious to buy separate saucers for their tea and coffee cups so these would be sold as 'trios'. There were usually eight or twelve such trios in a coffee and tea service, together with a *sucrier* (sugar bowl), a milk jug, slop basin, teapot with its cover and stand, and a couple of cake plates. This was absolutely standard. In general, wealthy Regency folk preferred their coffee pots in silver.

I was slightly bemused twenty years ago how often such services then turned up at auction, but they were rarely complete. On the whole we tended to shun breakages, chips, cracks and discoloration: it limited the choice enormously. But we would take repairs with rivets in our stride, regarding them as honorable scars.

It was not long before we had a space problem. Those parts of our house which had housed catalogues for the Sotheby history background filled up with boxes containing our new purchases. What was sad was that we could not display them. It became clear that we would either have to find premises elsewhere, or build a 'China Store' near our house. We decided on the latter, and so began the great adventure of planning a suitable building and getting it constructed. We persuaded a disbelieving district council planning committee that we were not surreptitiously devising a 'granny annexe'. The external design had to blend in with our principally Tudor home. It worked. We even won an award for the best new construction beside a 'listed' building.

By the time Bloomsbury Book Auctions no longer took up the lion's share of my time, our collection had grown to such an extent that our simple manual cataloguing in a host of old style account books needed desperately to be computerised, so we used the extra time that had become available to tackle the work. We proceeded with the help of an expert in the field, with whom we had become particularly friendly and whose knowledge was much greater than ours. The detailed scrutiny – and photography – of the collection revealed a host of things we had completely forgotten about. It was Patricia's patience and determination that saw us through: I am pretty certain I would never have persevered on my own. People began to tell us, and there could be little doubt that, despite occasional dispersals, such a collection as ours existed nowhere else.

*

There had been another project, not long ago, that kept us occupied. During my membership of the Travellers Club, I had noticed at the centre table of the dining room (known as the Coffee Room) that members would not only chit-chat on current events but would often recall stories of their adventures earlier in life as diplomats, explorers, bankers, barristers, solicitors, sailors, journalists or simply travellers. My publisher's ear kept prickling.

Eventually I suggested to the concatenation of committees that run such institutions as gentlemen's clubs, that it might be fun to get some of the storytellers to write down their experiences and to let us publish them as a collection we could call *Travellers' Tales*, travellers in both senses of the word – as members of the Club and as people who ventured to distant places. To my amazement the idea was accepted with enthusiasm. Clubs on the whole are rather averse to divulging details about their membership. I was chairman of our Library Committee at the time. Joining me as fellow editor was the chairman of our Wine Committee, Michael Allen, whose whole career had been devoted to organising and issuing classical records. His stars had been Maria Callas, Yehudi Menuhin, Otto Klemperer,

Simon Rattle and a host of the world's best-known conductors. So we were both experts at extracting contributions from sometimes unwilling creative talents. As it was, the Club membership included such well-known writers as Sir Wilfred Thesiger, Hugh Carless, Patrick Leigh Fermor, Terry Waite, Simon Winchester and Douglas Hurd. All of them contributed. We assembled some eighty pieces in all. Patricia became the chief editorial co-ordinator and undertook the onerous task of converting the individual contributions into a cohesive entity while preserving the diversity of styles by our many authors. The finished article, with charming endpapers by David Gentleman who had already made drawings of parts of the Club, was received with enthusiasm by its many reviewers. The book became a popular seller as a Christmas present in several major London bookshops. One of its features that went down particularly well was the potted biographies of the authors we included at the end. People enjoyed coupling those with the reading of the relevant pieces.

Sadly, our publisher became seriously ill soon after the book came out and the Club had to take over the role of publisher itself. Now there is a movement to consider the publication of a second volume. In publishing terms it is a bit of a conundrum because it was the originality of the idea that carried it through the first time.

And so it goes on. Once a publisher, the involvement never seems to cease even though my knowledge of what is left of the trade is sadly deficient. The number of manuscripts or publishing ideas that reach me hardly gets any less.

*

The reader will have noticed that I have enjoyed the adventure of diversity in an age of constant change, and that I like mingling my activities. Throughout my career I have never ceased to feel that occasionally one needs to sit down, away from all distractions, and make a conscious effort to THINK, to work out in one's own mind what should happen next, if one is to survive, and even flourish. I notice in my own children this same propensity for planning. In this age of total and instant communication one becomes, and needs to become, an observer of trends and tendencies, particularly as the speed of change seems to accelerate. Last year's booming economy becomes this year's deep recession – despite what all the pundits may have said to the contrary. So one must learn to recognise and seize opportunities before they become past history.

My generation has witnessed a degree of change that seems barely credible: not only in the technological sense but also in social attitudes, economic values and an ever increasing degree of political interference and loss of the ultimate freedoms. But we adapt, like the kestrels over the motorways (and urban foxes).

I can't help reminding myself from time to time that my own great-grandmother, with whom I chatted for hours on end as a small boy, was born 160 years ago (and that we are still using the bed- and table-linen she had received as part of her dowry!); that a newspaper which, after World War II, cost 2d now costs ten shillings (50p); that threats will continue in whatever form they take – be it fascism, war, the cold war or terrorism. For much of my life, when it came to strife between an individual and the so-called corporation, the corporation always won. Now I am not so sure. A determined individual can rapidly build up strength, and the withdrawal of talent from the one-time employer soon makes itself felt.

The sense of obedience that was drilled into me early in life and lasted until I was well into my thirties, is a thing of the past, so that for me the break into real independence meant more than it could ever do for my children's generation. I remember being regarded as a bit of an eccentric because I changed careers from time to time. In today's uncertain faster-moving business world such an attitude has been reversed: fairly frequent career changes are regarded with approbation. I have the great advantage now that I can remain in the background and pick and choose from the old habits or the new.

Index

Page numbers in *italic* indicate illustrations